GREATER LONDON COUNCIL

BEHIND THE

BLUE PLAQUES

OF LONDON

1867-1994

The Complete Guide
by Alan Symons

First published by Polo Publishing 1994

ISBN 0 9523751 09

Printed and bound by Holmes & Son (Printers), 10 High Street, Andover, Hampshire SP10 2NY

Cover designed by Anthony Maher

For Jennifer, Mitchell and Gillian

"We cannot eat the fruit while the tree is in blossom" Disraeli

BEHIND THE BLUE PLAQUES OF LONDON

It is a fact, that London is the city most people want to visit. One reason for London's popularity is its' traditions and one of these traditions is The Blue Plaques.

The Blue Plaques are an acknowledgment of what we owe to those who have helped to shape today's world. They include scientists, artists, soldiers, politicians, sociologists; men and women who made their mark on society. Whilst the majority of the 600 plus names you will find in this guide are British, there are many, from all over the world, who lived for some time in London and have been commemorated by a Blue Plaque.

The Blue Plaques are so called because, quite simply, they have a blue background and are plaques! In 1865, following an anonymous letter in 'The Journal of the Royal Society of Arts', William Ewart, a member of Parliament, endorsed the notion of commemorating the houses in London, where the famous lived, stating . . . 'the places which have been the residences of the ornaments of their history cannot but be precious to all so thinking Englishmen'.

The idea was taken up by the Royal Society and a committee established to 'promote the erection of statues or other memorials of persons eminent in the Arts, Manufactures and Commerce.'

The decision to fix plaques, at first floor level, to the front walls of houses, was partially in order to give some pleasure to passengers on public transport and alleviate their boredom!

The first plaque was in 1867, commemorating the birthplace of Lord Byron at 24, Holles Street, Westminster. The Royal Society erected some 35 plaques, they were not always blue and not always round but, in 1901 London County Council took over the scheme and gradually brought about the uniformity we know to-day; a 20 inch circular blue and white plaque of glazed earthenware.

Between 1901 and 1965, the LCC erected some 300 plaques before handing over responsibility to the Greater London Council.

The GLC broadened the scheme to cover Greater London and over the next 20 years, some 260 Blue Plaques were erected until in 1985 English Heritage assumed responsibility. There are now over 600 plaques in existence and English Heritage is increasing this number by around 12 a year, but not without some justified criticism.

It is claimed that English Heritage selection ignores well known people, in favour of some who are barely recognisable. Also there is, and always has been, a lack of plaques commemorating women's achievements and it is felt that in this day and age English Heritage have a duty to redress the balance.

'**Behind the Blue Plaques of London**' provides a wonderful opportunity to delve into the past and imagine the enviroment of old London.

HOW NAMES ARE SELECTED

The main criteria for selection has remained broadly the same:

1. The person proposed shall have been dead for 20 years or until the centenary of their birth, whichever is the earlier.
2. The belief that subjects would be regarded as eminent by a majority of members of their own profession or calling.
3. They shall have made some positive contribution to human welfare or happiness.
4. They shall have had such exceptional and outstanding personalities that the well informed passer-by immediately recognises their names.
5. They deserve recognition.

Conditions 4 and 5 should provide readers with much amusement and interest as they attempt to link up the achievement with names they are unlikely to know.

It is the main reason why this guide is a must for the London visitor because here you will find what lays behind the bland, 'actor lived here'. Our concentration is on the honoured person rather than where they lived; sometimes for only a few months. This guide gives you an insight into hundreds of lives, many of whom you will never have heard about but whose achievements you will recognise. Some will perhaps surprise you and make you wonder why they ever received a Blue Plaque.

Visiting the places, absorbing the atmosphere where your favourites lived, should prove an interesting pastime and introduce you to many parts of London that are off the beaten track and wouldn't normally be included in your itinerary.

Included are lists to make your decisions easier. 'List of People by Occupation', 'Which Tube Stations Serve Which Place', 'A List of Counties or Countries Where the Person was Born'.

'**Behind the Blue Plaques of London**', besides being a fascinating tourist guide, is also an ongoing historical record . . .

THE BLUE PLAQUES
(Listed alphabetically)

ADAM, Robert (1728-1792) 1-3, Robert Street, Adelphi, WC2.
'architect; Thomas HOOD (1799-1845), poet; John GALSWORTHY (1867-1933), novelist and playwright; Sir James BARRIE (1860-1937), dramatist; and other eminent artists and writers lived here'
Robert Adam, born in Kirkcaldy, Scotland, and his brother James, were the architects responsible for the creation of ADELPHI TERRACE. Here many famous artists lived and worked including: David Garrick, Actor; Richard d'Oyly Carte, the Gilbert and Sullivan promotor; Thomas Hardy, novelist and George Bernard Shaw, following his marriage to Charlotte Payne-Townshend in 1898. The original London School of Economics and the Savage Club also occupied buildings in the Terrace which was demolished in 1936. Robert Adam was involved in the design of many of London's famous buildings including Fitzroy Square and Kenwood House in Hampstead. Adelphi Terrace was a speculative development which didn't sell as well as the brothers imagined. Down to very low finances they sold off portions by organising a lottery. Plaque erected 1950. Nearest tube station = Embankment.

ADAMS, Henry Brooks (1838-1918) 98, Portland Place, Marylebone, W1
'United States Embassy/Henry Brook ADAMS (1838-1918), US historian, lived here.'
Adams was born in Boston, the great-grandson of John Adams, the second president of the USA. He lived at Portland Place, between 1861 and 1868 during which time it was the United States Embassy and his father, Charles Francis ADAMS, was ambassador to Great Britain, appointed by President Lincoln at the time of the Civil War. Henry Adams wrote extensively on the association between art and religion, in the middle ages, and came to be regarded as an authority. Plaque erected 1978. Nearest tube station = Regent's Park.

ALEXANDER, Sir George (1858-1918) 57, Pont Street, Knightsbridge, SW1.
'actor-manager, lived here'
Alexander born in Reading, Berkshire, moved to Pont Street in 1896 and stayed until 1909. He is best remembered for the original productions of two great Oscar Wilde plays, "Lady Windermere's Fan" (1892) and "The Importance of Being Earnest" (1895). He also produced and acted in Pinero's, "The Second Mrs Tanquery". These productions took place at the St. James Theatre. As plain George Samson, he started out as an actor at the Adelphi Theatre. How or why he acquired the surname of Alexander isn't known. Plaque erected 1951. Nearest tube station = Knightsbridge.

ALLENBY, Field Marshal Edmund Henry Hynman, Viscount. (1881-1936)
24, Wetherby Gardens, South Kensington, SW5.
'lived here 1928-1936'
Allenby, born in London and educated at Haileybury and Sandhurst, lived here,
following his retirement from the army in 1928. Famous for his exploits during
WW1, when he commanded the British Expeditionary Force that invaded
Palestine and liberated Jerusalem from the Turks (with some help from
T.E.Lawrence). In 1919 he was created a Viscount and promoted to Field Marshal.
In the same year he was appointed High Commissioner for Egypt, a post he held
until 1925. Probably the most positive thing he ever did was to establish an aviary
in the garden of number 24. Plaque erected 1960. Nearest tube station =
Gloucester Road.

ALMA-TADEMA, Sir Laurence, OM (1836-1912) 44, Grove End Road,
St.John's Wood, NW8.
'painter, lived here 1886-1912'
Alma-Tadema was born in Dornrijp, Holland and studied art in Antwerp,
Belgium. He settled in England in 1870 and took British nationality. His
paintings, many of which are scenes from Greek and Roman mythology, are an
acquired taste. He is probably better known for the theatrical sets he created for
Actor/Manager, Henry Irving. Alma-Tadema spent a lot of time and money
restoring this house but the unusual features he created have been lost as the
house was converted into self contained flats shortly after WW2. However, the
front gate piers still have his initials intertwined. Plaque erected 1975. Nearest
tube station = St.John's Wood.

ARKWRIGHT, Sir Richard (1732-1792) 8, Adam Street, Aldwych, WC2.
'industrialist and inventor, lived here'
Arkwright, born in Preston, Lancashire was the youngest of the 13 children born
to his impoverished parents. He received no formal education but developed a
mechanical spinning process, in Nottingham, and patented it in 1769. His
invention provided the basis for mass production in the cotton industry and his
factory in Cromford was the first to use steam power. Whilst this meant new
employment for much of the working population of Lancashire, and a fortune for
himself, it also required additional slaves being despatched to the plantations of
the United States in order to produce more of the raw material. As time went on
the increased use of mechanical power lessened the need for manual labour in
the mills. In 1779, his large mill at Chorley was destroyed by an out of work mob.
He lived here from 1780 to 1789. Plaque erected 1984. Nearest tube station =
Embankment.

ARNE, Thomas (1710-1778) 31, King Street, Covent Garden, WC2.
'composer, lived here'
Arne, born in London and educated at Eton, wrote several operas, some with Shakespearean settings, which are rarely performed although his admirers describe his music as tuneful. His main claim to fame however is that he wrote the opera "Alfred" in which "Rule Britannia" features. In his opera 'Judith', it was the first time women appeared in a choir on stage. So far as King Street is concerned, modernists might care to know it is where the British Communist Party operated until recently. Arne's son Michael, (1740-1786) was also a musician and composer and wrote the song "Lass with the delicate air". Arne Senior lived here from 1760 to 1775. Plaque erected in 1988. Nearest tube station = Leicester Square.

ARNOLD, Sir Edwin (1832-1904) 31, Bolton Gardens, South Kensington, SW5.
'poet and journalist, lived and died here'
Arnold born in Gravesend, Kent spent the last ten years of his life in Bolton Gardens. In 1852 he won the Newdigate prize for poetry at Oxford and taught at King Edward's School, Birmingham. He became an exponent of Eastern culture and a devotee of Buddha. In 1879 he published "The Light of Asia", a blank verse poem which set down his thoughts and feelings for what was then an unknown culture. He was also responsible for translating into English much Oriental literature. Plaque erected 1931. Nearest tube station = Gloucester Road.

ARNOLD, Matthew (1822-1888) 2, Chester Square, Victoria, SW1.
'poet and critic, lived here'
Arnold was born in Laleham, nr Staines. His father Thomas, was the reforming headmaster of Rugby School (1827-42). Arnold, educated at Winchester, Rugby and Balliol College, Oxford won the Newdigate prize for poetry in 1843 with a poem about Cromwell. He was later acknowledged as a major figure in the English critical tradition. He held, "that only by an appreciation of poetry could the rising tide of Victorian materialism be curbed". His poems include, "The Scholar Gypsy" (1853) and "Thyrsis" (1866). His work "Essays in Criticism" published in two volumes 1865 and 1888 were especially admired. He acted as private secretary to Lord Lansdowne whilst he was President of The Council before becoming Professor of Poetry at Oxford (1857-1867). He lived here from 1871 to 1883. Plaque erected in 1954. Nearest tube station = Victoria.

ASHFIELD, Albert Henry Stanley, Lord Ashfield (1874-1948) 43, South Street, Mayfair, W1.
'first Chairman of London Transport, lived here'
Ashfield was born in Derby. Later his American father took the family to the States and Albert was educated at American colleges and technical schools. Prior to 1907 he was General Manager of U.S.Electric Railways then he voyaged to England to take up the post of General Manager of Metropolitan District Rail and Tube. In 1912 the whole system was re-organised and became known as London Transport; with Ashfield as Chairman. In 1926 he became a Peer and on occasion sat in the House of Lords. He lived here from 1930 to 1941 moving to the country when the German blitz on London started. Plaque erected 1984. Nearest Tube Station = Green Park.

ASQUITH, Herbert Henry, Earl of Oxford (1852-1928) 20, Cavendish Square, Marylebone, W1.
'statesman, lived here'
Asquith, together with his second wife Margot Tennant, lived here from 1895 to 1908. The house was later the home of the Cowdray Club and grew by the addition of two further floors. Asquith was born in Morley, Yorkshire and educated at the City of London School and Balliol College, Oxford. Before entering politics, he qualified and practised as a lawyer. As the Liberal Chancellor of the Exchequer, he introduced old-age pensions. He became Prime Minister in 1908 but resigned, in favour of Lloyd George, in 1916 following criticisms of his handling of World War One. He continued in politics until his bitter quarrel with Lloyd George over the 1926 General Strike. He completed his autobiography, "Memories and Reflections" a month before he died. Plaque erected in 1951. Nearest tube station = Oxford Circus.

ASTAFIEVA, Princess Seraphine (1876-1934) The Pheasantry, 152, King's Road, Chelsea, SW3.
'ballet dancer, lived and taught here'
Princess Astafieva, born in Tsarist Russia, lived and worked at the Pheasantry from 1918 onwards. She arrived in London, with Diaghilev, in 1910. Following her retirement from dancing, in 1913, she created a ballet school and her pupils included Markova, Dolin and Fonteyn. The Pheasantry is now a restaurant and office block. Plaque erected 1968. Nearest tube station = Sloane Square.

ASTOR, Nancy, (1879-1964) 4, St.James's Square, St.James's, SW1.
'first woman to sit in Parliament, lived here'
Nancy Astor lived here from 1919 to 1925. She was born in Danville, Virginia and had the good sense to marry into the Astor family which gave her priviledge and wealth. She accompanied her husband to London, when he was appointed to look after the family business, and became interested in British politics with the result that Nancy, in 1919, became the first woman to sit in the House of Commons. She influenced Conservative policy, mostly via the house parties she gave at Clivedon, her country house on the banks of the Thames in Berkshire. She became Lady Astor when her husband succeeded to the title of Viscount, originally granted to his grandfather. Lady Astor continued to sit in the Commons until 1945 and her verbal exchanges with Winston Churchill in particular, were a delight for members of all Parties. One of the best examples is when Astor claimed that "if Churchill were her husband she would poison his coffee," Churchill's reply of "Madam, If I were your husband I would drink it" brought the 'House' down. Plaque erected in 1987. Nearest tube station = Piccadilly.

ATTLEE, Richard Clement, (1883-1976) 17, Monkhams Avenue, Woodford Green, Essex.
'Prime Minister, lived here'
Attlee was born in Putney, London, and educated at Haileybury and University College, Oxford. He lived here prior to WW2. Prime Minister of the first post war government, he defeated Winston Churchill, in a Labour landslide in 1945, and put into effect a number of radical measures including the public ownership of The Bank of England, the coal mines, civil aviation, railways, steel, and road transport. In addition, the Health Service was introduced, India granted independence, Palestine evacuated, leading to the creation of the State of Israel and much else in one Parliament. Attlee had served in Cabinet during the 1924 and 1929 Labour governments and, during the war time coalition, was deputy Prime Minister. He retired in 1955 after losing the 1951 election. He became Lord Attlee and took an active part in the House of Lords until ill health forced him to bow out of active politics. During the Spanish civil war (1936-1939) he organised a British contingent, known as the 'Major Attlee Brigade' to fight on behalf of the Spanish government against Franco and the fascists. In 1954 he published his autobiography; "As It Happened". Plaque erected 1984. Nearest tube station = Woodford.

AVEBURY, Sir John Lubbock, Bt. (1834-1913) 29, Eaton Place, Belgravia, SW1.
'scientist, born here'
Avebury was born in London the son of the astronomer, Sir J. W. Lubbock. He left Eton at 14 and began a career that was the most varied imaginable. He started out as a banker, and was largely responsible for the reforms that led to the present system of bank accounts. He became a politician in 1870, and introduced Bank Holidays and the Shop Hours Act (1889). Then he achieved recognition as a naturalist when, in 1874, he published 'Origin and Metamorphoses of Insects.' Plaque erected 1935. Nearest tube station = Sloane Square.

BADEN-POWELL, Robert, (1857-1941), 9, Hyde Park Gate, Knightsbridge, SW7.
'Chief Scout of the World, lived here'
Baden-Powell lived at Hyde Park Gate, from 1860 to 1876. He was born in London the son of an Oxford professor of geometry. Educated at Charterhouse he joined the army at 19. Following his promotion to major-general, after the relief of Mafeking in 1900, he became interested in the welfare of young boys and as a result founded the Boy Scout movement in 1908, following publication of his book "Scouting for Boys". His work, rewarded by a baronetcy in 1909 and the OM in 1937, is now a world-wide organisation. The parallel organisation for girls was established in the UK in 1910. Baden-Powell died in Nyere, Kenya and is buried there. Plaque erected in 1972. Nearest tube station = High Street Kensington.

BAX, Arnold (1883-1953), 13, Pendennis Road, Streatham, SW16.
'Composer was born here'
Bax was born in London and studied piano at the Royal Acadamy of Music. He became an admirer of all things Celtic and this was apparant in his early compositions. He wrote seven symphonies that expressed a wide variety of moods. He also wrote a number of choral works especially 'Mater Ora Filium' (1921) . His tome poem "Tintagel" (1917) is still popular. He was appointed Master of the King's Musick in 1942 and knighted in 1950. His autobiography "Farewell my Youth" was published in 1943. Plaque erected 1993. Nearest Tube Station = Streatham

BAGEHOT, Walter, (1826-1877), 12, Upper Belgrave Street, Belgravia, SW1.
'writer, banker and economist, lived here'
Bagehot was born in Langport, Somerset and graduated in mathematics at University College, London. He was called to the bar in 1852 but didn't practise. He lived here for only nine years from 1861, but during this time he published his great classic on the interpretation of government, "The English Constitution". He wrote "Physics and Politics" in 1872 and was editor of "The Economist" (1860-1877). In 1870 he advocated the reform of the House of Lords by the creation of life peers. Of Queen Victoria he once said . . . "Magic should not be exposed to the light of day". How the present royals must wish this sentiment remained. Plaque erected 1967. Nearest tube station = Hyde Park.

BAILLIE, Joanna, (1762-1851), Bolton House, Windmill Hill, Hampstead, NW3.
'poet and dramatist, born 1762, died 1851, lived in this house for nearly fifty years'
Joanna Baillie, born in London, lived in this distinguished house for over fifty years. The commanding position provided one of the finest views of Old Hampstead and the sprawl of London beyond. She was only a minor literary figure but her house became one of the first literary salons in London. Wordsworth and Walter Scott were frequent visitors. Joanna Baillie had a small career as a playwright and one of her plays was performed by Sarah Siddons, the greatest actress of her day, at the Drury Lane Theatre. Plaque erected 1900. Nearest Tube Station = Hampstead.

BAIRD, John Logie, (1888-1946), 3, Crescent Wood Road, Sydenham, SE26. 'television pioneer, lived here' AND 22, Frith Street, Soho, W1. 'first demonstrated television in this house in 1926'
How many children rushing home from school to watch TV know what they owe to Baird. For that matter how many of their parents realise Baird is generally known as the Father of Television. He was born in Helensburgh, Scotland and studied electrical engineering at Glasgow University. Poor health forced him to live in the South, at Hastings, where he began his experiments. On Friday January 27 1926, he gave his first demonstration to 40 members of The British Institution in the attic of 22, Frith Street. He was 34. Following his successful demonstration, he received sufficient funds to continue his research. He set up the Baird Television Development Company Ltd, experimented with colour and transmitted trans Atlantic pictures. In 1932, Baird sold out to the BBC and, following his marriage to Margaret Albo, came to live in Crescent Wood Road remaining until his death in 1946. In 1939, Baird successfully demonstrated a TV transmission in colour. Baird, a great inventor and scientist never profited financially from his success or rewarded with a Peerage or The Order of Merit; all of which he richly deserved. Plaque erected 1977. Nearest station = Sydenham Hill; BR./Frith Street; Tottenham Court Road.

BAIRNSFATHER, Bruce (1888-1959) 1, Sterling Street, South Kensington, SW7.
'cartoonist, lived here'
Bairnsfather was born in Murree, India and probably had the oddest title in the British Army. During WW1, following recovery from wounds received at Ypres, Bairnsfather was promoted to Captain and created Officer-Cartoonist. He established the characters, "Old Bill" and "Bert and Alf", who were meant to typify soldiers fighting a war they no longer believed in. The magazine 'The Bystander' was the journal that published his cartoons during and after the war. His wartime characters carried over into civvy street and depicted the problems ex-servicemen had in finding jobs and homes. He lived and worked from Sterling Street from 1919 to 1921. During WW2 he was an official war cartoonist and attached to the US Army in Europe. Plaque erected 1981. Nearest tube station = Knightsbridge.

BALDWIN, Stanley (1867-1947) 93, Eaton Square, Belgravia, SW1.
'Earl Baldwin of Bewdley, Prime Minister, lived here'
Baldwin, born in Bewdley Shropshire and educated at Harrow and Trinity College, Cambridge lived at Eaton Square from 1913-1924. He moved from there to Downing Street, first at No. 11, when he became Conservative Chancellor of the Exchequer and then to No.10 in July 1923 when he succeeded Bonar Law as Prime Minister. He stayed on as Prime Minister for three terms before resigning in 1937. He mismanaged the abdication crisis involving Edward VIII and Mrs Simpson and didn't appear to have much appetite in curbing the rising tide of Fascism. His son, Oliver, in 1929 became a Labour MP whilst his father was Conservative prime minister. Plaque erected 1969 Nearest tube station = Sloane Square.

BALFE, Michael William (1808-1870) 12, Seymour Street, Marylebone, W1.
'musical composer, lived here'
Balfe born in Dublin came to England as a boy. He resided in Seymour Street
from 1861-1864. In 1843 he wrote what was to become his best known opera, "The
Bohemian Girl" followed by "The Puritan's Daughter", "Blanche de Nevers" and
"The Armourer of Nantes". His later operas failed to live up to his earlier
promise so he wisely invested the wealth he had earned from "The Bohemian
Girl" in a Hertfordshire estate from where he played the role of a gentleman
farmer. Plaque erected 1912. Nearest tube station = Edgware Road.

BALLANTYNE, Robert Michael (1825-1894) 'Duneaves', Mount Park Road,
Harrow, Middx.
'author of books for boys, lived here'
Ballantyne was born in Edinburgh and educated at Edinburgh Academy. He
went off to Canada and worked as a clerk in the Hudson Bay Company. He
returned in 1848 to Edinburgh and came South when his two sons went to Harrow
School. Ballantyne built 'Duneaves' and then spent the rest of his life churning
out children's books in a desperate attempt to pay the builders and school fees.
He died of overwork having written over 80 books in under 40 years. His only
work of note was "The Coral Academy" in 1857. Plaque erected 1979. Nearest tube
station = Harrow-on-the-Hill.

BANKS, Sir Joseph (1743-1820) 32, Soho Square, Soho, W1.
'President of the Royal Society; and Robert BROWN (1773-1858) and David
DON (1800-1841) botanists, lived in a house on this site. THE LINNEAAN
SOCIETY met here 1820-1857.'
Banks was born in London and went to both Harrow and Eton before Christ
Church College, Oxford. He became a naturalist who, when aged 24, accompanied
James Cook on his voyages to the South Pacific. In 1777, Banks moved into Soho
Square and established a varied collection on natural history subjects together
with an extensive library. He became President of the Royal Society in 1778.
Banks enjoyed eating and drinking too much, with the result, he died of an attack
of gout, following the shock of having his house attacked by rioters, protesting
against the Corn Laws. It was Banks who brought bread-fruit from Tahiti to the
West Indies. ROBERT BROWN, born in Montrose, Scotland, became an assistant
to Banks and accompanied Matthew Flinders on his voyage to Australia and on
his return invited DAVID DON to assist him. As a result Brown and Don formed
the Linneaan Society which continued meeting until 1857. 32 Soho Square was
demolished in 1936. Plaque erected 1938. Nearest tube station = Tottenham Court
Road.

BARLOW, William Henry (1812-1902) 'Highcombe', 145, Charlton Road, Charlton, SE7.
'Engineer lived and died here'
Born in London, Barlow was educated at the Engineering School of H.M.Dockyard, Woolwich. He worked for some time at the Ordnance factory, gaining practical experience before being seconded, by the Admiralty, to go to Turkey and work on their emerging engineering industry (1832). He returned to England in 1842 and took up the appointment of resident engineer to the Midlands Counties Railway. Barlow was responsible for creating a practical railway station from the eyesore of St.Pancras, originally envisaged as a cathedral. He had track laid, rebuilt much of the main building, and provided essential services in order to create a viable and valuable London railway station. He was a past president of the Institute of Civil Engineers and much admired by his colleagues. Plaque erected 1991. Nearest Station = Charlton

BARNADO, Dr Thomas John (1845-1905) 58, Solent House, Ben Jonson Road Tower Hamlets, E1.
'began his work for children in a building on this site in 1866'
Barnado, born in Dublin, is universally recognised as the man who, seeing the horrors of destitute children in London during the prosperous Victorian times, did something positive to alleviate their sufferings. He lectured, pleaded and demanded the aid that he thought was due. It resulted, in 1867, in the opening of the first Dr.Barnado's Home. Throughout his adult life Barnado's guiding principle was that no destitute child should ever be refused admission. Over the intervening years, hundreds of thousands of children have benefited from his original efforts. Today, all over the world, there are over a hundred homes catering for homeless and needy children. Plaque erected 1953. Nearest tube station = Stepney Green.

BARNETT, Dame Henrietta (1851-1936) Heath End House, Spaniards Road, Hampstead, NW3.
'founder of Hampstead Garden Suburb, and Canon Samuel BARNETT (1844-1913), social reformer, lived here'
Henrietta Barnett, born in London, was a visionary responsible for one of the most interesting and far reaching projects of her time. She imagined a residential suburb, in a country like atmosphere, where poor people from the slums of London could live and enjoy their environment. So the Hampstead Garden Suburb was created to greet the 20th century. She also opened a school. But a school with a difference, being a grammar school for girls. Today, Henrietta Barnett is one of the top girl's schools in Britain. Unfortunately the cottages are no longer rented at low affordable rents, they were sold off years ago and now change hands for sums to-day's poor could never hope to afford. The dream has gone but the result remains. Hampstead Garden Suburb is still there but it no longer serves the poor as Dame Henrietta envisaged. She lived here from 1910. Plaque erected 1983. Nearest tube station = Golder's Green.

BARRIE, Sir James, M. (1860-1937) 100, Bayswater Road, Bayswater, W2.
'novelist and dramatist, lived here'
Barrie was born in Kirriemuir, Scotland, the son of a weaver. He was educated at Dumfries Academy and Edinburgh University. After a stint of two years, in Nottingham as a journalist, Barrie came to London to work on the "St.James's Gazette". Barrie lived here from 1902 to 1909 and during this time, on his frequent walks in Kensington Gardens, he met the Llewelyn Davies boys who became his inspiration for "Peter Pan". This he wrote in 1904 whilst working in a small summer house sited at the bottom of his garden. Here he also wrote his well known play (later a popular film) "The Admirable Crichton". All the royalties earned from "Peter Pan" go to the Great Ormand Street Hospital for Sick Children. Plaque erected 1961. Nearest tube station = Lancaster Gate.

BARRY, Sir Charles (1795-1860) The Elms, Clapham Common North Side, Clapham, SW4.
'architect, lived and died here'
Barry, born in London and educated privately, became a leading architect and responsible for designing the Houses of Parliament (1840-1846), after the original building burnt down in 1834. During his period in Clapham, Barry also designed Pentonville Prison. Unfortunately the prison hasn't altered much since it was designed and still reflects the sanitation methods of Victorian times. Plaque erected 1950. Nearest tube station = Clapham Common.

BASEVI, George, (1794-1845) 17, Saville Row, Mayfair, W1.
'architect, lived here'
Basevi born in London lived in Saville Row from 1829-1845. He was a gifted architect whose most important commission led to his death. He designed the Fitzwilliam Museum in Cambridge and whilst on an inspection tour there, was asked to have a look at the bell-tower of nearby Ely Cathedral. Clambering around on the roof he slipped and fell to his death. His brother, Nathaniel (1792-1869), became the first Jewish born barrister to practise in England. Plaque erected 1949. Nearest tube station = Piccadilly.

BAYLIS, Lilian Mary (1874-1937) 27, Stockwell Park Road, SW9.
'manager of the Old Vic and Sadlers Wells Theatres, lived and died here'
Lilian Baylis was born in London the daughter of Jewish parents both of whom were musicians. The family emigrated to South Africa in 1890 where Lilian became a music teacher. In 1898 she returned to London to spend the rest of her working life in theatre management. After serving an apprenticeship under her aunt, Emma Cons, Lilian took over the running of The Old Vic in 1900. With that theatre well established, she turned her attention to the neglected Sadler's Wells Theatre which she re-opened in 1931 with a performance of Shakespeare's "Twelfth Night". That both theatres have managed to survive two world wars and countless recessions is a reflection of the strong foundations she laid. She lived here from 1917 to 1937. Plaque erected 1974. Nearest tube station = Stockwell

BAZALGETTE, Sir Joseph William (1819-1891) 17, Hamilton Terrace, St.John's Wood, NW8.
'civil engineer, lived here'
Bazalgette, born in London, was a very busy civil engineer. His biggest achievement was the design and build of London's drainage system. Over 80 miles long, it took ten years to complete but it has stood the test of time. With minimum additions and modernising it is still London's main system but is now considered to be in urgent need of major repair and overhaul. Bazalgette also constructed Putney and Battersea bridges and the Albert, Chelsea and Victoria Embankments. If he has descendants they are still able to see and use everything he built 100 years later. He was knighted in 1874 and lived here from 1879 to 1889. Plaque erected 1974. Nearest tube station = Maida Vale.

BEARD, John, (c1717-1791) Hampton Branch Library, Rose Hill, Hampton, Middx.
'singer'
No-one is certain the date of birth of John Beard who, after training as a singer at King's Chapel, decided to become an actor. He first appeared at Drury Lane Theatre as Sir John Loverule in "Devil to Pay" (1737). A couple of plays later and he decided to switch to his first love, singing. He appeared as Mackheath in the "Devil's Opera" at Covent Garden (1743). This became his favourite role and he never tired of it. In 1761, he gave up performing for management and took on the role as manager of the Covent Garden theatre until his retirement in 1780. Plaque erected 1992. Nearest Station = Hampton.

BEARDSLEY, Aubrey (1872-1898) 114, Cambridge Street, Belgravia, SW1.
'artist, lived here'
Beardsley was born in Brighton and only 26 when he died. During his short life he revolutionised the world of art. In particular, his sometimes grotesque black and white drawings brought the wrath of the establishment down upon him. The result was that he became close to Oscar Wilde and illustrated his "Salome". He later worked with Max Beerbohm to produce, in 1894, "The Yellow Book". Beardsley's work epitomized the onset of Art Nouveau. He lived here, with his sister, from 1893 and died from tuberculosis. Plaque erected 1948. Nearest tube station = Victoria.

BEAUFORT, Sir Francis (1774 1857) 51, Manchester Street, Marylebone, W1.
'admiral and hydrographer, lived here'
Everyone who goes to sea blesses Francis Beaufort, for it was he who gave the maritime world the method of measuring the force of wind velocity. From 0 for calm and to 12 for hurricane force, the "Beaufort Scale" is known throughout the world. Beaufort, born in Navan, County Meath joined the navy and became an admiral. Following a brilliant naval career during which time he saw much action in the wars against Spain, he decided to become a hydrographer and, in 1829, was appointed Hydrographer to the Royal Navy. He lived here from 1833-1854. Plaque erected 1959. Nearest tube station = Baker Street.

BEECHAM, Sir Thomas (1879-1961) 31, Grove End Road, St. John's Wood, NW8.
'conductor and impresario, lived here'
Beecham born in St. Helens, Lancs, was the son of the 'pill millionaire' and educated at Rossall School and Wadham College, Oxford. He decided against the family business and opted for music. His boisterous personality and sometimes outrageous statements caused thousands to listen to classical music who perhaps might not otherwise have done. As he didn't have to worry where his next penny was coming from he retained an independent attitude. He was an excellent musician who commanded and received respect from all who came under his conductor's baton. He founded two orchestras, The London Philharmonic in 1932 and the Royal Philharmonic in 1947; both are alive and doing well. He lived here after WW2. Plaque erected 1985. Nearest tube station = St. John's Wood

BEERBOHM, Sir Max (1872-1956) 57, Palace Garden's Terrace, Kensington, W8.
'artist and writer, born here'
Beerbohm was born here, the son of a Lithuanian corn merchant, and educated at Charterhouse and Merton College, Oxford. Following a literary career he succeeded Bernard Shaw as drama critic on the "Saturday Review". He is remembered as a co-founder of the elitist Aesthetic movement and dining night after night at the Cafe Royal in the company of such celebrities as Oscar Wilde and Aubrey Beardsley. After the death of these two friends he married Florence Kahn, the American actress, and lived for some time in Italy, before returning to England and a journalistic career that ignored the past and pursued the present. His only novel "Zuleika Dobson" (1912) was well received as were his radio programmes from 1935 to 1939. Like many other well known figures, longevity forgave an indiscreet youth. Plaque erected 1969. Nearest tube station = High Street Kensington.

BELLOC, Hilaire (1870-1953) 104, Cheyne Walk, Chelsea, SW3.
'poet, essayist and historian, lived here 1900-1905'
Belloc was born in France the son of a French barrister. He lived most of his life in England, where he became well known for his humorous writings. In 1906 he entered Parliament as a Liberal MP but in 1910 decided not to seek re-election. In marked contrast to his relaxed literary style and imaginative writings, e.g. "Cautionary Tales", were his outspoken attacks on Jews and Protestants whilst advocating his Roman Catholic beliefs. His comments demeaned him and somewhat diminished his appeal. He later wrote several books on French historical figures. Plaque erected 1973. Nearest tube station = South Kensington.

BENEDICT, Sir Julius (1804-1885) 2, Manchester Square, Marylebone, W1. 'musical composer, lived and died here'
Benedict was born in Stuttgart into a middle class Jewish family and studied music under Hummel and Weber. In 1836 he settled in London and lived here from 1845 until his death 40 years later. A musician and composer, his most successful work was the opera "The Lily of Killarney" which featured Jenny Lind. Following the London production, Benedict took the opera and Jenny Lind to the USA. In 1840, on the occasion of the first Reform synagogue in London, he set to music Psalm 84. He wrote the biographies of Mendelssohn (1853) and Carl von Weber (1881). He was knighted in 1871 for services to music. Plaque erected 1934. Nearest tube station = Baker Street

BENES, Dr Edward (1884-1948) 26, Gwendolian Avenue, Putney, SW15. 'President of Czechoslovakia, lived here'
Benes was born in Kozlany the son of a farmer. He qualified as a Doctor of Law in 1908. In 1918 he entered politics becoming President in 1935. Following his exile from Czechoslovakia in 1938, when Hitler and the Germans took over his country, Benes and his nephew came to live here. After the war he returned to Prague and in 1945 once again led his country. He resigned in 1948 when the Communist Party took over and died soon after by falling out of a window; or was he pushed? To-day his country has embraced Capitalism and is no longer united. It has been split in two in order for the Czechs and the Slovacks to develop independently from one another. Benes must be turning in his grave. Plaque erected 1978 Nearest station = East Putney.

BEN-GURION, David (1886-1973) 75, Warrington Crescent, Maida Vale W9. 'first Prime Minister of Israel, lived here'
Ben-Gurion was born David Green in Plonsk, Poland. During WW1 he was active in raising the Jewish Legion that fought with the Allies and in which he served. After WW1, Ben-Gurion lived here whilst attempting to persuade the British government to honour the Balfour Declaration and create a Jewish State. His plea fell on deaf ears. Not until a quarter of a century later, the death of six million Jews and demands from the United Nations did the British Government give up their Mandate and leave the way clear for the creation, in 1948, of The State of Israel. Ben-Gurion became it's first Prime Minister, in a Labour party administration. Except for a two year break, 1953-5, he remained PM until his retirement to his kibbutz in 1963. Plaque erected 1986. Nearest tube station = Warwick Avenue.

BENNETT, Arnold (1867-1931) 75, Cadogan Square, Belgravia, SW1.
'novelist, lived here'
Bennett was born in Hanley, Staffordshire the son of a solicitor. He was educated locally and at London University. He started as a solicitor's clerk but took up journalism before turning to writing books. He made enough money from his two novels, "The Old Wives Tales" and "Anna of the Five Towns" to afford a lease on 75, Cadogan Square. This was in 1922. The idyll lasted until the lease ran out in 1930 at which time he and his mistress, the actress Dorothy Cheston, together with their daughter, moved to Chiltern Court; a bright new block of flats developed by London Transport over Baker Street underground station. He wrote many of the favourite stories of the first half of the 20th century and still found time to work as a critic under the name "Jacob Tonson" for the journal "New Age". His final novel, "Imperial Palace", was published a week before his death. Plaque erected 1958. Nearest tube station = Knightsbridge.

BENTHAM, George (1800-1884) 25, Wilton Place, Belgravia, SW1.
'botanist, lived here'
Bentham born in Stoke, Plymouth was the nephew of Jeremy Bentham the boy wonder who entered Queen's College, Oxford when only 12 and admitted to Lincoln's Inn at 15. George was secretary to his uncle before leaving to pursue his career as a botanist. He lived here for the last twenty years of a long and distinguished life. A botanical expert, Bentham was one of the leading advisors to Kew Gardens and his contribution to an encyclopedia of all known flowering plants of the greatest importance. In 1858 he published "The Handbook of British Flora" a best seller in its' day. Plaque erected 1978. Nearest tube station = Hyde Park Corner.

BENTLEY, John Francis (1839-1902) 43, Old Town, Clapham, SW4.
'architect, lived here'
Bentley lived here between 1876 and 1894. Born in London he was an architect who specialised in designing churches. Whilst living in Clapham he designed his best known work, Westminster Cathedral. Plaque erected 1950. Nearest tube station = Clapham Common.

BERLIOZ, Hector (1803-1869) 58, Queen Anne Street, Marylebone, W1.
'composer, stayed here in 1851'
Berlioz didn't exactly live here, he stayed for a few months, in 1851 whilst acting as a judge of musical instruments being presented during the Great Exhibition. This house was also home to the Beethoven Quartet Society and Berlioz was reported as "hugely enjoying myself with wonderful music and poisoning myself with terrible food". Berlioz, born in Cote-Saint-Andre, was French not only in gastronomic terms but also as the exponent of French romantic music. His best known work is probably "Symphonie Fantastique". Plaque erected 1969. Nearest tube station = Bond Street.

BESANT, Annie (1847-1933) 39, Colby Road, Dulwich, SE19.
'social reformer, lived here in 1874'
Annie Besant, nee Wood, was born in London of Irish parents. She was tried for immorality, following publication in 1877, of a pamphlet on birth control. She was acquitted. Earlier, in 1873, she lost her religious faith and left her vicar husband to his church in Sibsey, Lincolnshire and moved into Colby Road. She didn't stay long, just long enough to write the "Gospel of Atheism", before moving on to India to preach Theosophy. She joined the Fabian Society, was present during the Trafalgar Square riot of 1886 and organised the Matchmakers strike a year later. Annie Besant was a social reformer ahead of her time. Plaque erected 1963. Nearest station = Gypsy Hill.

BESANT, Sir Walter (1836-1901) Frognal End, Frognal Gardens, Hampstead, NW3.
'novelist and antiquary, lived and died here'
Besant was Annie Besant's brother-in-law. Born in Portsmouth he studied at King's College, London and Christ's College, Cambridge. He is best remembered for founding "The Society of Authors" and the magazine "Author" which he edited. He also specialised in novels with an historical slant . Another interest was his house at Frognal which he built in 1893. On the fanlight of his study he had written "Work while it is day, for the night cometh when no man can work". In 1887, following his pleas for social change, the 'People's Palace' opened in East London as a place for popular recreation. Plaque erected 1925. Nearest tube station = Hampstead.

BLIGH, William (1754-1817) 100, Lambeth Road, Lambeth, SE1.
'Commander of the "Bounty", lived here'
Bligh was born in Plymouth the son of a Customs officer and went to sea at 15. Bligh of the 'Bounty'. Blessed by actors Charles Laughton, Trevor Howard and Anthony Hopkins. The mutiny however happened five years before Bligh and his family moved into Lambeth Road in 1794. Bligh has, in every film to a greater or lesser degree, been shown to be cruel and sadistic. What the films failed to show was that the times were cruel. In reality, and without the navigational aids seamen now have, Bligh brilliantly and successfully navigated dangerous seas, without charts or compass. In a period of three months he covered 4,000 miles, an achievement never equalled; given the same circumstances. He is buried in St. Mary's Lambeth. Plaque erected 1952. Nearest tube station = Lambeth North.

BLISS, Arthur (1891-1975) East Heath Lodge, 1 East Heath Road, Hampstead, NW3
'Composer lived here'
Bliss was born in London and studied at the Royal college of music under Holst, Stanford and others. He served in WW1 after which he became professor of composition at his old college. He resigned to become director of music at the BBC (1942-4). He wrote the film music for HG Wells' "Things to Come". He wrote the ballet "Checkmate" (1937). Following the death of Arnold Bax he was appointed Master of the Queen's Musick and knighted in 1960. Plaque erected 1993. Nearest tube station = Hampstead

BLUMLEIN, Alan Dower (1903-1942) 37, The Ridings, Ealing, W5.
'electronics engineer and inventor, lived here'
Blumlein, born in London, lived here during the Thirties. He was an inventor
who died a hero's death. During WW2 he invented an extension of Radar. It
meant that RAF Bomber Command could, by use of the radar map Blumlein
developed, accurately pinpoint enemy targets. Whilst testing his project in battle
conditions, his Halifax bomber was shot down when returning from a raid over
Germany. Plaque erected 1977. Nearest tube station = Hanger Lane.

**BLUNT, Wilfred Scawen (1840-1922) 15, Buckingham Gate, Belgravia,
SW1.**
**'diplomat, poet and traveller, founder of Crabbet Park Arabian stud, lived
here'**
Blunt was born in Petworth, Sussex. Although known for his travel writing and
anti-imperialist propaganda, he is best remembered for his poetry particularly,
"Love Sonnets of Proteus", published in 1880. He travelled throughout the Near
and Middle East and promoted the cause of Egyptian nationalism. In 1858, he
married Anne Noel and they began breeding horses here. Plaque erected 1979.
Nearest tube station = St. James's Park.

**BONAR LAW, Andrew (1858-1923) 24, Onslow Gardens, South Kensington,
SW7.**
'Prime Minister, lived here'
Bonar Law was born in Canada. Educated in Glasgow he became an iron
merchant before entering parliament. He became Leader of the House of
Commons when Balfour resigned in 1911. He served in the coalition governments
under Lloyd George 1915-1921, eventually succeeding him as Prime Minister in
1922. In 1923 he resigned because of ill health and moved to Onslow Gardens
where he died a few months later. Plaque erected 1958. Nearest tube station =
South Kensington.

BOOTH, Charles (1840-1916) 6, Grenville Place, South Kensington, SW7.
'pioneer in social research, lived here'
Booth was born in Liverpool but settled in London in 1875. It was whilst living in
Grenville Place, 1875-1890, that Charles Booth undertook his great research into
the poverty and deprivation that permeated London. A 17 volume work entitled,
"Life and Labour of the People of London", was published 1891-3. Booth, after
researching some 4,000 cases, concluded that the cause of poverty due to low or
irregular wages was 62%; illness or large families was 23%; and squandered on
drink or refusing to work was 15%. What would have Booth made of the Tory
government's rejection in 1993 of the Common Market's Social Charter and the
principal of a minimum wage and maximum hours? He was a Privy Councillor
and married to Mary Macaulay, the niece of the historian. Plaque erected 1951.
Nearest tube station = Gloucester Road.

BORROW, George (1803-1881) 22, Hereford Square, South Kensington, SW7.
'author, lived here'
Borrow was born in East Dereham, Norfolk, the son of an army recruiting officer working on commission. Educated at Norwich Grammar School Borrow eventually became a well known novelist using Gypsies as his main theme e.g., "The Bible in Spain", 1843, "The Romany Rye" 1857. In 1860, he and his family left the Norwich area for London and Hereford Square. It was a mistake, his literary output suffered as did his health and wealth (and the wealth of his wife). He became an agent for the British and Foreign Bible Society and used their funds to travel Europe but he was a poor salesman. In 1872 he cried quits, rented out the house and returned to East Anglia. Plaque erected 1911. Nearest tube station = Gloucester Road.

BOSWELL, James (1740-1795) 122, Great Portland Street, Marylebone, W1.
'biographer, lived and died in a house on this site'
Boswell was born in Edinburgh the eldest son of Judge Lord Auchinleck. He was educated privately and at the University of Edinburgh before studying law at Glasgow. Probably the most famous biographer who has ever lived and published. Boswell is synonymous with Johnson. They go together like strawberries and cream or Laurel and Hardy. Boswell lived and worked in Edinburgh and only saw Johnson when he came South. He was the original gatecrasher of social events. He had many love affairs including one with Rousseau's mistress, Therese Le Vasseur before finally marrying, in 1769, his cousin, Margaret Montgomerie. It wasn't until Johnson was dead did Boswell move to London and Great Portland Street. He spent the last five years of his life here and used the first two to write his, "Life of Johnson". That task completed, he spent his time and money drinking to excess. Thomas Carlyle was particularly scathing in his opinion of Boswell ". . . a wine bibber and gross liver. . . vain, heedless a babbler". Boswell was the perfect example of how you can't please all of the people . . . In 1927 additional manuscripts by Boswell were found at Malahide Castle in Ireland. . . Plaque erected 1936. Nearest tube station = Regent's Park.

BOW STREET, 19-20 , Bow Street, Covent Garden, WC2.
Bow Street is now most famous for its' Magistrates Court, the venue where many well known people have been arraigned. Bow Street was thus named because the street is bent like a bow. The houses of Bow Street, during the 17th and 18th centuries, were where many notables lived and worked. Probably the best known resident was Henry Fielding who, besides being a famous novelist, was a magistrate who created the Bow Street Runners. At No 1 Bow Street was "Wills Coffee House" a venue that attracted many of the intelligentsia of the day. Dryden and Macaulay and others spent much time eating, drinking, discussing and debating issues of the day. Plaque erected 1929. Nearest tube station = Covent Garden.

BRADLAUGH, Charles (1833-1891) 29, Turner Street, Stepney, E1.
'advocate of free thought, lived here 1870-1877'
Bradlaugh was born in London and self educated. He lived here, in an East End slum. Long before it became fashionable Bradlaugh, an associate of Annie Besant, was fighting for women's suffrage and urging birth control. He was an ardent advocate of trade unionism and social reform and hated by the church, who objected to his work in opposing the blasphemy laws. In 1880 he was elected MP for Northampton but as he refused to take the oath he wasn't allowed to take his seat. He regularly stood for Northampton was elected and expelled. In 1886 he relented, took the oath and annoyed the House by his pleas for birth control to be legal practise. Plaque erected 1961. Nearest tube station = Whitechapel.

BRAILSFORD, Henry Noel (1873-1958) 37, Belsize Park Gardens, Hampstead, NW3.
'writer, champion of equality and free humanity, lived here'
Brailsford was born in Yorkshire and completed his education at Glasgow University. He later joined the staff of his college as assistant professor of Logic. In 1897 he left to join the Greek Foreign Legion in the war with Turkey. He describes his experiences in, 'The Broom of the War God', (1898). He was an international socialist and joined the Independent Labour Party. He edited 'The New Leader' (1922-1926) and became a leader-writer on such papers as 'The Guardian' and 'The Daily Herald'. He wrote books on several subjects connected with International socialism. He lived here after WW2. Plaque erected 1983. Nearest Tube Station = Belsize Park.

BRANGWYN, Sir Frank (1867-1956) Temple Lodge, 51, Queen Caroline Street, Hammersmith, W6.
'artist, lived here'
Brangwyn was born in Bruges, Belgium and after an English education was apprenticed to William Morris for four years. He then travelled the world and on his return concentrated on painting murals. His best known work is 'British Empire Panels' (1925), commissioned for the House of Lords. These were rejected by their Lordships and now rest at the Guildhall, Swansea. There is a Brangwyn museum in Bruges. He lived here from 1923 to 1937. Plaque erected 1989. Nearest tube station = Hammersmith.

BRIDGE, Frank (1879-1941) 4, Bedford Gardens, Kensington, W8.
'composer and musician, lived here'
Bridge was born in Brighton, Sussex and trained under Stanford. He played the viola in many leading orchestras until appointed to conduct the New Symphony Orchestra, from its inception at Covent Garden. He often conducted the Proms and held master classes. One of his better known pupils was Benjamin Britten. He lived here from 1924 to 1932 and his best known work is his 'Sea Suite'. Plaque erected 1989. Nearest tube station = Kensington, High Street.

BRIDGEMAN, Charles 54, Broadwick Street, Soho, W1.
'landscape gardener, lived here 1723-1738'
Charles Bridgeman's date of birth and parentage is unknown. It is thought that his father might have been 'old Charles Bridgeman', head gardener at Wimpole. What is known is that young Charles worked and lived on the estate of Robert Harley, 1st Earl of Oxford, and later became his protege. In 1717 Bridgeman married Sarah the daughter of John Mist, the King's Pavior, and from here onwards he began to secure positions that soon brought him into great demand as a landscaper. He became known as 'The Heroic Poet' for the manner in which he cast aside old ideas for new. He banished verdant sculpture, so long the stand by for formal gardens. He introduced areas of wilderness within those formal parts. He preferred open gardens to walled gardens and in pursuance introduced the Ha! Ha!, a device that opened the way to true landscape gardening. The great Ha Ha at Stowe (1725), is a good example. Bridgeman was an artist and accepted as such by more conventional artists. His great works include, Marble Hill, Twickenham (1724). King's College, Cambridge (1725). Compton Place, Sussex (1728) and Wibledon House (1732-1735). For all his talent the financial rewards were meagre. He never received more than £150 for a commission that would involve an enormous amount of work designing, supervising and controlling. Eventually he became Surveyor to the Royal Gardens at a salary of £2,200 p.a. and a house at Hampton Court. Plaque erected 1984. Nearest tube station = Tottenham Court Road.

BRIGHT, Sir Richard (1789-1858) 11, Saville Row, Mayfair, W1.
'physician, lived here'
Bright was born in Bristol and studied at Edinburgh, London, Berlin and Vienna. If it's an honour to be remembered for having a disease named after you then Sir Richard Bright is one of a select few. Bright's Disease, a malfunction of the kidneys, is still around and Bright who lived here from 1830 until his death, did a lot of his research on the fourth floor he built as his scientific workshop. In 1818 he published, 'Travels from Vienna through Lower Hungary', an account of Gypsy living. Plaque erected 1979. Nearest tube station = Bond Street

BROOKE, Sir Charles Vyner (1874-1963) 13, Albion Street, Bayswater, W2.
'last Rajah of Sarawak, lived here'
Brooke's Great Uncle was Sir James Brooke, better known as the White Rajah of Sarawak, a British colony over which Brooke ruled as though he owned it. In some peculiar way he did, for after helping the Sultan to suppress a revolt, the area was ceded to Brooke and the colony downgraded to a Protectorate. It enabled the Brooke family to amass a great fortune from bauxite and rubber. Sir Charles, born in London, whose father had changed his name from Johnson to Brooke upon his inheritance, continued the family tradition until 1946 when the Malayan troubles broke out and the fighting reached Sarawak. Brooke promptly handed the place back to the British Government and returned to London leaving the British Army to fight the Communists who reckoned they could run the place better than the Brookes' family. Plaque erected 1983. Nearest tube station = Lancaster Gate.

BROWN, Ford Maddox (1821-1893) 56, Fortess Road, Kentish Town, NW5.
'painter, lived here'
Brown was born in Calais, France but his two most famous paintings are associated with England. "Work", showing a Hampstead street scene and "The Last of England". He lived here for 6 years, from 1856 and during this period he gave freely of his time to the newly emerging Working Men's Colleges, founded by his friend F. D. Maurice. Just before his death, he completed twelve frescoes for Manchester Town Hall. Plaque erected 1976. Nearest tube station = Tufnell Park.

BROWNING, Elizabeth Barrett (1806-1861) 99, Gloucester Place, Marylebone, W1.
'poet, lived here' AND AT,
50, Wimpole Street, Marylebone, W1.
'poet, lived in a house on this site 1838-1846'
Elizabeth Barrett was born in Coxhoe Hall, Durham but brought up in Herefordshire. The family lived at 50, Wimpole Street (since redeveloped). As depicted in the film, "The Barretts of Wimpole Street" her tyrannical father, played by Charles Laughton, forbade his invalid poet daughter, played by Norma Shearer, from marrying Robert Browning, played by Fredric March. But marry they did, in 1846, and went off to live in Florence from where she published, "Sonnets from the Portuguese", a series of love poems to Robert, six years her junior. Later, together with their son they lived for a brief time at Gloucester Place. Her book, 'Poems', included a poem called, 'The Cry of the Children', a protest against the employment of young children in factories. Plaque erected 1924. Nearest tube stations, Wimpole Street = Regent's Park. Gloucester Place = Marble Arch.

BRUMMELL, George Bryan (Beau) (1778-1840) 4, Chesterfield Street, Mayfair, W1.
'leader of fashion, lived here'
George Bryan Brummell was born in London the son of Frederick Brummell, secretary to Lord North. Educated at Eton and Oxford Brummell adopted the forename of Beau and Beau Brummell was, in his day, the arbiter of men's fashion. He was fortunate in having the Prince Regent, who later became George IV when his lunatic father eventually died, as his close associate. This opened all doors and Beau became rich and popular and he lived here during this time. Unfortunately it all went to his head and he became pompous and conceited. His world ended when he lost the patronage of George and the rest of the Royal Court snubbed him. He lost his fortune gambling and died in a pauper's lunatic asylum at Bon Sauveur in Caen, France. Plaque erected 1984. Nearest tube station = Green Park

BRUNEL, Sir Marc Isambard (1769-1849) 98, Cheyne Walk, Chelsea, SW3.
'and Isambard Kingdom BRUNEL, (1806-1859), civil engineers, lived here'
Marc was born in Hacqueville, near Rouen and during the French Revolution
escaped to America in 1793. He returned to Europe in 1799 married and settled in
London. Isambard arrived six years later in Portsmouth. The Brunels began
living in Chelsea in 1808. At the time Marc was working for the Admiralty but he
got involved in commerce with the result he became bankrupt and imprisoned
for debt (1814). Thanks to a gift of £5,000, from the Duke of Wellington, Brunel
cleared his debts, stayed in England, instead of taking a job in Russia and
together with his son built the Rotherhithe Tunnel under the Thames. They went
to New York and built the Bowery Theatre. Later, Isambard Kingdom built much
of the Great Western Railway and designed some of the biggest steamships of the
day viz, "The Great Western" 1838 and "The Great Eastern" 1858. He also built
the Clifton suspension bridge at Bristol as well as the docks there and at Cardiff
and Milford Haven. Plaque erected 1954. Nearest tube station = Sloane Square.

BURGOYNE, General John (1722-1792) 10, Hertford Street, Mayfair, W1.
'lived and died here'
Burgoyne was born in London and educated at Westminster School. He spurned
university for the Army and in 1740 purchased a commission. He had the most
varied life imaginable. It encompassed the Army, Parliament as an MP, Theatre
as a playwright and a leader of London's social life. As an Army general he is best
remembered as the British General who was defeated at Saratoga during the
American War of Independence (1777). On a happier note, he wrote two
successful plays, both produced by David Garrick. "Maid of the Oaks" in 1775 and
the "Heiress", in 1786. It didn't exactly harm his career by marrying into the
Derby family, albeit not with their immediate approval having eloped with their
daughter in 1743, long before his exploits revealed himself as an admirable son-in-
law. Plaque erected 1954. Nearest tube station = Green Park

BURKE, Edmund (1729-1797) 37, Gerrard Street, Soho, W1.
'author and statesman , lived here'
Burke was born in Dublin and educated at a Quaker boarding school before
graduating from Trinity College, Dublin. He only spent 3 years here in Gerrard
Street, but they were very important years. During this time he was heavily
involved with bringing impeachment proceedings against Warren Hastings. He
broke with the Whig party in 1791 over the French Revolution, which he
denounced in his book, "Reflections on the Revolution in France" (1790). He
wrote much and with a common theme; advocating wise and liberal measures.
He ranks as a foremost political thinker who had the misfortune to be poor. He
must be especially remembered for the manner with which he reduced
Bolingbrooke's ideas of society to one of, 'reductio and absurdum', in his
'Vindication of Natural Society' (1756). Gerrard Street is now the centre of
London's thriving Chinese community. Plaque erected 1876. Nearest tube station
= Piccadilly Circus.

BURNETT, Frances Hodgson (1849-1924) 63, Portland Place, Marylebone, W1.
'writer, lived here'
Frances Burnett nee, Hodgson, although known as an American writer, was born in Manchester. Her family emigrated to Tennessee in 1865 but she returned to England and Portland Place in 1893. Her most famous novel was, "Little Lord Fauntleroy" (1886), followed by, "The Little Princess (1905) and "The Secret Garden" (1909). She later divorced her husband and became famous for her lavish parties and intelligent guests. Plaque erected 1979. Nearest tube station = Regent's Park.

BURNEY, Fanny (Madame D'Arbly), 11, Bolton Street, Mayfair, W1.
'authoress, lived here. Born 1752, died 1840'
Fanny Burney was born in King's Lynn, Norfolk and educated herself by reading English and French literature and by observing the distinguished people who frequently visited her father. Her most famous novel was "Evelina" (1778). It was published anonymously but recognised by her father. The book, describing a country girl's introduction to court, was a great success and her father, together with Dr. Johnson, persuaded her to continue writing. She wrote many more books but none lived up to her original promise. She married the French Count D'Arbly in 1793 but continued writing. Her book 'Letters and Diaries' (1846) published after her death showed great ability in reporting events of the day. She lived here from 1818 to 1826. Plaque erected 1885. Nearest tube station = Green Park.

BURNS, John (1858-1943) 110, North Side, Clapham Common, SW4.
'statesman, lived here'
Burns was born in London of Scottish parents. He began work as an engineer, before socialist politics took over his life and he became a labour leader. He led the great docks strike of 1889, in support of a minimum wage of 6d an hour. He was MP for Battersea 1892-1918. He became a cabinet minister in the Liberal government of Campbell Bannerman but resigned because he was opposed to the 1914 declaration of war against Germany. It is ironic perhaps that he died in 1943 as a direct result of a German air raid, near his home. Burns had the distinction of being the first working class man to become a cabinet minister. He lived here from 1914. Plaque erected 1950. Nearest tube station = Clapham Common.

BUTT, Dame Clara (1873-1937) 7, Harley Road, Hampstead, NW3.
'singer, lived here 1901-1929'
Clara Butt was born in Southwick, London and became one of the most famous singers of her day. She and her husband, Robert Rumford, built the house at Harley Road in 1901 after Dame Clara had taken London by storm in Elgar's "Sea Pictures" especially written for her. Her most famous piece was her rendering of "Abide With Me" which was constantly in demand. She was created a Dame on the insistence of Queen Mary, wife of George V and grandmother of the present Queen. Plaque erected 1969. Nearest tube station = Swiss Cottage.

BUTTERFIELD, William (1814-1900) 42, Bedford Square, Bloomsbury, WC1.
'architect, lived here'
Butterfield born in London, became, a leading architect and moved here in 1886 appreciative that here was a style he could live and work in. He specialised in building churches and his two most famous are still to be seen and appreciated. All Saints', in Margaret Street behind Oxford Street and St. Augustine, at Queen's Gate. He was also responsible for many controversial restorations which, when he had finished with them, were barely recognisable. Associated with the Oxford Movement he was an ardent advocate of a Gothic revival. Plaque erected 1978. Nearest tube station = Tottenham Court Road.

CALDECOTT, Randolph (1846-1886) 46, Great Russell Street, Bloomsbury, WC2.
'artist and book illustrator, lived here'
Caldecott left his native Manchester as a young man, where he was working as a bank clerk, for London and lived in Great Russell Street for many years. He gradually created a name for himself as an illustrator of books, particularly children's books. He published two every year for the last ten years of his short life. Since 1938, the Caldecott Medal has been awarded annually to the best American artist-illustrator of children's books. Plaque erected 1977. Nearest tube station = Tottenham Court Road.

CAMPBELL, Colen (1676-1729) 76, Brook Street, Mayfair, W1.
'architect and author of "Vitruvius Britannicus", lived and died here'
Campbell was born in Argyll, Scotland and spent the last three years of his life here. The house went with the job. It was owned by Sir Richard Grosvenor and Campbell was his architect working on the great Mayfair estate. Not that Campbell couldn't have afforded to buy a house for himself. He was one of the earliest architects who made sure that whilst designing large houses for the wealthy his fees were of the same dimensions. He built all over the country, Shawfield Mansion, Glasgow: Merewith Castle, Kent; Stourhead, Wiltshire and much more. He also found time to write and compile a book on Roman architecture in Britain. "Vitruvius Britannicus" (1712). Plaque erected 1977. Nearest tube station = Bond Street.

CAMPBELL-BANNERMAN, Sir Henry (1836-1908) 6, Grosvenor Place, Belgravia, SW1.
'Prime Minister, lived here'
Campbell-Bannerman born in Glasgow and educated at Trinity College, Cambridge, lived here, 1877-1904. During this time he held many high offices of state and only left Grosvenor Place to take up residence at 10, Downing Street. There, as Prime Minister, he oversaw the independance of South Africa and sought to minimise the great differences that occurred between Parliament and The Lords. Ill health caused him to resign as Prime Minister on April 4th 1904 and he died a week later. He was 36 when he added Bannerman to his name. Plaque erected 1959. Nearest tube station = Hyde Park Corner.

CANAL, Antonio (Canaletto) (1697-1768) 41, Beak Street, Soho, W1.
'Venetian painter, lived here'
When Canaletto, born in Venice, lived in London between 1746 and 1756 Beak Street didn't exist. This spot was known as Silver Street and renamed Beak Street some years later. However, London and England didn't appear to do a lot for the artist. His style became stilted and didn't recover until he visited Dresden and Warsaw and returned to Venice. The best selection of his paintings are to be seen in the Queen's Collection. Plaque erected 1925. Nearest tube station = Piccadilly.

CANNING, George (1770-1827) 50, Berkeley Square, Mayfair, W1.
'statesman, lived here'
Canning was born in London the son of a pauper who died when George was a year old. Fortunately he had a rich uncle who had him educated at Eton followed by Christ Church, Oxford. A leading light in the Tory party, Canning spent many years as foreign secretary. During this time he organised the defeat of the Danish fleet in 1807 and later advocated free trade and Catholic emancipation. He became Prime Minister in 1827 and died in office. He only lived here for a year as he claimed the place was haunted. Plaque erected 1979. Nearest tube station = Green Park.

CARLILE, Wilson, Prebendary (1847-1942) 34, Sheffield Terrace, Kensington, W8.
'founder of the Church Army, lived here'
Carlile was born in Buxton, Derbyshire. He founded the Church Army in an effort to relieve the suffering of tramps and ex-prisoners in an evangelistic atmosphere. He established homes and training centres all over the country and lived at Sheffield Terrace 1881-1891, an area of affluence that was in sharp contrast to the districts housing his down and outs. Plaque erected 1972. Nearest tube station = Notting Hill Gate.

CARLYLE, Thomas (1795-1881) 33, Ampton Street, Bloomsbury, WC1.
'essayist and historian, lived here'
Carlyle was born in Ecclefechan, Dunfries the son of a strict Calvinist stonemason. He was educated at the village school and Edinburgh University. He would today be termed an "oddbod". There is no doubt that in his time he was held in high esteem as a philosopher and historian but he distrusted democracy and his views as expressed in "French Revolution", 1837 were unfortunate. His strange ideas were continued in, "Heroes and Hero Worship", 1841. In "Past and Present" 1843, he wrote an account of how the Jews of Bury St Edmonds were exploited and murdered in 1190, the first revelation of such facts. Carlyle lived at Ampton Street for only a short while before moving to 24, CHEYNE ROW, SW3 in 1834. Here he continued to live and work until, in 1863, his wife Jane was knocked down by a carriage and left bedridden until she died in 1866. For the last fifteen years of his life Carlyle continued living in Cheyne Row but he was a lonely sad man who had lost the will to live. The house in Cheyne Row was taken over by the National Trust to prevent it falling into disrepair. Plaque erected 1907. Nearest tube stations/Ampton Street = King's Cross and Cheyne Row = Sloane Square.

CASLON, William (1692-1766) 23, Chiswell Street, Finsbury, EC1.
'the foundry established by William Caslon, typefounder stood on this site 1737-1909'
Caslon was born in Cradley, Worcestershire. Until the end of the 18th century printers were still using Caslon's types for printing based on the early Dutch style. Here was where Caslon had his foundry and a house at the rear. The foundry continued long after his death and the building survived until demolished in an air-raid during WW2. Plaque erected 1958. Nearest tube station = Old Street.

CASTLEREAGH, Viscount (1769-1822) Loring Hall, Water Lane, North Cray.
'statesman, lived and died here'
Castlereagh was born in Ireland and educated in Armagh and Cambridge where he was sent down after a year. He became prominent in politics during the Napoleonic wars and served Conservative interests provided they didn't conflict with his own. He fought a duel with George Canning, who supported Catholic emancipation, and was slightly wounded. The present troubles in Northern Ireland are a direct result of Castlereagh's evil influences. In 1807 he became War Minister and responsible for the ill fated Walcheren expedition. He committed suicide whilst in office as foreign secretary. He was so disliked that when his coffin was being carried into Westminster Abbey there were shouts of gladness from the crowd. Plaque erected in 1989.

THE CATO STREET CONSPIRACY, February 23rd 1820. Discovered at 1a, Cato Street, Paddington, W1.
'discovered here, 23 February 1820'
The years, following the Napoleonic wars, were hard on the working population. Through the influence of the Duke of Wellington, harsh measures were brought about which led Arthur Thistlewood, born in Lincoln (and whose name should have been added to this plaque) to organise a revolution, in order to achieve aid for the poor and alleviate their sufferings. Thistlewood hatched his plan to fellow conspirators at a house in Cato Street. There he explained how they would murder as many members of the Cabinet as possible, as they met at the home of Lord Harrowby at 44, Grosvenor Square, W1, on the evening of February 23. In the event, they were betrayed by a paid police informer, and as a result, the police (Bow Street Runners) arrested the group in Cato Street, before they could achieve their objective. One of the Cabinet they were after was the notorious Castlereagh. The trial did not bring credit on the British legal system, the conspirators were accused of treason but did not receive a fair trial. They were refused permission to appeal their harsh sentences and Thistlewood and four others were hanged. The remainder were transported to Australia. Plaque erected 1977. Nearest tube station = Edgware Road.

CAVELL, Edith (1865-1915) London Hospital, Stepney, E1.
'pioneer of modern nursing in Belgium and heroine of the Great War, trained and worked here 1896-1901'
Edith Cavell was 50 years old when she faced a German firing squad in Belgium during WW1. She was born in Swardeston, Norfolk the second daughter of the local Rector. Whilst working as the Matron of a nurses' training institute in Brussels, occupied by German forces, she was accused of being a British spy and aiding some 200 Allied prisoners to escape over the border into Holland. She didn't deny the charges and the Military Tribunal found her guilty. Despite pleas for clemency from international leaders the sentence was carried out. Plaque erected 1988. Nearest tube station = Aldgate East.

CAVENDISH, The Honourable Henry (1731-1810) 11, Bedford Square, WC1.
'natural philosopher, lived here, born 1731 died 1810'
Henry Cavendish was born in Nice, France and went to Peterhouse College, Cambridge; leaving without a degree. He richly deserves his commemorative plaque. Although without a degree, he became a first class scientist and measured the density and mass of the Earth. He converted oxygen and hydrogen into water and involved himself in balloon experiments. Although later a recluse, he created a large library at his home which was open to all his friends and colleagues. It was once reckoned that he probably spoke less words in the course of a long life than any other man, save possibly a Trappist monk. Plaque erected 1903. Nearest tube station = Tottenham Court Road.

CAYLEY, Sir George (1773-1857) 20, Hertford Street, Mayfair, W1.
'scientist and pioneer of aviation, lived here'
George Cayley was born in Scarborough, Yorkshire. In 1839 Cayley co-founded the Regent Street Polytechnic which is probably the most famous of all "Polys". His principle interest was in aviation and, in 1853, he built the first successful glider that carried a man a short distance across what is now Regents' Park. He lived at Hertford Street, when his duties as an MP demanded his attendance at the Commons. As a result of the Battle of Waterloo (1815) he became interested in the manufacture of artificial limbs. Plaque erected 1962. Nearest tube station = Green Park

CECIL, Viscount, of Chelwood (1864-1958) 16, South Eaton Place, Belgravia, SW1.
'creator of the League of Nations, lived here'
The Cecil dynasty reaches back to the 14th century. Robert Cecil, born in London, was educated at Eton and University College, Oxford. He was called to the bar in 1887 and entered parliament in 1903. As under-secretary for foreign affairs he helped, in 1919, to create the League of Nations. He lived to see it replaced, in 1945, by to-day's United Nations. He was awarded the Nobel Prize for Peace in 1937. Cecil, who was the third son of the Marquess of Salisbury, lived here from 1922 until he died. It is said that his humanitarian work began during WW1 when he witnessed the great suffering that war caused. Plaque erected 1976. Nearest tube station = Sloane Square.

CECIL, Robert Gascoyne (1830-1903) 3rd Marquess of Salisbury. 21, Fitzroy Square, W1.
'Prime Minister, lived here'
Cecil was born at Hatfield House, educated at Eton and Christ Church, Oxford and was only 23 when he became an M.P. The whole family was, one way or another, involved not just in politics but running the country. The Cecil influence was more than any one family had the right to expect. Robert Cecil was an extreme right-winger who fought every piece of reformist legislation. He went on to become Prime Minister three times. (1885, 1886-92, 1895-1902) His main interest was South Africa and he was in power during the Boer Wars. He resided here for only four years, 1858-1862. He was once described by Disraeli as . . . 'a great master of gibes and flouts and jeers'. Parties were held to celebrate his retirement from public life in 1902. Plaque erected 1965. Nearest tube station = Warren Street.

CHADWICK, Sir Edwin (1801-1890) 5, Montague Road, Richmond, Surrey.
'Public Health Reformer lived here'
Chadwick, born in Manchester, was called to the bar in 1830. Two years later he was appointed an assistant poor-law commissioner. His report in 1833 concerning his work, laid the foundation for future systems of government inspection. His main interest, besides poor law, was health. Influenced by the writings of Jeremy Bentham, who once stated, 'that the proper objective of all conduct and legislation is the greatest happiness of the greatest number', Chadwick brought about the Public Health Act of 1848 and was himself a commissioner of the Board of Health from 1848-1854. He was knighted for his work and came to live here during his retirement. Plaque erected 1992. Nearest Tube Station = Richmond.

CHAMBERLAIN, Joseph (1836-1914) 188, Camberwell Grove, SE5 AND 25, Highbury Place, N5.
'statesman, lived here'
Chamberlain was born at Camberwell Grove, London. When he was 9 years old the family moved to Highbury Place where they remained for 20 years. He was educated at University College School, Hampstead. On behalf of his father, Joseph moved to Birmingham and ran the Nettlefold ironmongery department. He entered politics and became M.P. for Birmingham and moved back to London in 1876. He was an Imperialist whose policies helped precipitate the Boer war. He resigned from Gladstone's cabinet in 1903. In 1902 he suggested to Theodor Herzl, the Zionist leader, that instead of Palestine becoming the Jewish National Home the Jews have Uganda in Africa. After some discussion Chamberlain's suggestion was turned down. Plaques erected 1915 and 1920. Nearest tube stations Camberwell Grove = Brixton. Highbury Place = Highbury and Islington.

CHAMBERLAIN, Neville (1869-1940) 37, Eaton Square, Belgravia, SW1.
'Prime Minister, lived here 1923-1935'
Neville Chamberlain followed in his father's Birmingham footsteps and entered politics in 1918 as Conservative M.P. for the Ladywood division. In 1923, when he became Chancellor of the Exchequer he moved into Eaton Square where he remained until, in 1937, he became Prime Minister. He was forced to resign in favour of Winston Churchill following the German invasion of Norway in 1940. Periodically he can be seen on T.V. waving the infamous piece of paper he received from Hitler, following their meeting in Munich. His declaration of war against Germany, broadcast on September 3rd 1939, has probably been heard more often than any other radio piece. Plaque erected 1962. Nearest tube station = Sloane Square.

CHELSEA CHINA, 16, Lawrence Street, SW3. (1745- 1784)
'this plaque is dedicated to the famous Chelsea China factory which existed somewhere in the vicinity of number 16.'
No-one is quite certain where the factory stood. The house, once the residence of the Duchess of Monmouth, was demolished in 1834. However this plaque also recalls TOBIAS SMOLLETT (1721-1771), the doctor and novelist who lived for some time in part of the house and who was imprisoned in 1760 for libel whilst editing, 'Critical Review'. It is interesting to recall that Dr. Johnson spent time at the factory being taught by the great craftsmen of Dresden and Venice how to turn a pot. However there are none of his examples amongst the Chelsea Pottery on show at the Victoria and Albert Museum. Plaque erected 1950. Nearest tube station = Sloane Square.

CHESTERFIELD, Philip, 4th Earl of (1694-1773) Rangers House, Chesterfield Walk, SE10.
'statesman and author, lived in this house'
Chesterfield was born in London and became M.P. for St. Germains, Cornwall in 1715. He developed Rangers House as a summer retreat however, following a series of illnesses and suffering from gout, he took up permanent residence in 1753. During his political career he acted as Britain's ambassador to The Hague and in 1731, negotiated the Second Treaty of Vienna. Today Chesterfield is best remembered for the letters of good advice he sent to his son Philip who, to his later detriment, scorned them. Rangers House is open to the public. Plaque erected 1937. Nearest station = Greenwich

CHESTERTON, Gilbert Keith (1874-1936) 11, Warwick Gardens, W14.
'poet, novelist and critic, lived here'
Chesterton G. K. was born in London and educated at St. Paul's School before studying art at the Slade. He was a widely read novelist and although his Father Brown stories, modelled on his friend Father O'Connor have proved most popular they are now perceived to be somewhat anti-social. Following the rise of Hitler, Chesterton became pro-fascist. He lived here, with his family, from the time he was seven and until he left to marry in 1901. Following his conversion to Catholicism, he wrote biographies on St. Francis of Assisi and St. Thomas Aquinas. Plaque erected 1952. Nearest tube station = High Street, Kensington.

CHEVALIER, Albert (1861-1923) 17, St. Ann's Villas, Kensington, W11.
'music hall comedian, was born here'
Chevalier who become one of Britain's greatest music hall artists was born here. He had a French father, who taught at the Kensington Grammar School, and a Welsh mother. They had no connection with 'show business' and did their best to dissuade Albert from pursuing the career he had set his heart on; following being taken to the Holborn Empire by a doting aunt. He achieved great fame with his songs, "My Old Dutch" and "Knocked Them in the Old Kent Road". He published his autobiography "Before I Forget", in 1901. Plaque erected 1965. Nearest tube station = Shepherds Bush.

CHIPPENDALE, Thomas (1718-1779) 61, St. Martin's Lane, WC2.
'The workshop of Thomas Chippendale and his son, cabinet makers, stood near this site 1753-1813'
Chippendale, born in Otley, Yorkshire, the son of a joiner became one of the most famous furniture designers of all time. He published his, 'The Gentleman and Cabinet Maker's Director' in 1754, which showed a predominance of styles in the Rococo style whilst not neglecting the contemporary taste for Gothic and Chinese. For reasons which appear unknown, the principle wood Chippendale used was dark mahogany. St. Martin's Lane is where his workshop was located. Following his death, the business was continued by his son until the Battle of Waterloo in 1815. Plaque erected 1952. Nearest tube station = Leicester Square.

CHISHOLM, Caroline (1808-1877) 32, Charlton Place, Islington, N1.
'philanthropist, "The Emigrants' Friend", lived here'
Caroline Chisholm was born in Northampton. In 1836 she married an officer in the army of the East India Company and went with him to Madras. Two years later Captain Chisholm was posted to Windsor, New South Wales where Caroline spent her time helping abandoned and impoverished immigrant women. In the 1840s she cared for and aided, over 11,000 women and children. She also eventually persuaded a reluctant British government to give free passage to 'relatives of convicts already transported'. In 1854 she made public the appalling conditions that existed in the gold mines of Victoria. Ill-health forced her, in 1866, to return to England where she was granted a life pension of £100 a year and came to live here. Plaque erected 1983. Nearest tube station = Angel.

CHOPIN, Frederick (1810-1849) 4, St. James's Street, St. James's, SW1.
'From this house in 1848 Frederic CHOPIN went to the Guildhall to give his last public performance'
Chopin, the Polish composer born in Zelazowa Wola and leader of the Romantic movement spent only a month here, in November 1848. He was already seriously ill and anxious to return to his mistress, George Sands. His reason for being in London was to give a concert at the Guildhall. Sadly, it proved to be his last but of course his music lives on. Plaque erected 1981. Nearest tube station = Green Park.

CHURCHILL, Lord Randolph (1849-1895) 2, Connaught Place, Bayswater, W2.
'statesman, lived here 1883-1892'
Churchill was born in Blenheim Palace, Oxfordshire the third son of the Duke of Marlborough. Educated at Eton and Merton College, Oxford he entered parliament in 1874 as MP for Woodstock; the same year he married. His wife, the American born Jennie Jerome chose this house as an alternative to living in draughty Blenheim Palace. It became known to their friends as, 'Tyburnia', because opposite, on the railings of Hyde Park, was a plaque marking the site of Tyburn Gate, once London's place of public executions. Churchill's political career reflected his bumptious personality. In 1880 he led, in parliament, a 'fifth column' group that became known as the 'Fourth Party'. Once he reached cabinet rank, he attempted to include in Conservative policy an increase in democracy. He eventually ended his career by resigning from the post of Chancellor of the Exchequer over the question of high military expenditure. He died young, from an undiagnosed mental illness. His enemies claimed it was VD. This family home was amongst the first to be lit by electricity. Plaque erected 1962. Nearest tube station = Marble Arch.

CHURCHILL, Sir Winston, KG (1874-1965) 28, Hyde Park Gate, SW7.
'Prime Minister, lived and died here'
Churchill, son of Lord Randolph, lived here for a large part of his later life. He, like his father, was born at Blenheim Palace. Educated at Harrow he decided on a military career and entered Sandhurst from where, in 1895, he was gazetted to the 4th Hussars. The Churchill that is praised by so many only came about in the late thirties. Prior to that time he was a failure. He did badly at school, was a poor soldier and during the Boer war his reports from South Africa, in his role as war correspondent, were ill considered. During WW1, his failure concerning the ill-fated and ill-conceived Dardanelles campaign, left him discredited. His confrontation with the miners during the Twenties, over their strike to earn a living wage did nothing to endear him to the working class. His influence in hiving off part of Palestine to form Trans-Jordan leads directly to the problems existing to-day in the Middle East. Then came Hitler and Churchill became 'Winnie'. The past was put to one side. Here was the man who had opposed appeasement and was now Britain's wartime leader. After WW2, he wrote "The Second World War" in 6 volumes, this magnificent effort won him, in 1953, the Nobel Prize for Literature. At this time he was once again Prime Minister. He retired in 1955 to write his "History of the English Speaking Peoples" in four volumes. If ever there was an example of someone fulfilling his destiny in later life it is Churchill. However, his career as a great war-time leader didn't persuade the electorate to vote for him. In 1945 Labour won by a landslide. Plaque erected 1985. Nearest tube station = Kensington High Street.

CLARKSON, Willy (1861-1934) 41-43, Wardour Street, Soho, W1.
'theatrical wigmaker, lived and died here'
Wardour Street, renowned as the home of the big film companies, was once dubbed the, 'only street shady on both sides'. Willy, born in London, continued the wig making business his father had started in 1817. He added theatrical costume designing to the already thriving business and moved in 1905 to Wardour Street and a specially designed building. Sarah Bernhardt laid the foundation stone and Clarkson had a flat over. Business flourished but ill health forced him to retire in 1930. Plaque erected 1966, Nearest tube station = Leicester Square.

CLEMENTI, Muzio (1752-1832) 128, Kensington Church Street, Kensington, W8.
'composer, lived here'
Clementi, although born in Rome, spent most of his adult life in England. He is recognised as the first composer to write specifically for the piano including composing the famous collection of studies, 'Gradus ad Parnassum'. He became rich from teaching and manufacturing pianos and famous from performing and conducting. In 1820 he sold his lease to the composer William Horsley and returned to Rome. Plaque erected 1963. Nearest tube station = Kensington High Street.

CLIVE of India, Lord (1725-1774) 45, Berkeley Square, Mayfair, W1.
'soldier and administrator, lived here'
Robert Clive was born in Market Drayton, Cheshire and brought up by his uncle in Eccles. In 1743 he joined the East India Company in Madras but was so miserable and homesick that he tried to commit suicide. By the time war had broken out with the French, Clive was able to organise the defence of Arcot and hold it, with only 56 Indian soldiers, for 53 days. He married a year later and returned to England and a hero's welcome. Clive of India, as he had become known, moved here after returning from his post as Governor of Bengal in 1761. The house was to remain in the Clive family until 1937. Clive achieved fame and fortune by accepting a commission in the private army run by the East India Company. He assisted in consolidating British power in India and of defeating the French and ousting them from the territory. From an early age he was addicted to laudanum, which he took in ever increasing doses, first for the lift it gave, later as a painkiller. In 1767, he was charged with accepting bribes from Indian princes. Although acquitted, he was widely believed, especially by a group led by Dr. Johnson, to be guilty, a belief they felt to be justified following Clive's eventual successful suicide. Plaque erected 1953. Nearest tube station = Green Park.

COBDEN, Richard (1804-1865) 23, Suffolk Street, St. James's, SW1.
'statesman, died here'
Cobden, born in Heyshott, Sussex became a politician who, together with John Bright, was a leader in the fight against the Corn Laws. This they achieved in 1846. In 1860 Cobden negotiated the tariff treaty with the French. Before his political days Cobden was involved in trade and became known as the 'Apostle of Free Trade'. In 1835, following his travels, he wrote "England, Ireland and America", followed a year later by, "Russia". Cobden didn't spend a lot of time at his London home: ill-health kept him at his country house. He was against the Crimean War and didn't mind the unpopularity he received from speaking out. He favoured the North over the South in the American Civil War, although the British government supported the South. In 1865, whilst taking part in a Commons debate concerning Canada, Cobden was taken ill and later died here. Plaque erected 1905. Nearest tube station = Leicester Square.

COBDEN-SANDERSON, Thomas James (1840-1922) 15, Upper Mall, Hammersmith, W6.
'founded the Doves Bindery and Doves Press in this house, and later lived and died here'
'Cobden-Sanderson was born in Alnwick, Northumberland and although trained as a barrister made his reputation and fortune as a bookbinder and publisher. He established Doves Bindery at his home and later Doves Press. In 1903, he produced the lovely "Dove's Bible". The business continued, until the first world war caused closure in 1916, and an angry Cobden-Sanderson threw his type into the Thames. The family continued living here, on the river, long after Cobden-Sanderson's death. Plaque erected 1974. Nearest tube station = Ravenscourt Park.

COCHRANE, Thomas, Earl of Dundonald (1775-1860) Hanover Lodge, Outer Circle, Regent's Park NW1.
'and later David, Earl BEATTY, OM (1871-1936), admirals, lived here'
Cochrane was born in Annsfield, Hamilton. This area of North West London contains the best examples of the work of John Nash. Cochrane, and later Earl Beatty (1871-1936), lived at Hanover Lodge from 1830 onwards. Cochrane joined the navy in 1793 and rose to be an admiral. The navy in those days allowed their line captains to keep a large share of the prize money they got from capturing foreign merchant ships. In the first six months of 1805, whilst working off the Azores, Cochrane's share was £75,000. Then he left the navy and went into commerce. In 1814 he was arrested and accused of partaking in a stock exchange swindle. It resulted in his being sentenced to a year in prison, a fine of £1,000 and an hour in the pillory. He was thought to have been framed and during his imprisonment was elected to Parliament. In 1818 he left England and became the Commander of Chile's navy. He saw that country reach independence and then ran the Brazilian navy with equal success (1823-5). Word was out and he was asked to command the Greek navy (1827-8). Fortunately, in 1831, he succeeded to the Earldom of Dundonald and a year later pardoned for past misdeeds. He re-joined the British navy, as a rear-admiral, and wound up getting buried in Westminster Abbey. EARL BEATTY, born in Nantwich, Cheshire, first saw action when as a captain, he was sent as part of a force to relieve Kitchener at Khartoum. On the outbreak of WW1, whilst commanding the 1st Battle Cruiser Squadron, he steamed into Heligoland Bight and destroyed three German warships. He became an Admiral of the Fleet and First Sea Lord in 1919. Plaque erected 1974. Nearest tube station = St. John's Wood.

COCKERELL, Charles Robert (C. R.) (1788-1863) 13, Chester Terrace, Regent's Park, NW1.
'architect and antiquary, lived and died here'
Cockerell was born in London. After graduating as an architect he spent many years in the Levant and Italy. He was appointed professor of architecture at the Royal Academy (1840-1857) and influenced future generations of architects to the continental style. He designed the Taylorian Institute at Oxford and the Fitzwilliam Museum at Cambridge. His father was Samuel Cockerell, the architect who designed Brunswick Square in London. Plaque erected 1989, Nearest tube station = Regent's Park.

COLE, Sir Henry (1808-1882) 33, Thurloe Square, Kensington, SW7.
'campaigner and educator. First Director of the Victoria and Albert Museum, lived here'
Cole was born in Bath and became assistant keeper at the Public Records office from 1838. He was responsible for the introduction of the penny postage system and invented the adhesive stamp. He also set up a system for preserving poorly kept records. He planned and organised the Great Exhibition of 1851 for which he was later knighted. In 1853 he became the director of the South Kensington Museum, later to be known as the Victoria and Albert Museum, and moved here. He stayed until 1873, when he retired and returned to Bath. Following the introduction of his penny post, Cole, under the pseudonym, 'Felix Summerley', published the first known Christmas cards. Plaque erected 1991. Nearest tube station = South Kensington.

COLERIDGE, Samuel Taylor (1772-1834) 71, Berners Street, W1.
"poet and philosopher, lived here'
AND at 7, Addison Bridge Place, Fulham, W14.
The first plaque to commemorate Coleridge was set in 1905. Then the premises were rebuilt and a new plaque was set in 1928. The present plaque at Berners Street dates from 1966. Coleridge was the son of the Vicar of Ottery St. Mary, Devon, where he was born. The youngest of a very large family there was little love or money left by the time he was born. Educated, by courtesy of a rich uncle, at Christ's Hospital and Jesus College, Cambridge, he was destined for the church but enlisted instead in the army. Bought out by the family he, together with Wordsworth, established English Romanticism. He is best remembered for "The Ancient Mariner" (1810) and "Kubla Khan" (1816), at which time he was living in Fulham. Although he wrote much more excellent work throughout his life, his health was poor, due to his ever increasing addiction to opium. He continued writing and published, "Biographia Literaria" in 1817. He wrote little after this, spending his time with Dr. James Gillman who tried to wean him off drugs. He remained with the Gillman family at 3, The Grove, Highgate, N6 until his death. During this long period he inspired many young poets, such as Keats, to greatness. Plaque at Fulham erected 1950. Nearest tube stations / Tottenham Court Road. /Fulham Broadway.

COLERIDGE-TAYLOR, Samuel (1875-1912) 30, Dagnall Park, South Norwood, SE25.
'composer of the "Song of Hiawatha", lived here'
Coleridge-Taylor was born in London of an English mother and a West Indian father. He spent most of his life in the Croydon area but only the first two years of married life here. Educated at the Royal College of Music his most notable and long lasting achievement was setting Longfellow's poem, "Hiawatha" to music. "Hiawatha's Wedding Feast", first performed in 1898, became a regular part of the Albert Hall programme. At the beginning of the century his popularity rivalled that of Elgar but he died a few years later in poverty, having sold the rights to "Hiawatha" for 15 guineas. Plaque erected 1975. Nearest station = Selhurst BR.

COLLINS, William Wilkie (1824-1889) 65, Gloucester Place, Marylebone, W1.
'novelist, lived here'
Born in London, Collins received most of his education in Italy, where his father was a doctor at the British embassy. Collins was called to the bar in 1845 but preferred writing. A well known novelist, he tended to be overshadowed by his friend Charles Dickens. He is however credited as the first writer of an English detective novel. "The Moonstone", was published in 1868. His best known work is the thriller, "The Woman in White" (1860). Success and money went to his head. He became a womaniser and although married, kept three mistresses in separate establishments. The arrangement didn't last long. He spent so much time on sex and so much money on opium, something had to go. It proved to be first the women and then his health. Plaque erected 1951. Nearest tube station = Baker Street

COLLIN'S MUSIC HALL. (1862-1958) 10-11, Islington Green, N1.
Collin's Music Hall, the home of variety, owed it's life to Sam Collins. He was born in London and started his working life as a twelve year old chimney sweep. He had a fund of Irish songs and turned the Landsdowne Arms into a music hall. The crowds flocked to it as did the stars of the times. Unfortunately Collins didn't live to see its biggest successes. He died three years after it opened at the age of 39. Before Collins closed in 1958, the greatest performers graced its stage. Little Tich, Marie Lloyd, Chaplin, Vesta Tilley, Champagne Charlie, The Lenos, Albert Chevalier, Gracie Fields, Tommy Trinder and many more. Plaque erected 1968. Nearest tube station = The Angel.

CONAN-DOYLE Sir Arthur (1859-1930) 12, Tennison Road, South Norwood, SE25.
'creator of Sherlock Holmes, lived here 1891-1894.'
Conan Doyle lived here for only three years. He was born in Edinburgh, studied medicine there and practised in Southsea before deciding to take up writing. The character SHERLOCK HOLMES first saw daylight in "A Study in Scarlet" (1887). (Holmes is probably fiction's best known character). Conan-Doyle also wrote historical novels and romances, "The White Company" (1891) being his best known. During the Boer Wars, Conan-Doyle was most supportive of Government policy towards South Africa, so much so he served as a doctor during the second Boer War (1899-1902). For his services and public support a grateful government awarded him a knighthood. Conan-Doyle's health began to fail, not least because of his addiction to Laudanum. As a result he gave up writing. His Sherlock Holmes stories were particularly missed and, by public demand, he resurrected the character and published his final Sherlock Holmes story in 1905. In 1909, he became a convert to spiritualism. Plaque erected 1973. Nearest Station = Selhurst BR.

CONRAD, Joseph (1857-1924) 17, Gillingham Street, Belgravia, SW1.
'novelist, lived here'
Conrad was born in Berdichev, Poland and came to Britain after serving as a sailor in British and French ships. He became a naturalised Britain and lived here from 1890 to become regarded as one of Englands' greatest novelists. His writings are mostly set at sea, concerned with man's ability to cope with testing situations. "Lord Jim" (1900), was followed by "Typhoon" (1903) and "Victory" (1915). His most intense work was, "Heart of Darkness", a book of short stories, based on his travels in the Belgian Congo. In 1896 he married and settled in Ashford, Kent. His autobiography, "A Personal Record", was published in 1912. Plaque erected 1984. Nearest tube station = Victoria.

CONS, Emma (1837-1912) 136, Seymour Street, Marylebone, W1.
'philanthropist and founder of the Old Vic, lived here'
Emma Cons, born in London, the elder daughter of a middle-class Jewish family, is best remembered as the founder of The Old Vic which opened in 1880, by courtesy of public subscription. It was meant to provide an escape for working class people and divert them from the pubs and an excess of drink. It took some time before poor people took advantage of the entertainment offered and it took the First World War before the project Emma Cons worked so hard for to take root. Sadly however, she didn't live to see it. She came to live here after her retirement in 1906. Plaque erected 1978. Nearest tube station = Marble Arch.

CONSTABLE, John (1776-1837) 40, Well Walk, Hampstead, NW3.
'painter, lived here'
It is strange to think of Constable, the great English landscape painter living anywhere but in his precious Suffolk, where he was born in East Bergholt, the son of a miller. Following his marriage, he spent considerable time in London. He had been living in Charlotte Street, a noisy dirty and smelly part of London until for his wife Maria's sake, he moved to this then rural part of Hampstead. In November 1828, after a long illness, which often reduced her husband to tears, Maria died. For five long years, during which time Constable rarely did more than sketch the immediate Heath, he looked after his children. After his family grew up he returned to his rooms at 76, Charlotte Street and died there in an attic bedroom. He left behind a great tradition of countryside painting. 'The Hay Wain' and 'View on the Stour', won gold medals at the 1824 Paris Salon Show. His observations of nature, and the way he captured the effects of changing light influenced French Romantic painters. Plaque erected 1923. Nearest tube station = Hampstead.

COOK, Captain James (1728-1779) 88, Mile End Road, E1,
'circumnavigator and explorer, lived in a house on this site'
Cook lived in a house on this site for only a brief period. Even in those days the district was unattractive. He probably lived here during his days as a naval officer the area being local for the London Docks. Cook was born in Marton, Yorkshire, the son of a labourer. He worked as an apprentice to Whitby ship-owners before entering the navy in 1755 and going on to achieve fame as a navigator. He surveyed and chartered the St. Lawrence river and the coasts of Newfoundland, Labrador and New Zealand. He later surveyed the entire length of the East coast of Australia. On his second great voyage (1772-5), he completed the exploration of the Southern Hemisphere and by coincidence found a cure for scurvy. His third voyage was to be his last. He discovered the Hawaiian Islands and went on to survey the West coast of America to beyond the Bering Straits. Then he decided to return to beautiful Hawaii only to be set upon and killed by hitherto peaceful natives. Plaque erected 1970. Nearest tube station = Mile End.

The County Hall, County Hall, London, SE1.
'the home of London government from 1922 to 1986; LCC 1889-1965, GLC 1965-1986'
County Hall was the home of London Government from 1922 to 1986. Until 1965, the ruling body for the Capital was known as the LCC (London County Council). Following the end of WW1, the LCC was responsible for the large number of council estates that spread throughout Central London and the Suburbs providing affordable housing for working people. Besides the City of London, the LCC embraced 32 London Boroughs. During WW2, the LCC undertook the vital Civil Defence forces that saved so much of the Capital from devastation and provided the essential services that kept London going. In 1965, a change in local government policy saw the change in London. Whilst County Hall remained the seat of administration the name was changed to GLC (Greater London Council). Gradually its' powers diminished until, in 1987, local London government was abolished. In 1992 it was reported that County Hall had been sold to Japanese business interests for development as a hotel, despite being wanted as a renewal for the London School of Economics. Plaque erected 1986. Nearest tube station = Waterloo

COX, David (1783-1859) 34, Foxley Road, Brixton, SW9.
'artist, lived here'
Cox, born in Birmingham, lived here from 1827 to 1841. He is acknowledged as one of the foremost artists of his day but recognition didn't come easy. His father, a blacksmith, wanted David to come into the family foundry business but David, who had been given a box of paints when he was a lad recovering from a broken leg, wanted to paint pictures. He spent some time painting scenery for the Birmingham Theatre, whilst taking lessons from the great Joseph Barber. In 1804 he went to London to paint scenery at Astley's Theatre in Lambeth. A year later he had two water colour landscapes accepted by the Royal Academy but acceptance by the 'Arty Establishment' didn't come until, in 1839 and aged 59, he started painting in oils and found the fluency that had been eluding him for so long. In 1841 he left for Harborne, near to where he was born and remained there until his death. It was whilst living here that Cox produced some of his best work. At the Tate there are examples of his craft and also at the Birmingham Art Gallery. Plaque erected 1951. Nearest tube station = The Oval

CRANE, Walter (1845-1915) 13, Holland Street, Kensington, W8.
'artist, lived here'
Crane was born in Liverpool the son of a portrait painter. This area of Kensington is still one of the loveliest and 13, Holland Street a handsome mansion of the time. Here Crane and his family lived and was where Crane had his studio. He had a varied career that spanned painting, illustrating children's books, designing stain glass windows, textiles and wallpapers. He is perhaps best known for his illustrated edition of Spencer's "Faerie Queen" (1894-6). He also found time to support William Morris's Kelmscott Press, an early supporter of Socialism. He was principal of the Royal College of Art (1898-1899). Plaque erected 1952. Nearest tube station = Kensington High Street.

CREED, Frederick George (1871-1957) 20, Outram Road, Addiscombe, Surrey.
'electrical engineer, inventor of the teleprinter, lived and died here'
Creed was born in Nova Scotia and came to Britain in 1897. After a brief spell in Glasgow he lived most of his life here during a lifetime of research into the practical and commercial possibilities that emerged following the invention of the telephone. At the turn of the 20th Century, he started work at nearby factory premises that had been adapted to produce the teleprinter he had invented and which newspaper offices all over the world eventually had installed. Plaque erected 1973. Nearest Station = Bingham Road BR.

CRIPPS, Sir Stafford (1899-1952) 32, Elm Park Gardens, South Kensington, SW10.
'statesman, born here'
Cripps was born in London and educated at Winchester and New College, Oxford. His aunt was Beatrice Webb and perhaps it was her encouragement that led Cripps to the Labour Party. There is little doubt that had Cripps not died at 53 he would have accomplished much. Instead he has gone down in history as an austere man who, as Chancellor of the Exchequer in the post war Labour government, had the unenviable task of creating the promised Welfare State from very limited funds. It was because of the penal austerity measures he took in the budgets of the late Forties that the foundation of British prosperity has been built. He was an early prophet on the dangers of German Nationalism and warned the Labour Party that Hitler was a deadly menace. He urged a common front, with the then strong British Communist Party, to resist Oswald Mosley and his British Fascists and to oppose Chamberlain's appeasement policy. The result was that in 1939 he was expelled from the Labour Party and not readmitted until 1945. Churchill however saw Cripps as a first class politician and in 1942 invited him to serve in his war-time coalition cabinet. Cripps was a Christian who believed that Christ was an early socialist. Plaque erected 1989. Nearest tube station = South Kensington.

CROOKES, Sir William (1832-1919) 7, Kensington Park Gardens, Notting Hill, W11.
'scientist, lived here from 1880 until his death'
Crookes, who was born in London, spent the last 38 years of his life here. Like many scientists he worked at home as well as in the laboratory. During a lifetime of achievement that followed his training at the Royal College of Chemistry, Crookes studied electrical discharges through rarefied gases which led to the development of Crookes Tube. He devised the radiometer which measured the intensity of radiation and discovered Thallium. He became a Fellow of the Royal Society in 1863, in recognition of his experiments in spectroscopy. He was later awarded the Order of Merit. Plaque erected 1967. Nearest tube station = Holland Park.

CRUIKSHANK, George. (1792-1878) 263, Hampstead Road, Regent's Park, NW1.
'artist, lived here from 1850 to 1878 b September 27th 1792, d. Feb 1st 1878'
Cruikshank born in London was to became the well known illustrator and feared caricaturist. He achieved instant fame, or notoriety, when in 1818, shocked by the sentence of death on two women found guilty of passing forged one pound notes, he published a cartoon attacking hanging as the punishment that had been passed on them. His efforts helped in saving them from the gallows and the punishment of a flogging and transportation to Australia substituted. Although he earned his money illustrating the works of Grimms and Dickens it was his satirizing of politicians generally and the Prince Regent in particular that were eagerly read. He had a long battle against the addiction of alcohol and only achieved total abstinence in 1847, following watching the death of a close friend from the effects of drink. Plaque erected 1885. Nearest tube station = Regent's Park.

CUBITT, Thomas (1788-1855) 3, Lyall Street, Belgravia, SW1.
'master builder, lived here'
Cubitt is acknowledged as the developer of Belgravia, most of which remains as he finished it. He was born in Buxton, Derbyshire but came to London at a young age and lived here for the final 8 years of his life. He had the satisfaction of knowing he was responsible for many of the fine buildings that altered London's residential lifestyle for the well to do. His firm uniquely employed craftsmen, in company owned workshops, to create the mouldings that distinguished his work. Although he built Osborne for Queen Victoria, he never received the peerage he thought he deserved. Plaque erected 1959. Nearest tube station = Sloane Square.

CURZON, George Nathaniel, Marquess Curzon (1859-1925) 1, Carlton House Terrace. SW1.
'statesman, Viceroy of India, lived here'
Curzon was born at Kedleston Hall in Derbyshire. He was educated at Eton and Oxford, where he failed to get an expected first in classics; although he was later made a Fellow of All Souls. He bought this house, designed by John Nash, following his forced resignation from the post of Viceroy of India in 1905. He hated Lord Kitchener and saw him as the exploiter of the Indian people for personal gain. Curzon remained semi retired until 1915, when he returned to politics and the Conservative party. He served as foreign secretary (1919-1924) a difficult period for the diplomacy that followed WW1. He is remembered for resolving Turkey's objections to the terms set by the Versailles Treaty of 1919. In 1923, following the resignation of Bonar Law, he expected to be chosen by his party as Prime Minister but was heartbroken when Baldwin was elected instead. His loss was also Britain's. Plaque erected 1976. Nearest tube station = Charing Cross.

DADD, Richard (1817-1886) 15, Suffolk Street, St. James's, SW1.
'painter, lived here'
The story of Dadd's life would make an excellent film. The outline goes something like this. Richard Dadd, born in Chatham, Kent lives with his father, a silversmith who specialises in picture frames, over the shop in Suffolk Street. He attends the Royal Academy School and becomes a passable painter but earns little money. Then in 1843, aged 26, he murders his father: for some petty reason and makes for France only to be brought back to face trial. His defence is that he was mad at the time. The judge orders that Dadd be detained at the 'Bethlem Hospital for the Criminally Insane' for the rest of his life. His mental condition constantly goes from normal to insane and back again. To-day this is known as, 'Paranoid Schizophrenia', but not in 1864. Dadd is amongst the first patients to be admitted to the newly created mental hospital at Broadmoor in Berkshire. There he is encouraged to use oils and paint whatsoever he wishes. Canvases and brushes are provided and Dadd proceeds, from out of his mad imagination and fantasy, to create his life's finest works. His fantastically detailed paintings of fairies feature in most of his paintings of which, "The Fairy Feller's Master Stroke", (1855-1864) is best known. Plaque erected 1977. Nearest tube station = Charing Cross.

DALE, Sir Henry Hallett (1875-1968) Mount Vernon House, Mount Vernon, Hampstead NW3.
'physiologist, lived here'
Dale, born in London, lived here from 1919 until 1942 when the London blitz drove him to settle for a quiet Cotswold village. His brilliant career in the world of science and medicine earned him a Fellowship of the Royal Society and in 1940 he became its President. In 1930, he shared the Nobel Prize for Physiology and Medicine, for his work in studying acetylcholine's role in the chemical transmission of nerve impulses. This lovely house dates from early 19th century and is listed. Plaque erected 1981. Nearest tube station = Hampstead

DANCE, George, the younger (1741-1825) 91, Gower Street, Bloomsbury, WC1.
'architect, lived and died here'
Dance, born in London, was an architect of unimaginative buildings. The best known of which was Newgate prison; thankfully demolished in 1902. He had some success with the squares he designed in North London, particularly Finsbury Square. He also designed John Wesley's house and chapel. Dance lived here from the time the house was built in 1790 and until he retired in 1815. George Dance senior, his father and also an architect designed and built the Mansion House, home of the Lord Mayors of London. Plaque erected 1970. Nearest tube station = Warren Street.

DARWIN, Charles (1809-1882) Biological Sciences Building, University College, Gower Street (site of 110), WC1.
'naturalist, lived in a house on this site 1838-1842'
Darwin was born in Shrewsbury and educated at the local grammar school before going to Edinburgh to study medicine. He described his house here '. . . a small commonplace London house with a drawing room in front and a small room behind and a garden that is as wide as the house and thirty yards long'. Darwin lived here from 1839 to 1842 and then moved to Downe, Kent where he wrote, "On the Origin of the Species" (1859) and "The Descent of Man" (1871). These were theories, which resulted from his observations during his voyages to the Pacific on the 'Beagle', about man's ancestry and principles of natural selection which were bitterly contested on theological grounds. He had two famous grandfathers. Erasmus Darwin, the physician and poet and Josiah Wedgwood the potter. Darwin is buried in Westminster Abbey. Plaque erected 1961. Nearest tube station = Warren Street.

DAVIES, Emily (1830-1921) 17, Cunningham Place, St. John's Wood, NW8.
'founder of Girton College, Cambridge, lived here'
Sarah Emily Davies born in Southampton, was another of those women who campaigned for women's rights long before it was fashionable. She lived here from 1862 to 1886 and during this time she started a campaign to allow women to sit university exams. In 1865 Cambridge became the first university to agree, with Oxford following five years later. Her biggest success was founding Girton College, Cambridge in 1873; following its' humble start in Hitchin. She was Mistress of Girton from 1873 to 75. Emily Davies long campaigned for women to be awarded degrees. This she achieved for London in 1874 but Cambridge didn't follow until 1921. Plaque erected 1978. Nearest tube station = St. John's Wood.

DEFOE, Daniel (1661-1731) 95, Stoke Newington Church Street, N16.
'novelist, lived in a house on this site'
Defoe, the son of a butcher, was born in a slum close to where he later lived in style. It is fanciful to suppose that young Daniel passed this mansion whilst delivering meat to his father's customers. Defoe Road now cuts through the grounds of the house that originally stood here. Defoe lived here for the final twenty years of his life enjoying the large twelve roomed house and its four acres of cultivated gardens. He had one room converted as a safe. It had seven locks and the windows carried heavy bars. This was the room in which he stored his papers. Although famous for the novels, "Robinson Crusoe" (1719) and "Moll Flanders" (1722) Defoe was constantly in fear of his life because of his dissenting attitude towards the State and, as a result, had suffered prison, fines and the pillory. He was also believed to be a spy for the Scots and as a result constantly watched. His thrice weekly journal, 'The Review', lasted from 1704-1713 and reflected his radical attitude. Defoe was a prolific writer, penning some 500 books during an adventurous lifetime. A versatile writer he is justly known as the founder of British journalism. Plaque erected 1932. Nearest station = Stoke Newington

DE GAULLE, General Charles Andre Joseph Marie (1890-1970) 4, Carlton Gardens, SW1.
'President of the French National Committee, set up the Headquarters of the Free French Forces here in 1940'
De Gaulle, born in Lille, arrived in London in 1940 following his refusal to join Petain in an armistice with Hitler. After declaring, 'France has lost a battle, she has not lost the war', he formed the Free French Forces and throughout WW2, 4, Carlton Gardens was his H.Q. Following his return to France in 1944, where he led the victory parade through Paris, De Gaulle served as interim President. He left politics in 1946 but in 1958 was recalled to head the Fifth Republic and end the colonial war with Algeria. His final resignation came after he was defeated in a referendum concerning regional and senate reforms (1969). Plaque erected 1984. Nearest tube station = Piccadilly.

DE MORGAN, William (1839-1917). DE MORGAN Evelyn (1855-1919) 127, Old Church Street, SW3.
'ceramic artist and novelist, and his wife, Evelyn DE MORGAN (1855-1919), artist lived and died here'
With his wife designing much of his work De Morgan, born in London, created the most beautiful ceramics. He had discovered the secret of medieval ceramics and worked with William Morris on tiles and plates in vivid colours. All his good work however made little money. So he took to writing novels and in 1906, now aged 66 he published, "Joseph Vance", an instant success to be followed by more. At the outbreak of WW1, De Morgan offered his services to the War Office following his researches into submarine and aircraft defence. His wife Evelyn whom he married in 1887, was a Pre-Raphaelite painter. Plaque erected 1937. Nearest tube station = Sloane Square.

DE QUINCEY, Thomas (1785-1859) 36, Tavistock Street, Holborn, WC2.
'wrote "Confessions of an English Opium Eater" in this house'
De Quincy was born in Manchester, the son of a merchant and educated at Manchester Grammar School. In 1802 he ran away from school to Wales where he wandered the countryside and lived with a young prostitute called Ann. They came briefly to London before he went to Oxford and Worcester College. There he developed the habit of taking opium. In 1816 he married Margaret Simpson. Over a twelve year period she gave birth to three daughters and five sons. He wrote several books but only, "The Confessions of an English Opium Eater" (1822) is considered of any consequence. After publication he moved to the Lake District where Wordsworth and his circle welcomed him. In 1828 he and his family moved again this time to Edinburgh where he remained alone, poor and eccentric; following the death of his wife and desertion by his eight children. Plaque erected 1981. Nearest tube station = Aldwych.

DEVINE, George (1910-1965) 9, Lower Mall, Hammersmith, W6.
'Actor. Artistic Director of the Royal Court Theatre 1956-1965, lived here'
Born in London, Devine began his career as an actor followed by teaching at the London Theatre Studio from 1936 to 1939. Following WW2, he became Director of the Old Vic School. In 1956 he founded the English Stage Company which he based at the Royal Court Theatre in Sloane Square. Here Devine staged Osborne's "Look Back in Anger" and Arden's, "Serjeant Musgrave's Dance". Devine continued the prestige of British theatre and encouraged new writers. In 1965 he returned to the stage in Osborne's, "A Patriot For Me". Following his death the "George Devine Award" was founded to be given to young theatre workers. Plaque erected 1992. Nearest tube station = Ravenscourt Park.

DICKENS, Charles (1812-1870) 48, Doughty Street, Holborn, WC1.
'novelist, lived here'
Dickens was born near Portsmouth the son of a navy pay clerk. When his father became redundant the family moved to London. Soon his father was in prison for debt and Charles, still only a boy, was sent to work in a blacking factory. Through the good offices of a family friend, Charles had three years of schooling at Hampstead Road Academy, after which he worked for a solicitor as an office boy. During this time, Dickens senior got himself a job as a reporter on the 'Morning Herald' and Charles decided to try his hand at journalism. Although Dickens only lived here for four years (1837-1841) it is open to the public. Dickens moved here from lodgings at Furnival's Inn in High Holborn; following publication of "The Pickwick Papers", he married Catherine Hogarth and was able to afford this upmarket residence in a private road guarded over by uniformed porters. Between 1837 and 1852, his wife bore him seven sons and three daughters. The only fly in the ointment was the death, at 17, of Mary his wife's only sister and with whom Dickens was infatuated. He wore her ring and when his marriage broke up in 1858, he surrounded his study at Gad's Hill Place, Rochester in Kent with her mementoes. He wrote, "Oliver Twist" whilst at Doughty Street followed shortly after by, "Nicholas Nickleby". It is said of Dickens that he worked himself to death. This is probably true because besides his vast literary outpourings he visited many European countries as well as the USA. He was prominent in many charitable causes and never forgot his poor origins or the imprisonment of his father for debt. His father was later to be the role model for Mr Micawber. Plaque erected 1903. He is buried in Westminster Abbey although his wish was to be interred in the grounds of his home at Gadshill near Rochester. Nearest tube station = Holborn.

DICKINSON, Goldsworthy Lowes (1862-1932) 11, Edwardes Square, Kensington, W8.
'This was the London home of Goldsworthy Lowes Dickinson, author and humanist'
The plaque states Dickinson, born in London, was a humanist and author. What is not stated is that he was the prime mover in what became, following the end of the first world war, The League of Nations. Dickinson, who lived here with his sisters from 1912 to 1920, worked behind the scenes to bring about his dream without thought of fame or acknowledgment. He was a lecturer at Cambridge from 1896 to 1920 and author of several popular books about life in general. Plaque erected 1956. Nearest Tube Station = Kensington High Street.

DILKE, Sir Charles Wentworth (1843-1911) 76, Sloane Street, Belgravia, SW1.
'statesman and author, lived here'
Dilke was born in Chelsea and lived here as a boy. After graduating from Trinity Hall, Cambridge he was called to the bar in 1866. He became a Liberal MP in 1868 and is credited with legalising the trade unions and limiting how many hours could be worked per week. He was a radical who grew up here in an area of privilege far removed from those he helped. He inherited his title from his father who in 1869 was murdered whilst on a diplomatic mission to St. Petersburg. Plaque erected 1959. Nearest tube station = Sloane Square.

DISRAELI, Benjamin, Earl of Beaconsfield (1804-1881) 22, Theobalds Road, Holborn, WC1.
'statesman, born here 1804'
AND 19, Curzon Street, Mayfair, W1.
'statesman, died here'
There are two plaques to Disraeli, the first commemorates where he was born the other where he died. However, close by Curzon Street is where he lived longest, 93, Park Lane, from 1839 to 1873. Following the publication of his last novel, 'Endymion' in 1880, Disraeli paid £10,000 for a nine year lease on 19, Curzon Street, a house he would only occupy for the last few months of a rich and varied life. Although baptised (he was thirteen at the time) Disraeli was born of Jewish parents, something he was most proud about and he never allowed any anti-semitic insult to go unchallenged. When in 1848 Baron Lionel de Rothschild was elected to parliament it was Disraeli who supported his right to be admitted without taking the Christian oath. He was born in London and educated privately in Walthamstow. He worked for some while in a solicitor's office and in 1826 his first novel was published. "Vivian Grey" caused a stir and Disraeli began getting noticed. He finally entered parliament in 1837, after four attempts. He was prime minister in 1868 and again in 1874 until his retirement in 1880. During his time he secured the Suez Canal (1875) and had Queen Victoria crowned Empress of India (1876). He was renowned as an author and published many books including the novels "Coningsby" (1844) and "Sybil" (1845). He was created Earl of Beaconsfield in 1876. History has shown how great a man he was. His foresight gave Britain the wealth and influence that carried her through two world wars. He once said . . . 'if I want to read a good book I write one'. He is buried at Hughenden, near High Wycombe, his country house from 1848. Towards the end of 1993 it has been revealed that Disraeli fathered two illegitimate children. Ralph, born in 1865 to Lady Walpole Nevill known as Dolly, and Kate, born a short time later, whose mother was presumed to have been a French lady; identity as yet unknown. Plaques erected 1948 and 1908. Nearest tube stations; Theobalds Road = Holborn. Curzon Street = Hyde Park.

DOBSON, Frank (1886-1963) 14, Harley Gardens, SW10,
'Sculptor lived here'
Born in London Dobson, as a child, was given modeling clay to keep him quiet. He left school at 14 and went as an assistant to an artist working in pottery. He went on to become a fully fledged sculptor and became associated with the London Group. For many years he was professor of sculpture at the Royal College of Art retiring in 1953. He had a style of his own that specified simplistic form that was best shown in his female studies. Probably his best known work is "The Man Child, Morning". Plaque erected 1993. Nearest tube station = Fulham Broadway

DOBSON Henry Austin (1840-1921) 10, Redcliffe Street, SW10.
'poet and essayist, lived here'
Dobson born in Plymouth was educated at Beaumaris, Coventry and Strasbourg, as an engineer. However he spent forty five years working as a civil servant at the Board of Trade and lived here from 1872-1879. What rescued him from his boring existence was his ability as a poet and essayist. His most notable work being, "The Vignettes of Rhyme" (1873). He published many monographs and several essays that were graceful and erudite. Plaque erected 1959. Nearest tube station = Fulham Broadway.

DOUGLAS, Norman (1868-1952) 63, Albany Mansions, Albert Bridge Road, Battersea, SW11.
'writer, lived here'
Douglas was born in Tilquhillie, Scotland and educated at Uppingham before joining the Foreign Office in 1894. Two years later he settled in Capri and joined the literary circle of Compton Mackenzie and DH. Lawrence. He only spent 1913 to 1917 at Albany Mansions. His writings included "Old Calabria" (1915) and "South Wind" (1917). He never tried to hide the fact that although married, he was a homosexual, with the result that to avoid persecution he spent much of his time in Italy. Here he wrote travel books about Capri. In 1933 his autobiography "Looking Back", was an unusual book consisting of a series of anecdotes about his friends and recalling their calling cards. He then related long or terse comments about them as the mood, at the time of writing, took him. Plaque erected 1980. Nearest tube station = Sloane Square.

DRYDEN, John (1631-1700) 43, Gerrard Street, Soho, W1.
'poet, lived here'
Dryden was born at the vicarage of Aldwinkle All Saints, Northamptonshire where his maternal grandfather was rector. Educated at Westminster School and Trinity College, Cambridge he was 36 years old before he left Cambridge and came to London to help Cromwell and the parliamentary cause. Following the death of Cromwell in 1658, Dryden came and worked here and his plaque is one of the oldest. However it is probably on the wrong house, number 44 is more likely. He worked on the ground floor, facing the street and enjoyed the distraction of passers by. In 1663 he married Lady Elizabeth Howard, the eldest daughter of the Earl of Berkshire. His works included, "Absalom and Achitophel" (1681) and the play, "All for Love" (1678). He was the first poet to have the title, 'Poet Laureate' (1668-1689). His outpourings were enormous and mostly outstanding. Plaque erected 1875. Nearest tube station = Piccadilly.

DRYSDALE, Dr Charles Vickery (1874-1961) 153a, East Street, Walworth, SE17 11
'a founder of the Family Planning Association, opened his first birth control clinic here in 1921'
Drysdale was not a medical doctor, which is probably surprising considering his association with family planning matters. He was born in Barnstaple, Devon the son of parents who were both doctors; medical ones. Charles went to engineering colleges and picked up a doctorate in that field. He was an inventor of several scientific instruments; the A. C. Pontentionmeter the Polyphase Wattmeter and more. His parents were leading lights in the Malthusian League as were Charles and his wife. When Drysdale senior died Charles took his place as chairman. The league had considerable influence on the emerging Family Planning movement. In 1930 Charles Drysdale became an executive member of the National Birth Control Council. He was awarded the OBE in 1920 and the CB in 1932. He gave up his association with family planning following the death of his wife. His daughter had died when she was only 13 and Drysdale spent his final years with a nephew in Bexhill. Plaque erected 1988. Nearest Station = Walworth.

DU MAURIER, George Louis Palmella Busson (1834-1896) 91, Great Russell Street, Holborn, WC1.
'artist and writer, lived here 1863-1868'
Du Maurier only lived here for five years but he lived at New Grove House, 28, Hampstead Grove, Hampstead, NW3 for far longer (1874-1895). Although born and educated in Paris he is well known as an English novelist and illustrator. He is remembered for illustrations in "Punch" and the novels, "Peter Ibbotson" (1892) and the enormously successful, "Trilby" (1894). His grandaughter, Daphne Du Maurier, wrote the popular novel, 'Jamaica Inn' (1936). Plaque erected 1960. Nearest tube station = Holborn.

DU MAURIER, Gerald (1873-1934) Cannon Hall, 14, Cannon Place, Hampstead, NW3.
'actor manager, lived here from 1916 until his death'
Gerald the youngest child of George Du Maurier was born in London and educated at Harrow. He started off as an actor and achieved some success in the role of Captain Hook in "Peter Pan", but it was as a theatre manager and producer that he reached prominence. Whilst living at Cannon Hall, an 18th century mansion that had once been Hampstead's Courthouse, he became manager of Wyndhams and from 1925, the St. James's Theatre also. In 1922 he was knighted for his services to the stage. Plaque erected 1967. Nearest tube station = Hampstead.

DYSON, Sir Frank (1868-1939) 6, Vanbrugh Hill, Blackheath, SE3.
'Astronomer Royal, lived here 1894-1906'
Dyson, born in Measham, Staffordshire was the Director of Greenwich Observatory from 1910 to 1933. During this time he inaugurated radio transmissions of Greenwich time, including the pips heard at the beginning of radio news broadcasts. He published his findings, following his study of stella motions and solar eclipses. Plaque erected 1990. Nearest Station = Maze Hill.

EARNSHAW, Thomas (1749-1829) 119, High Holborn, WC1. (site of)
'Site of the business premises of Thomas Earnshaw noted watch and chronometer maker'
Unless you are madly interested to see the rather tired area where the modern marine chronometer was created you would be better off visiting the Science Museum. Plaque erected 1948. Nearest tube station = Holborn.

EASTLAKE, Charles (1793-1865) 7, Fitzroy Square, Marylebone, W1
'painter and first Director of the National Gallery, lived here'
Eastlake was born in Plymouth. Although a painter of some renown, his best known works being two full length portraits of Napoleon, Eastlake is commemorated as the first director of the National Gallery at Trafalgar Square. He was responsible for collecting the art treasures of Britain in order to create a national picture collection. He opened the doors of the Gallery in 1824 with the purchase of the Angerstein collection and oversaw the main building works which were completed in 1838. He was knighted in 1842. Plaque erected 1985. Nearest tube station = Leicester Square.

EDDINGTON, Sir Arthur, OM (1882-1944) 4, Bennett Park, Blackheath, SE3.
'mathematician and astrophysicist lived here'
Eddington was born in Kendal. He lived here in 1906 whilst assistant to the Astronomer Royal. He then took up the appointment as Plumian Professor of Astronomy at Cambridge. There he made theoretical studies of the structure of the stars, predicting enormous temperatures of their interiors. He also lectured on his early predictions concerning the theory of relativity and gravitation. He is considered the greatest modern English astronomer and wrote several books on the subject including, "Mathematical Theory of Relativity" (1923). Plaque erected 1974. Nearest Station = Blackheath

EDWARDS, John Passmore (1823-1911) 51, Netherall Gardens, Hampstead, NW3.
'journalist, editor and builder of free public libraries, lived here'
Edwards was born in Kennington, London where his father worked as a gravedigger. Although poor, Edward's parents encouraged his education. He worked hard at school and went on to university. He became a journalist and later an editor. He assisted William Ewart who, with his committee, was working for the establishment of free libraries throughout Britain. This was achieved in 1850 and thereafter Edwards spent much of his working life touring large towns and cities looking for likely library sites. Plaque erected 1988. Nearest tube station = Finchley Road.

ELDON, John Scott, Lord. (1751-1838) 6, Bedford Square, Holborn, WC1.
'Lord Chancellor, lived here'
Eldon, born in Newcastle, was one of the most unpopular politicians of his day. He was Tory lord chancellor (1801-6)(1807-27) and often dominated the cabinet. He was opposed to reforms of any kind and wanted hanging kept for the most trivial offenses. He opposed liberal reform and Catholic Emancipation. In 1815 a London mob, protesting against the Corn Laws, made Eldon's home in Bedford Square the object of their hatred. They attempted to fire it but Eldon met them on the steps and harangued them so fiercely they left. In the Leeds Grammar School case of 1805, he held that the teaching of foreign languages was not in keeping with the aims of grammar schools, which were meant for the teaching of reading grammatically. His findings were based on the powers the schools had. However he didn't rule out that school governors could, if they wished, seek permission to alter the syllabus. Plaque erected 1954. Nearest tube station = Tottenham Court Road.

ELEN, Gus (1862-1940) 3, Thurleigh Avenue, Balham, SW12.
'music hall comedian, lived here '
In his heyday Elen, born in London, was a star as big as any to-day. His appearances at music halls brought out crowds of fans who thrilled at the way he put over his cockney songs. He moved to Balham with his wife in 1934 where he spent his last years. Plaque erected 1979. Nearest tube station = Balham.

ELGAR, Sir Edward (1857-1934) 51, Avonmore Road, Baron's Court, W14.
'composer, lived here 1890-1891'
Elgar, born in Broadheath, Worcester is probably the greatest English composer ever. He lived here for only a year, although he spent 10 years living at 42, Netherall Gardens in Hampstead, a house designed by Norman Shaw and demolished in 1938. Elgar spent most of his working life in Malvern where he wrote the major part of his large output. Musically he was largely self-taught and played, not very well, the bassoon and violin. In 1889 he married and moved to London whilst still retaining his Malvern home. He has the distinction of being the first musician to receive the Order of Merit (1911). During the First World War, Elgar was censored for being more concerned about the treatment of horses at the front, than about the soldiers. He was knighted in 1904 on the occasion of the Elgar Festival. Elgar always hated a lyric being put to part of his "Pomp and Circumstance" to create "Land of Hope and Glory". Following the death of his wife in 1920 he wrote very little. His appointment in 1924 as Master of the King's Musick was largely honourary. Plaque erected 1962. Nearest tube station = West Kensington.

ELIOT, George (Mary Ann Cross, nee Evans) (1819-1880) Holly Lodge, 31, Wimbledon Park Road, SW18.
'novelist lived here'
AND 4, Cheyne Walk, SW3.
'novelist died here'
George Eliot was the pen name Mary Evans used to circumvent the difficulties women had in getting published. She was born on Arbury Farm, Astley, the daughter of a Warwickshire Land Agent. Following her mother's death the family moved to Coventry in 1841. Here she met Charles Bray, a writer on philosophy whose ideas had a great effect upon her. She finally came to London in 1849 and met the Talmudic scholar Emanuel Deutsch. From him she learnt Hebrew and for some while considered conversion to Judaism. Her novel "Daniel Deronda" (1874) reflects her interest on the subject. In 1850 she began writing for the "Westminster Review". At Holly Lodge she wrote "Mill on the Floss" (1860) and lived openly with George Lewes, causing her to be regarded as a wanton. She was most concerned about the social conditions she saw around her and "Silas Marner" (1861) and "Middlemarch" (1872) reflects this concern. She was much influenced by the rationalist theology of Herbert Spencer. In 1880, following the death of her beloved Lewes, she married his friend John Cross, twenty years younger and went to live at Cheyne Walk. However it would only be three weeks before she too died. She is buried at Highgate cemetery in a grave next to Lewes. As a novelist she is amongst the greats. Her descriptions of the lower and middle classes as well as of market traders, especially in the Midlands, are particularly effective. Plaques erected 1905 and 1949. Nearest Tube Stations = Southfields and Sloane Square.

ELIOT, T. S. OM (1888-1965) 3, Kensington Court Gardens, Kensington, W8.
'poet lived and died here'
Eliot was born in St. Louis, USA and educated at Harvard and Oxford. He settled in England in 1915 and, following his naturalisation in 1927, is recognised as an English writer. He lived in Kensington for many years and died here. He spent some time teaching and worked for Lloyds bank for several years. He went into publishing and became a director of Fabers. He was an ardent admirer of Ezra Pound and for a time supported his fascist views. His early work was published by the Hogarth Press, owned by Virginia and Leonard Woolf. He wrote much that was brilliant and justified the Nobel Prize he received in 1948 for literature. However some of his work and public comments were marred by intemperate anti-semitic comments which, following the advent of Hitler, he regretted. He received the Order of Merit in 1948. His place in English literature is assured if only because of "Murder in the Cathedral" (1935) and "The Cocktail Party" (1950). Plaque erected 1986. Nearest tube station = Kensington High Street.

ELLIS, Henry Havelock (1859-1939) 14, Dover Mansions, Canterbury Crescent, Stockwell, SW9.
'pioneer in the scientific study of sex, lived here'
Ellis born in Croydon, Surrey was the son of a sea captain and lived here towards the end of the 19th century. He travelled to Australia, New Zealand and the Americas before taking his medical degree at St. Thomas's Hospital. He gave up the idea of private practise in favour of writing technical books on sexual scientific studies. His "Studies in the Psychology of Sex" in 7 volumes and published between 1898-1928 was the first scientific examination of sexuality ever. These books were, for several years, banned in Britain. His autobiography published in 1940 was entitled "My Life". A title that was not uncommon. Plaque erected 1981. Nearest tube station = Brixton.

ENGELS, Frederick (1820-1895) 121, Regent's Park Road, NW1.
'political philosopher, lived here 1870-1894'
Engels was born in Barmen, Germany but lived in England from 1842. He had been sent by his father to Manchester to work in the family textile business and there he met Moses Hess. Through Hess, Engels became involved with the Owenite and Chartist movements. In 1844, he moved to London and published "The Condition of the Working Classes in England". This brought him to the notice of Karl Marx and together they worked in Paris to organise an international socialist movement. Then they worked on the "Communist Manifesto" published in 1848. Following the death of Marx in 1883, Engels devoted the rest of his life to producing and translating Marx's writings and revising "Das Kapital". Plaque erected 1972. Nearest tube station = Camden Town.

ESSEX STREET, Essex Hall, Essex Street, WC2.
At Essex Hall will be found a plaque that commemorates the creation, in 1675, of Essex Street named after the Earl of Essex whose mansion was demolished in order for the street to be built, by Nicholas Barbon, in ever expanding London. Here lived and worked many famous people of the time. Lawyer Sir Orlando Bridgeman (1606-1674), Novelist Henry Fielding (1707-1754). The Rev Theophilus Lindsey (1723-1808) founded the Essex Street Chapel and Dr Samuel Johnson a drinking club, known as the "Essex Head", in 1783. Essex Street to-day serves as an adjunct to neighbouring Middle Temple, home and workplace to many barristers. Plaque erected at Essex Hall rebuilt 1962, to mark the historical connection with the whole street. Nearest tube station = Temple.

EWART, William (1798-1869) 16, Eaton Place, Belgravia, SW1
'reformer, lived here'
The reason you are browsing through this book is because Ewart, born in Liverpool had, in 1863, suggested erecting plaques to commemorate famous men and women... Whether he had in mind his own commemoration isn't known but to him goes the credit for the imaginative idea. The government of the day however didn't exactly jump at the suggestion but the Royal Society of Arts decided, in 1864, to form a committee to... 'promote the erection of statues or other memorials of persons eminent in the Arts, Manufactures and Commerce'. Ewart was a barrister who in 1827 became an MP. His most important act was not the erection of plaques to remember the famous but the enactment of the Public Libraries Act of 1850 which led to a free library service for everyone. He was also responsible for the abolition of capital punishment for many minor criminal acts and hanging prisoners whilst still wearing their chains. Ewart lived here from 1830 to 1838. Later in his life he lived at Rose Hill, Hampton the scene of the present Hampton Branch Library and where in 1992 a Blue Plaque was erected. Plaque erected 1963. Nearest tube station = Sloane Square.

FABIAN SOCIETY, The White House, Osnaburgh Street, Regent's Park, NW1.
This is the site of 17, Osnaburgh Street, now a hotel, where in 1884 the Fabian Society was founded. 'A British socialist organisation which aimed to achieve socialism through a gradual reformist policy rather than through revolution'. The Fabians were instrumental in establishing the Labour Party, ably assisted by such luminaries as G. B. Shaw and Beatrice and Sydney Webb. The Society still flourishes and continues its work of political research. Plaque erected 1985. Nearest tube station = Great Portland Street.

FARADAY, Michael (1791-1867) 48, Blandford Street, Mayfair, W1.
'man of science apprentice here, b. 1791, d. 1867'
For a man who was to achieve much eminence Faraday's origins were most humble. He was born in Newington Butts, London, but his father a blacksmith soon moved to Jacob Well Mews, close to Baker Street, and all the family lived in two rooms at the rear of the smithy. Close by was a bookshop owned by George Riebau. Here in 1804 aged 13, Faraday started as an errand boy. He progressed first as a bookbinder then as a bookseller but all the time Faraday was aware of the books around him and the knowledge they contained. This was his university until he started evening classes. Later he attended lectures by Sir Humphrey Davy of the Royal Institute. Davy found the boy eager to learn and appointed him his assistant. His faith was rewarded when in 1831, Faraday read his paper about magneto-electric induction, a forerunner to electricity, to the Royal Society. In recognition of his great work he was, in 1835, granted a life pension and in 1858 given a house at Hampton Court. In 1862 he suggested to the Trinity House that they use electricity in their lighthouses. Faraday is probably the greatest of all investigative physicists. Plaque erected (by the Royal Society) 1876. Nearest tube station = Marble Arch.

FAWCETT, Dame Millicent Garrett (1847-1929) 2, Gower Street, Bloomsbury, WC1
'pioneer of women's suffrage, lived and died here'
Millicent Fawcett nee Garrett was born in Aldburgh, Suffolk. She, together with her elder sister, Elizabeth Garrett Anderson, was a leader in the women's suffrage movement. A woman of limited education it was her marriage to Henry Fawcett, a Professor of Economics at Cambridge and M.P. for Brighton, that enabled her to develop. Because Henry was blind, it was her task to see that his correspondence was maintained and his papers prepared. She also came into contact with the radical influences of 19th century politics. It all served her well in her role as a formidable champion of women's rights who went on to found Newnham College, Cambridge. In 1920 she wrote "The Women's Victory - and After". Plaque erected 1954. Nearest tube station = Euston Square.

FENTON, Roger (1819-1869) 2, Albert Terrace, Primrose Hill, Regent's Park, NW1.
'photographer lived here'
Fenton was born in Lancashire and studied painting in Paris. Between 1849 and 1851 he exhibited at the Royal Academy. Then he laid down his brushes and took up photography. He went off to Russia in 1852, took lots of pictures and showed them in London. This resulted in his founding the Photographic Society which later became 'Royal'. Fenton invited Queen Victoria to become the Society's patron which of course resulted in an invitation to photograph the family. In 1855 he packed his bags and his newly acquired film equipment and went off to the Crimea, so becoming the world's first official war photographer. In 1862 he laid aside his films and plates and became a lawyer. Plaque erected 1991. Nearest tube station = Swiss Cottage.

FERRIER, Kathleen (1912-1953) 97, Frognal, Hampstead, NW3.
'contralto lived here'
Kathleen Ferrier, who was born in Higher Walton, Lancashire, didn't start serious musical study until 1940. Following the end of WW2 Ferrier's career took off. Her full rich voice brought her international fame and Britten wrote the title role of "Rape of Lucretia" for her. She lived here, at 2 Frognal Mansions, throughout the war years and until she died from cancer aged only 41. Her greatest success was in Mahler's, "The Song of the Earth", which she performed at the 1947 Edinburgh Festival. Plaque erected 1979. Nearest tube station = Hampstead.

FIELDING, Henry (1707-1754) Milbourne House, Barnes Green, SW13.
'novelist, lived here'
Fielding was born at Sharpham Park near Glastonbury, Somerset the son of an army officer and grandson of a judge. After his last term at Eton he spent some time at Lyme Regis where he fell in love with a young heiress and tried to kidnap her. He was bound over to keep the peace and went to London. He only spent four years, during the latter part of his life here. Even to-day it is a delightful part of suburban London, during the 18th century it was open countryside. Milbourne House was built during the 17th century and first occupied by William Milbourne. Fielding spent most of his working life writing books, plays and political satires. It was his satires on Walpole that brought an end to his playwriting. In 1737 the Theatrical Licensing Act was brought in and Fielding decided to become a barrister. In appreciation of his work he was granted the dubious honour of being appointed Magistrate at Bow Street (1750). It was one of the most crowded and criminally infested parts of London. With its surrounding narrow alleyways, courtyards and lanes it was open season for thieves, muggers and murderers. The area was wholly given over to organised crime. It was against this tyranny that Fielding had to operate. He persevered for four years, mostly countering the bribery within his Bow Street Runners. When his health collapsed he retired to Lisbon, where he died some months later. Probably his most famous work was "Tom Jones" (1749). Plaque erected 1978. Nearest Station = Barnes.

FILDES, Sir Samuel Luke (1844-1927) 31, Melbury Road, Fulham, W14
'artist, lived here 1878-1927'
Fildes was born in Liverpool and soon realised that an artist who was fashionable could make a lot of money. Fildes was such an artist. His charm exceeded his ability but it was enough for him to accumulate sufficient wealth in order to commission Norman Shaw, the fashionable designer, to build him a house. Melbury Road was adjacent to Holland Park and one of the newest parts of London in which to live. The family remained here long after Fildes died in 1927. Plaque erected 1959. Nearest tube station = Kensington High Street.

FISHER, Admiral of the Fleet, Lord OM (1841-1920) 16, Queen Anne's Gate, St. James's, SW1.

'lived here as First Sea Lord 1905-1910'

Fisher's Christian names were John Arbuthnot but his friends called him Jacky. He had the unusual distinction, for those stuffy days of being popular with both officers and men. He was born in Ceylon and joined the navy in 1854 and eventually lived here whilst First Sea Lord (1905-1910). During his period of office he introduced the 'Dreadnought' class of battleships which came on stream in time to participate in WW1, particularly in The Battle Of Jutland (1916). In 1915 he resigned, following a row with Winston Churchill the First Lord of the Admiralty, over the planning of the Dardanelles campaign which Fisher thought ill conceived. Events proved him to be tragically right. Plaque erected 1975. Nearest tube station = St. James's.

FITZROY, Admiral Robert (1805-1865) 38, Onslow Square, Kensington, SW7.

'hydrographer and meteorologist lived here'

Fitzroy, born at Ampton Hall near Bury St. Edmunds in Suffolk, was that odd combination of scientist and religious fanatic. He somehow conceived the idea that because he commanded the ship 'HMS Beagle', that took Charles Darwin to the Galapagos Islands and as a result led him to formulate the ideas that became germain to his theory of evolution, meant he had betrayed God and the bible. In 1865, some thirty years after the voyage, he committed suicide in the attic of this house. During the intervening years however, he developed a portable barometer and instituted a system of storm warnings that were a forerunner to weather forecasting. Plaque erected 1981. Nearest tube station = South Kensington.

FLAXMAN, John (1755-1826) 7, Greenwell Street, Mayfair, W1.

'sculptor lived and died here b. 1755, d. 1826'

Flaxman was born in York. He was a delicate and slightly deformed child who showed an early ability to paint and draw. In the event he became a neo-classical sculptor and worked briefly for Wedgewood. Following a visit to Rome, he decided on a career as a monumental sculptor. His subsequent works include Mansfield in Westminster Abbey, William Collins in Chichester Cathedral, Nelson in St. Pauls and Robert Burns in Westminster Abbey. He also gained a reputation for a series of outline drawings illustrating Greek mythology. Plaque erected 1876. Nearest tube station = Great Portland Street.

FLECKER, James Elroy (1884-1915) 9, Gilmore Road, Blackheath, SE13.
'poet and dramatist, was born here'
Educated at Uppingham, Flecker went on to Trinity College, Cambridge to study oriental languages. He then entered the diplomatic service and was posted to the Lebanon. More poet than diplomat he wrote most poetically about his Eastern travels. He is best known for his exotically lyrical "The Golden Journey to Samarkind" (1913). Plaque erected 1986. Nearest Station = Hither Green.

FLEMING, Sir Alexander (1881-1955) 20a, Danvers Street, Chelsea, SW3.
'discoverer of penicillin lived here'
Fleming was born in Loudoun, Ayrshire and educated at Kilmarnock. Before embarking on a career in medicine, he spent several years as a shipping clerk in the City of London. He joined the medical school of St. Mary's Hospital Paddington and after qualifying, found a place at Sir Almroth Wright's bacteriological laboratory. He lived here, in a flat, from 1929. As many will know Fleming is accredited with the discovery of penicillin, what might not be so well known is whilst Fleming first noticed the effect of penicillin on bacteria, by accident in 1928, he didn't fully appreciate what had been discovered until Dr. Ernst Chain and Dr. Howard Florey succeeded in making pure penicillin in quantities large enough for practical purposes. In 1940 penicillin was used medically for the first time; on allied war wounded. In 1945 the three men shared the Nobel Prize for Physiology and Medicine and all three received knighthoods. Fleming is credited as the first doctor to use anti-typhoid vaccines on humans. Plaque erected 1981. Nearest tube station = Sloane Square.

FLEMING, Sir John Ambrose (1849-1945) 9, Clifton Gardens, Maida Vale, W9.
'scientist and electrical engineer lived here'
Fleming was born in Lancaster. He lived here from 1892, whilst Professor of Electrical Engineering at University College London. It is now part of a hotel. Fleming invented the thermionic valve (1904) which in turn led to the development of telecommunications, electric light, radio, TV and electronics. A mild unassuming man, he was content to let others profit from his work while he was satisfied in remaining at University College for some 40 years. In his retirement he was knighted. Plaque erected 1971. Nearest tube station = Maida Vale.

FLINDERS, Captain Matthew, RN (1774-1814) 56, Fitzroy Street, Soho, W1.
'explorer and navigator lived here'
Flinders, born in Donington, Lincolnshire, spent only a year here; from 1813. He was the first man to circumnavigate Tasmania (1798). He also circumnavigated Australia (1801-1803) and charted the coastline. Flinder's first voyage was under Captain Bligh to the West Indies (1790). Following his imprisonment in Mauritius, where he was suspected by the French of spying, he died of malaria. Flinders river, in Queensland, is named after him. Plaque erected 1973. Nearest tube station = Warren Street.

FLYING BOMB. Railway Bridge, Grove Road, Bow, E3.
On the 13th June 1944, the first flying bomb against London fell here. The flying bomb or V1 was a jet propelled winged bomb which fell to earth when its engine stopped. The launching sites were all along the French, Belgian and Dutch coasts and some 8,000 pilotless planes were launched against the Southern part of England until the sites were captured by Allied troops following D-Day, June 6th 1944. The Germans had no way of targeting their weapons, they were purely used to create terror amongst the civilian population. Many V1s were shot down by fast RAF fighters before they reached London but a lot got through and many civilians died from these and the later, faster, deadlier rocket, the V2. Von Braun was the nazi responsile for the creation of these terror rockets. Instead of being brought to trial for war crimes against humanity, he was taken by US Intelligence officers to America where he lived in luxury and worked in comfort, developing the US space programme. Plaque erected 1988. Nearest tube station = Bethnal Green.

FORD, Ford Madox (1873-1939) 80, Campden Hill Road, Kensington, W8.
'novelist and critic lived here'
Madox Ford, originally Ford Hermann Hueffer, was born in Merton, Surrey. He published his first book when he was only 18, a fairy story called "The Brown Owl". He followed this with a novel that appeared the following year, "The Shifting of the Fire". In 1894 he eloped and married Elsie Martindale. They lived here for many years, whilst Ford was editor of "The English Review", and all through WW1. Although he was in the army and often away in France, he managed to write many novels which reflected the war including, "The Good Soldier" (1915) and "Parade's End" (1924-1928). The house is better known as South Lodge and was often the haunt of fellow writers; H. G. Wells, Wyndham Lewis and Ezra Pound. In a busy career he wrote over seventy books and co-authored several more. Plaque erected 1973. Nearest tube station = Notting Hill Gate.

FORESTER, C. S (1899-1966) 58, Underhill Road, Dulwich, SE22.
'novelist lived here'
Forester, born in Cairo, was best known for creating the character Horatio Hornblower, the naval officer featured in stories about the Napoleonic wars. He also wrote, "The African Queen" (1935) and "The Ship" (1943). He joined the navy as a midshipman but soon left the service to study medicine. In 1926 his book, "Payment Deferred" was published and was an immediate success. He gave up medicine for full time writing. He lived and worked for most of his adult life here. He was fascinated by Nurse Edith Cavell, executed by the Germans as a spy and, together with Bechofer Roberts, wrote a play about her. Plaque erected 1990. Nearest Station = West Dulwich.

FORSTER, E. M. (Edward Morgan) (1879-1970) Arlington Park Mansions, Sutton Lane, Turnham Green, Chiswick, W4.
'novelist lived here',
Forster was born in London and educated at Tonbridge School which he loathed and King's College, Cambridge which he loved. Halfway through his adult life, Forster gave up writing novels in favour of essays on politics and criticisms. This was a great pity because his novels were quite superb, "Where Angels Fear to Tread" (1905), "Howards End" (1910), "A Passage to India" (1924) great novels and a godsend to the Merchant Ivery team who turned them into excellent films. He lived here from the time WW2 broke out in 1939. From his top floor flat, during the blitz, he had a grandstand view of London's dockyards burning. In 1946 he was elected a Fellow of Kings and in 1951 collaborated with Eric Crozier on the libretto for Britten's opera, "Billy Budd". Forster was a private homosexual who only allowed his novel "Maurice" to be published after his death. Plaque erected 1983. Nearest tube station = Turnham Green.

FOX, Charles James (1749-1806) 46, Clarges Street, Mayfair, W1.
'statesman lived here'
Fox, born in London and educated at Eton and Hertford College, Oxford, lived here for the last two years of his life. Elected to Parliament at 19 he became a brilliant orator. He was also a 'man about town' which included gambling, drinking and whoring. The Prince Regent admired him but George III hated him. He was a true Whig radical. He fought against the harsh measures being used in America and supported their war for independence. Later, he supported the aims of the French Revolution and demanded abstention from involvement. In 1806, as foreign secretary, he advocated political rights for dissenters and Catholics. A leading light in the abolition of the slave trade, it was only finally achieved in 1807, a year after he died. He is buried in Westminster Abbey, alongside Pitt, with whom Fox had a long and bitter struggle. Burke once said of Fox '. . . the greatest debater the world ever saw . . . ' and he should know. Plaque erected 1950. Nearest tube station = Green Park.

FRAMPTON, George (1860-1928) 32, Queen's Grove, St. John's Wood, NW8.
'sculptor lived and worked here 1894-1908'
Frampton was a sculptor born in London who specialised in statues of Queen Victoria. These can be seen throughout Britain and parts of what is now the Commonwealth, especially India and Canada. In 1901 he was asked to design the commemorative medal for the Coronation of Edward VII. So much royal patronage, it wasn't surprising he was awarded a knighthood in 1908. Following this honour he moved from here in favour of the rural scene where his recent elevation would mean something to the crawling locals. Other examples of his work include, "Peter Pan" in Kensington Gardens and the Edith Cavell statue in London. Plaque erected 1977. Nearest tube station = St. John's Wood.

FRANKLIN, Benjamin (1706-1790) 36, Craven Street, Strand, WC2
'American statesman and scientist, lived here'
In America he was accused of being too much an Englishman and in England too much an American. Franklin, born in Boston, was much in demand as a diplomat in the years leading to the American Declaration of Independence. He lived here from 1724 to 1726 and had a large circle of friends, including David Garrick and Adam Smith. Although his diplomatic efforts were well received it is as a scientist for which he was renowned. His erection of lightning rods on St Paul's Cathedral being particularly spectacular and for which he was made a Fellow of the Royal Society. He finally left London for America in 1772, but returned to Europe in 1776 as Ambassador to France, where he remained until 1784. Franklin was also a meteorologist who discovered the course of storms over the North American continent; the course of the Gulf Stream, its high temperature, and the use of the thermometer in navigating it. Plaque erected 1914. Nearest tube station = Charing Cross

FRANKLIN, Rosalind (1920-1958) Donovan Court, Drayton Gardens, Fulham, SW10.
'1920-1958, pioneer of the study of molecular structures including DNA lived here 1951-1958'
Rosalind Franklin was the daughter of Ellis Franklin, a member of a distinguished Jewish family that arrived in Portsmouth from Germany, in 1784. Rosalind was born in London and studied chemistry at Cambridge before working in London and Paris. In 1951, she joined a research group at King's College, London where she worked on X-ray diffractions. This led to her work on DNA and was of the greatest value in determining a full structure DNA and its relation to modern molecular biology. She was working on new methods of cancer treatments when she died at only 38. Two years after her death her co-workers were awarded the Nobel Prize for their part in discovering DNA. Unfortunately the Prize is never awarded posthumously. Plaque erected 1992. Nearest tube station = Gloucester Road.

FREAKE, Sir Charles James (1814-1884) 21, Cromwell Road, Kensington, SW7.
'builder and patron of the arts, lived here'
Freake lived here in style from 1860. He was a 'self made man', which relieved God of much responsibility, who ingratiated himself with the Prince of Wales. Born in London, the son of a coal merchant, he was a lucky builder who was building houses in London at a time of prosperity, following years of stagnation. He made a fortune and indulged himself. This house was built to his specifications and included a large ballroom where theatrical performances were staged. He knew the way to social acceptance, was to buy a knighthood through the well trodden path of charitable donations to causes that royalty were associated with. The Prince of Wales was most interested in music, therefore Freake, who was tone deaf, built the National Training School for Music. The knighthood came shortly after; 'expensive but worth every note', commented a wag of the day. Plaque erected 1981. Nearest tube station = Gloucester Road.

FREUD, Sigmund (1856-1939) 20, Maresfield Gardens, Hampstead, NW3.
'founder of psychoanalysis, lived here in 1938-1939'
Freud only lived here a short while. He fled from Vienna where, in 1938 because he was a Jew, his books were publicly burnt and psychoanalysis banned. Unable to get their hands on him, the Germans found his four sisters and butchered them. Maresfield Gardens, now open to the public, became his sanctuary. Although racked with pain from cancer, he continued seeing patients and conducting psycho-analysis. He was born in Freiburg, Moravia and studied medicine at Vienna. He became Professor of the Therapeutics of Neurotic Diseases and of Neurology in Vienna (1902). His work on hysteria led him to believe that symptoms were expressions of repressed sexual energy. He devised the technique of 'free association' to discover repressed experiences. Amongst his many works were, "The Interpretation of Dreams", (1900), "The Ego and Id" (1923), "Moses and Monotheism" (1938) and "The Outline of Psycho-Analysis", published after his death. In 1933, together with Albert Einstein, he wrote, "Why War?" Two of his grandsons are the brothers Lucian and Clement Freud; they haven't spoken to one another for thirty years. Plaque erected 1956. Nearest tube station = Finchley Road.

FRIESE-GREENE, William Edward (1855-1921) 136, Maida Vale, W9.
'pioneer of cinematography lived here'
Friese-Greene was born in Bristol where he studied chemistry at Bristol University. He arrived in London in 1885 and experimented in making moving pictures. In 1888 he brought his wife and child from Bristol, rented this house and stayed three years. He successfully proved his invention of using celluloid in the making of moving films and was granted a patent in 1889. He later experimented with colour film and 3D. Unhappily he was ahead of his time, there were little financial rewards and he died penniless. Plaque erected 1954. Nearest tube station = Warwick Avenue.

FRITH, W. P. (1819-1909) 114, Clifton Hill, St. John's Wood, NW8.
'painter lived and died here'
Frith, and his family, came to live here in 1896 and stayed. He was born in Aldfield and as a child revealed his talent as an artist. There was a time, in the 1860s and 70s when his paintings were so successful, that he was feted wherever he went and became the richest painter of his day. At the Royal Academy, crush barriers had to be erected, so popular were his paintings of contemporary life. But, as with all fashion, the public moved on. Frith, however, stood still. His reputation lessened and the fire left him. Plaque erected 1973. Nearest tube station = Maida Vale.

FROUDE, James Anthony (1818-1894) 5, Onslow Gardens, Kensington, SW7.
'historian and man of letters lived here'
Froude, born in Dartington, Devon was educated at Westminster and Oriel College, Oxford. At times he appeared to be obsessed with Thomas Carlyle whom he first met in 1849. It led him to be Carlyle's literary executor and his biographer (1882-4). In his own right he established himself, in the eyes of the Establishment, as a great master of prose, with the publication of the 12 volumes of "A History of England from the fall of Wolsey to the Spanish Armada" (1856-1870). He wrote much else besides and in 1892 became Professor of Modern History at Oxford. He lived here from 1865 until 1888, when he retired to Devon. Plaque erected 1934. Nearest tube station = South Kensington.

FUSELI, Henry (1741-1825) 37, Foley Street, Soho, W1.
'artist lived here 1788-1803'
There is little doubt that William Blake was influenced by Fuseli. Fuseli, born in Zurich, came to London in 1764. He soon had a reputation for 'wild paintings', which earned him the title, 'wild Swiss man'. His painting, 'The Nightmare', caused great excitement as did his illustrations of Milton and Shakespeare. His private life was similarly wild. He had an ongoing affair with Mary Wollstonecraft, which his wife Sophia tolerated, until one day, she rebelled and refused Mary admittance to the house. In 1804 Fuseli left here and took up the appointment as Keeper of The Royal Academy, with official apartments at Somerset House. Plaque erected 1961. Nearest tube station = Goodge Street.

GAINSBOROUGH, Thomas (1727-1788) 82 Pall Mall, St. James's, SW1.
'artist lived here'
Gainsborough, born in Sudbury, Suffolk, lived here from 1744 onwards. For a man who preferred his own company it must seem surprising he needed a house so large. He only used it to the full once a year, when he held an exhibition of his works. Other artists made use of the Royal Academy, not Gainsborough. Backed by George III he could afford to distance himself from his contemporaries. Although Joshua Reynolds was his great rival, Reynolds was present at Gainsborough's death and later delivered the obituary lecture, praising him to the hilt. Gainsborough's famous landscapes often represent Eastern England. His portraits are legend, 'Blue Boy', 'Mrs Siddons' and members of the Royal Family. In 1745, he married one of his models, the illegitimate daughter of the Duke of Beaufort. This one act provided him with a loving wife and entree into society. He was considered an elegant painter in the style of Van Dyck but with the added dash of Rubens. Plaque erected 1951. Nearest tube station = Green Park.

GAITSKELL, Hugh (1906-1963) 18, Frognal Gardens, Hampstead, NW3.
'statesman lived here'
Gaitskell was born in London and educated at Winchester and New College, Oxford. He lived here towards the end of his life. It was the General Strike of 1926 that convinced Gaitskill that Socialism was the only answer to Britain's ills. He became MP for Leeds South in 1945 and only ten years later was leader of the Labour party. In the interval he was Chancellor of the Exchequer (1950-1) and responsible for bringing in national health charges. Gaitskell remained leader until his untimely death and it was under his aegis that the party began the watering down of socialism that has continued to the present day. Labour's defeat in the 1992 General Election can perhaps be found in the policies started by Gaitskell. Plaque erected 1986. Nearest tube station = Hampstead.

GALSWORTHY, John (1867-1933) Grove Lodge, Admiral's Walk, Hampstead, NW3.
'novelist and playwright lived here 1918-1933'
Galsworthy, born in Coombe, Surrey and educated at Harrow and New College, Oxford, spent the last thirteen years of his life here. He became a barrister (1890) but preferred writing. He was a tall athletic looking man of over 6ft, who could be seen striding the adjacent Heath in all weathers. His special enjoyment was to hear his wife, Ada, play the piano; even whilst he was working. Success came with his play, "The Silver Box" (1906). The work for which he is best remembered is, "The Forsyte Saga" (1906-1922). He also wrote Ibsenesque plays about social injustice, "Strife" (1909), "The Skin Game" (1920) but these were not well received. He was awarded the Nobel Prize for Literature in 1932. He was a lifelong friend of Joseph Conrad. Plaque erected 1950. Nearest tube station = Hampstead.

GALTON, Sir Francis (1822-1911) 42, Rutland Gate, Knightsbridge, SW7.
'explorer, statistician and founder of eugenics lived here for fifty years'
Galton was born in Birmingham and educated at King Edward's school before studying medicine at Birmingham Hospital and King's College, London. He lived here from 1858 onwards and can fairly be described as one of Britain's great scientists. Here he lived and worked and produced the results of experiments and studies. He introduced the basis of much of the meteorology we use to-day, as well as the terms used, e.g. 'anti-cyclone'. His work was published in, "Methods of Mapping the Weather" (1863). He founded and coined the term for Eugenics, the movement to improve species through hereditary factors. A noted anthropologist, he developed statistical correlation and questionnaire techniques which he used to great effect in advancing the theories of his cousin, Charles Darwin. Plaque erected 1959. Nearest tube station = Knightsbridge.

GANDHI, Mahatma (1869-1948) Kingley Hall, Powis Road, Bow, E3.
'philosopher and teacher stayed here in 1931' AND
20, Baron's Court Road, W14.
'lived here as a law student'
There are two commemorative plaques to Gandhi, the first is where he stayed for only three months, whilst representing the Indian Congress at talks in London concerning constitutional government. As the British government had foreseen, there was so much controversy within the native political parties it was simply a question of 'divide and rule' and the trade rape could continue. The Baron's Court address is where Gandhi lived whilst a law student. He became a Barrister-at-Law and admitted to the Inner Temple in 1890. Although born in Pornbandar, India, he chose to live in South Africa where he tried to use the legal system against the laws that disadvantaged non-whites. He remained there for 21 years before returning to India to play the major part in securing independence (1947). He was assassinated by a Hindu fanatic as he was leaving his Delhi home. His autobiography, 'The Story of my Experiment With Truth' was republished in 1949. Gandhi represents the ultimate in passive resistance. Plaques erected 1954 and 1986. Nearest Tube Stations = Bow Road and Baron's Court.

GARRETT ANDERSON, Elizabeth (1836-1917) 20, Upper Berkeley Street, Marylebone, W1.
'the first woman to qualify as a doctor in Britain, lived here'
Although born in London, Elizabeth Garrett was brought up in Aldeburgh, Suffolk. She returned to London to study medicine and whilst living here (1860-1874) qualified, in 1865, to practise medicine. The first woman in Britain to do so. It was a victory she and her friend, Dr Sophia Jex-Blake, had long fought for. In 1886, she opened a small clinic for women and children, in London, which quickly grew to become a fully fledged hospital: 'The New Hospital for Women'. It was later known as 'The Elizabeth Garrett Anderson Hospital'. Her younger sister was Millicent Fawcett, the famous suffragette. In 1908, Dr. Anderson returned to Aldeburgh, where she was elected Mayor; the first woman mayor in England. A double first? Plaque erected 1962. Nearest tube station = Marble Arch.

GARRICK, David (1717-1779) Garrick's Villa, Hampton Court Road, Richmond-upon-Thames.
'actor, lived here'
Garrick was born in Hereford and educated at Litchfield, where he met Samuel Johnson, who agreed to take him on as a pupil. In 1737, the two men set off for London to seek their fortune, Garrick with the idea of becoming a barrister. Instead he, together with his elder brother opened a wine shop. It closed in 1740 and Garrick devoted the rest of his life to the theatre, first as an actor then as a manager. Garrick lived here from 1754 and gave many parties for his fellow actors and others connected with the theatre. Dr. Johnson was a prominent visitor who remarked on one occasion, 'how proud I am of my creation'. Garrick first set foot on the London stage in 1741, in the role of Richard III and became famous overnight. He gave up acting in 1747 to concentrate on management. He took over the Drury Lane theatre where he remained until 1776. In 1749 he married Eva Violeti, a Viennese dancer who survived him by 43 years. He is buried in Westminster Abbey. Plaque erected 1970. Nearest Station = Hampton

GASKELL, Mrs Elizabeth Gleghorn (1810-1865) 93, Cheyne Walk, Chelsea, SW10.
'novelist born here'
Elizabeth Gaskell nee Stevenson was born here. Because her father was constantly changing his work Elizabeth was taken, shortly after her birth, to live with her aunt in Knutsford. He was, in succession, teacher, preacher, farmer, boarding-house keeper, writer and keeper of the records to the Treasury. Later, when married to the Reverend William Gaskell, she lived in Manchester. Her first published novel was "Mary Barton" (1848) which caused some controversy. It had been published anonymously but it soon emerged who had written it and she was feted by those whose grievances she had aired, namely poor people living in the poverty of Northern England. She was however vilified by those who wanted no exposure of these terrible facts. She then went on to write a series of pamphlets that were later published as "Cranford" (1853). She wrote many novels that were generally well received and continued doing so until the day before she died. In 1857 she wrote the controversial biography of "The Life of Charlotte Bronte". Plaque erected 1913. Nearest tube station = Sloane Square.

GAUDIER-BRZESKA, Henri (1891-1915) 454, Fulham Road, Fulham, SW6.
'sculptor and artist lived here'
A short life but an explosive one. He was a founding member of the Vorticists and was emerging as a leading sculptor when WW1 broke out. Born in St. Jean de Braye, France, Gaudier (Brzeska was added when he married) joined the French army and was killed in action in 1915 at Neuville-Saint-Vaast, near to where he was born. He was living here, in a small studio, when he left for the war. Plaque erected 1977. Nearest tube station = Fulham Broadway.

GERTLER, Mark (1891-1939) 32, Elder Street, Stepney, E1.
'painter lived here'
This is where Mark Gertler lived, together with his family, from 1911 to 1915. He was one of the first romantic painters to emerge following the wave of Jewish immigration into Britain during the 19th century. Until he went to school at the age of 8 he spoke only Yiddish. He left school at 14 and began evening classes in art whilst working for a firm of glass painters. In 1908, Sir William Rothenstein of the Jewish Educational Aid Society, sent him to the Slade School of Art. Before he was 20 he painted one of his finest works "The Artist's Mother", now in the Tate. He left the Slade in 1912 and began a career of portrait painting. Handsome, volatile and an excellent conversationalist he seemed destined for greatness. However, with advancing ill health came decreasing success, which in turn led to money problems. Depressed by reports of Hitler's purge of artistic Jewish life, led him to commit suicide at his Highgate home in 1939. Plaque erected 1975. Nearest tube station = Moorgate.

GIBBON, Edward (1737-1792) 7, Bentinck Street, Mayfair, W1.
'historian, lived in a house on this site 1773-1783'
Gibbon was born in Putney the son of a country gentleman in an area that has changed somewhat. He was educated at Westminster and Magdalen College, Oxford. This is the site of where Gibbon lived for his last ten years in England. He left here for Switzerland where he completed the final volumes of "Decline and Fall of the Roman Empire" (1788), acknowledged as one of the world's great historical works. Previously he had been an MP and, influenced by Samuel Johnson, had become Commissioner of Trades and Plantations. Gibbon was fortunate to have been the heir to a wealthy father; it meant he had a staff of servants to look after him; a housekeeper, valet, butler, two cooks and four maids and he lived alone! In 1753, whilst in Switzerland he met and fell in love with the daughter of a Calvinist minister. His father objected strongly to the proposed marriage and Edward returned to England alone . . . "I sighed as a lover, I obeyed as a son". His idea of history was as . . . "little more than the register of the crimes, follies and misfortunes of mankind". How very true. Plaque erected 1964. Nearest tube station = Bond Street.

GILBERT, Sir W. S. (1836-1911) 39, Magdalene Gardens, Kensington, SW7.
'dramatist lived here'

He was given the names of William Schwenck but is known as WS. Born in London, he was educated at King's College, London where he studied for the Bar. Unable to make a living at the law he turned to humorous writing, mostly for "Punch" . He lived here for seven years, until 1890. During this time he wrote "The Mikado" , "The Yeoman of the Guard" and "The Gondoliers" . The house was equipped, for the times, with some unusual features; central heating, a bathroom on each floor and a telephone. He, and of course Sir Arthur Sullivan, were very rich. The songs from their light operas were the great hits of the day, and their appeal has never diminished. But it might never had happened. In 1838, whilst travelling with his parents through Naples, he was kidnapped by robbers who demanded £25 for his release. Happily all ended well, the parents paid up and the two year old was released. The Gilberts moved to Grimsdyke, Harrow Weald in 1890. To-day excerpts of the operas are regularly performed; whilst the audience eat their dinner. The great row, between Gilbert and Sullivan, was sparked off over the cost of a carpet for their theatre, The Savoy. The carpet has long gone but their music survives. Plaque erected 1929. Nearest tube station = Gloucester Road.

GISSING, George (1857-1903) 33, Oakley Gardens, Chelsea, SW3.
'novelist, lived here 1882-1884'

Gissing spent 14 years in London but only lived here for a year, and that was one of his longest dwellings. He was born in Wakefield and died in St. Jean du Luz, France. In between, he had a varied, often crazy life. He won scholarships to two universities; Manchester and London, lived with a prostitute, Nell Harrison, from whom he contracted a venereal disease. In order to support her he stole from the coat pockets of his fellow students. He was caught, given a month in prison and expelled from his college. His father, a pharmacist, packed him off to America, where he wrote about his abject poverty 'New Grub Street' (1891). He returned to England, married Nell and continued to live in poverty. Nell died in 1888, was buried in a pauper's grave and Gissing continued writing, "Born in Exile" (1892), "The Odd Women" (1893) and his 'spoof' autobiography, "The Private Papers of Henry Pyecroft" (1903). In 1890 he married another prostitute, Edith Underwood, had two sons, many rows and left. He spent the last five years of life living with Gabrielle Fleury, his French translator, in the South of France. Few writers have pursued their career with such single mindedness as Gissing. In 1982, "The Diary of George Gissing, Novelist" was published. Plaque erected 1975. Nearest tube station = Sloane Square.

GLADSTONE, William Ewart (1809-1898) 11, Carlton House, Terrace, SW1.
'statesman, lived here'
Gladstone spent some 20 years here. During this period he enjoyed the highest offices of state possible. He was born in Liverpool and educated at Eton and Christ Church, Oxford. Although known as a great reformer Gladstone had a blind spot; he was anti Irish Catholics. So much so he resigned in 1845 rather than agree to a grant for R.C. education in Ireland. It is possible that his zeal for reform was in some way to atone for the fortune his family made from the Liverpool slave trade. He was a great orator and the parliamentary battles between he and Disraeli, when one or the other was Prime Minister or Leader of the Opposition, always ensured a full house. He claimed to have strong morals and that it was in pursuance of these objectives that he was constantly found in those parts of London populated by prostitutes. He was also a literary figure and in 1858 published "Studies in Homer and the Homeric Age". Towards the end of his life he had a change of heart over Irish affairs and in 1893 he got his Home Rule bill passed in the Commons, only to see it rejected by the Lords. He is buried in Westminster Abbey. Plaque erected 1925. Nearest tube station = Charing Cross.

GLAISHER, James (1809-1903) 20, Dartmouth Hill, Blackheath, SE10.
'astronomer, meteorologist and pioneer of weather forecasting, lived here'
Glaisher, born in London, spent thirty years here. He worked at the Greenwich Observatory and organised the system of weather forecasting that, with some updating, is still used today. He was also a balloonist and made some spectacular trips, the greatest of which was ascending to over seven miles, in order to study the higher strata of the atmosphere; without breathing apparatus. He wrote several books on his subject. Plaque erected 1974, Nearest Station = Greenwich.

GODLEY, John Robert (1814-1861) 48, Gloucester Place, Marylebone, W1.
'founder of Canterbury, New Zealand, lived and died here'
Godley, born in London, is generally known as the founder of New Zealand. He was in charge of a group who pledged themselves to establish a Church of England society in New Zealand. It represented all classes, except the Maoris whose country it was. In 1850 Godley was appointed Governor. There were protests about his behaviour with women. Forced to return to London and work at the war office, he lived here. Plaque erected 1951. Nearest tube station = Baker Street.

GODWIN, George (1813-1888) 24, Alexander Square, Chelsea, SW3.
'architect, journalist and social reformer, lived here'
Godwin, born in London, spent nearly a quarter of a century here. During this time he designed local churches and the general design of The Boltons, which still retains its original charm. He edited "The Builder" from 1844 to 1883 and used his influence to promote decent sanitary conditions in working class houses. Plaque erected 1969. Nearest tube station = South Kensington.

GOSSE, Philip Henry (1810-1888) 56, Mortimer Road, N1.
'Here lived Philip Henry GOSSE (1810-1888), zoologist; and Sir Edmund GOSSE (1849-1928), writer and critic, born here'
This plaque commemorates both father and son (Edmund). Both were born in London. Philip Gosse was a zoologist who, save for his "History of British Sea-anemones and Corals" (1860), made little impression. His temper and fanatical religious fervour did. The household were in daily fear and loathing of him. It was perhaps because of his frightening upbringing that led Edmund on his career as a writer. His "Father and Son" (1907) gives a graphic detail of what happened. Later he translated Ibsen into English and brought the new drama here. For this and other services to literature Edmund was knighted. Between 1888 and 1920 he wrote several biographies the best known of which is "Donne" (1899). Plaque erected 1983. Nearest Station = Dalston Junction

GOUNOD, Charles (1818-1893) 15, Morden Road, Blackheath, SE3.
'composer, stayed here in 1870'
A very brief stay appears to have warranted a plaque. His creation of the opera "Faust" in 1859 is of course his main claim to fame. There is however, no evidence that the four weeks he spent here, to escape the Franco-Prussian war, ever influenced his future work. Plaque erected 1961. Nearest Station = Blackheath.

GRACE, W. G. (1848-1915) 'Fairmount' Mottingham Lane, Eltham, SE9.
'cricketer lived here'
Grace lived here from 1909 onwards. During this time he was still playing 'the game'. He was born in Downend, Glos. and became a doctor. He practised for some time in Bristol until, in 1870, he started playing for Gloucestershire. His cricket career continued until 1914, when he was 66 years old. During this time he captained England 13 times, took over 2,800 wickets and scored over 54,000 runs, including 126 centuries. Notwithstanding the long interval between 1915 and to-day, Grace is still probably the greatest cricketer of all time. Two of his brothers were test players and played with him for Gloucester. Plaque erected 1966. Nearest Station = Mottingham.

GRAHAME, Kenneth (1859-1932) 16, Phillimore Place, Kensington, W8.
'author of "Wind in the Willows", lived here 1901-1908'
Grahame was a kindly man with a great insight to what children enjoyed. He was born in Edinburgh and educated at St. Edward's School, Oxford. Grahame and his wife lived here whilst he worked for the Bank of England. In 1909 the family moved to Cookham Dean where Grahame took up writing full-time. The story of how "Wind in the Willows" came about is worth telling. Grahame's son, Alistair then aged 8, was being told a series of bedtime stories, made up by his father, that featured such characters as Mr Toad, Water Rat and Mole. Then came the time when the family were to leave for a holiday at Littlehampton but father was so busy at the bank it was impossible for him to get away. Alistair refused to go, if it meant being away a whole month without the breathtaking adventures of Mr Toad. It was only when his father faithfully promised to forward the next instalment of the story each day by post, did Alistair agree to leave. What Grahame wrote, in the ensuing month, became the genesis for one of the most delightful books for young and old. Unhappily Alistair was killed by a train whilst an undergraduate at Christ Church, Oxford. It was a sadness from which his father never recovered. Plaque erected 1959. Nearest tube station = Kensington High Street.

GRAINGER, Percy (1882-1961) 31, King's Road, Chelsea, SW3.
'Australian composer, folklorist and pianist, lived here'
Grainger was born in Melbourne, Australia. After studying under Pabst and Busoni in Italy he settled in America in 1915. A great admirer of Grieg, he followed his example of including folk songs in his compositions. "Molly on the Shore", "Mock Morris" and "Shepherds Hey" are some examples. He lived here during the thirties whilst promoting his music. Plaque erected 1988. Nearest tube station = Sloane Square.

GRAY, Henry (1827-1861) 8, Wilton Street, Belgravia, SW1.
'anatomist, lived here'
Gray who was born in London and who lived here for most of his life, must surely be the youngest man ever elected a Fellow of The Royal Society. He was just 25. He published, in 1853, what is still the medical student's standard textbook on the subject, viz. "Anatomy". At the age of 34 he contracted smallpox from a child and died. Plaque erected 1947. Nearest tube station = Victoria

THE 'GREAT EASTERN' (launched 1858) Burrells Wharf, 262, West Ferry Road, Isle of Dogs, E14.
'Largest steamship of the century was built here by I. K. Brunel and J. Scott Russell.'

GREAVES, Walter (1846-1930) 104, Cheyne Walk, Chelsea, SW10.
'artist, lived here 1855-1897'
Greaves was an artist who specialised in paintings of the Thames. His father was a boatman who, for a living, transported things and people up, down and across the river. Greaves was only a young lad when the family moved here from Battersea where he was born. One of their neighbours was James Whistler, the American artist, who always made a point of using the Greaves Water Taxi service. Whistler soon saw that young Walter had a good eye and could paint. Greaves made a name for himself on the back of his patron but, as is often the case, it wasn't long before tutor and pupil fell out. Greaves outlived his mentor by some thirty years yet his manner and mode of dress reflected the dandyness of the master. Greaves's best known works are "Chelsea Regatta" and "Boat Race Day, Hammersmith Bridge". Plaque erected 1973. Nearest tube station = Sloane Square.

GREEN, John Richard (1837-1883) St. Philip's Vicarage, Newark Street, Stepney, E1. AND 4, Beaumont Street, Marylebone, W1.
'historian of the English people lived here'
Green was born in Oxford and educated at Magdalen School and Jesus College, Oxford. After a false start, as Vicar of St. Philips, Green found his forte as an historical writer, but not until he left the East End and crossed to the West in 1869. After many years of dedicated work his "Short History of the English People" was published in 1874. It was an immediate success and brought him offers from many universities. Green's rejection of Trinity College, Cambridge's offer was typical . . . "My winters abroad make it impossible for me to accept". He was in failing health, from tuberculosis, and needed to winter in the sun. He died before he was fifty but left a great legacy. Plaques erected 1909 and 1910. Nearest Tube Stations = Aldgate East and Baker Street.

GREENAWAY, Kate (1846-1901) 39, Frognal, Hampstead, NW3.
'artist, lived and died here'
Kate Greenaway was born in London and studied art at the Slade School of Art. She had her first exhibition at the Royal Academy in 1877. In 1885, she moved here to live in the house specifically designed for her by Norman Shaw. She was a watercolour artist of distinction who specialised in children's subjects. Her depiction of children in quaint early 19th century costume, e.g. "Mother Goose, Birthday Book", influenced children's fashion. The Greenaway medal is awarded annually for the best British children's artist. Plaque erected 1949. Nearest tube station = Hampstead.

GREET, Sir Philip Ben (1857-1936) 160, Lambeth Road, Lambeth, SE1.
'actor-manager lived here 1920-1936'
Greet, born in London, lived here with the Keys family for over fifty years. It was close to the Old Vic which he managed, for a time, with Lilian Baylis. He launched his open air theatre to bring Shakespeare to the attention of working class people. He was knighted in 1929 for services to education and drama. Plaque erected 1961. Nearest tube station = Lambeth North.

GREY, Sir Edward, Viscount Grey of Falloden (1862-1933) 3, Queen Anne's Gate, St. James's, SW1.
'Foreign Secretary lived here'
Born in London and educated at Winchester and Balliol College, Oxford, Grey was a natural diplomat. Foreign Secretary in the Liberal government of 1905 - 1916, he was an ardent worker for peace. In 1907, he established the Triple Entente between France, Russia and Britain. This agreement vitally proved itself when, in 1914, the first German war started. In 1916 he and Asquith resigned over the manner in which the war was being run. He was chancellor of Oxford University from 1928. He lived here from 1906 to 1912. In the House of Lords, just weeks before he died, Grey warned, to those who would listen, of the dangers of Hitler and fascism. Plaque erected 1981. Nearest tube station = St. James's Park.

GRIMALDI, Joseph (1778-1837) 56, Exmouth Market, Finsbury, EC1.
'clown, lived here 1818-1828'
Grimaldi, born in London, is arguably the greatest English clown ever. He was a master of song, dance, acrobatics, mime and an astute manager. He lived here for the last decade of an eventful popular and well rewarded life. The songs he made popular long outlived him. Plaque erected 1989. Nearest tube station = Farringdon.

GROCER, Reverend St. John (1890-1966) Royal Foundation of St. Katherine, 2 Butcher Row, E14.

'priest and social reformer lived here'

Born in Australia, Grocer became a cattle drover before coming to England and entering a seminary. He was ordained in time to become an Army Chaplain at the outbreak of WW1. A few months later, whilst in Flanders, he was awarded the Military Cross for aiding and comforting the wounded whilst under fire. He was later reprimanded for giving Holy Communion to enemy POW's. His response was to repeat the offence. He spent much time, after the war, in working with the East End poor. His support wasn't restricted to spiritual matters; in 1926, during the General Strike, he was in the workers midst and on the their street marches. On one of these marches he was assaulted by the police, during one of their infamous baton charges against defenceless unemployed workers, their wives and children. Whilst recovering from his injuries he voiced his criticism of the Church, charging them with being unconcerned about social justice. During WW2, he was still in the East End, an area of London that suffered the worst of Hitler's night bombing. He spent the nights comforting the poor whilst they sought refuge in cold damp air raid shelters. He was part of the group that pleaded for the London Underground to be kept open during the night in order Londoners might sleep on the platforms; warm and safe. Grocer was always the diplomat trying to solve the problems of his parish by conciliatory means. There was the time when the Red Flag flew over the Council offices, a mob tore it down and put up the Union flag in its place. After the Reverend Grocer stepped in the Union and the Red flag flew side by side. From 1943 to 1962 he was Master of the Royal Foundation of St. Katherine, one of the poorest, deprived and neglected parts of London; a very different place to what it is to-day. Plaque erected 1990. Nearest tube station = Stepney East.

GROSSMITH, George, Senior (1847-1912) 28, Dorset Square, Marylebone, NW1.

'actor and author lived here'

Grossmith, born in London, lived here for some fifteen years only moving out to go to an old age home where he died two years later. Together with his brother, Weedon, he wrote, "Diary of a Nobody" (1894) for PUNCH. It was an instant success in comic writing. George also appeared in D'Oyly Carte productions and was well known for his interpretations of Gilbert and Sullivan characters. Plaque erected 1963. Nearest tube station = Marylebone.

GROSSMITH, George, Junior (1874-1935) 3, Spanish Place, Marylebone, W1.

'actor-manager, lived here'

For many years Grossmith, born in London, lived and worked in the United States. In 1909 he moved here and stayed until he died. Grossmith decided, soon after his move, that he preferred to be a theatrical manager rather than an actor. His biggest achievement was in 1925 when the Drury Lane Theatre presented 'No! No! Nanette' and it ran and ran and ran. He was also a useful songwriter. Plaque erected 1963, Nearest tube station = Marble Arch.

GROTE, George (1794-1871) 12, Saville Row, Mayfair, W1.
'historian died here'
The Grote family moved here in 1848 and George turned the front rooms into his offices. Born in Beckenham, Kent and educated at Charterhouse, he would spend his entire day working on Greek history, although he managed to find time to act as MP for the City of London, (1832-1841). His small dog, Dora, would sit on his foot whilst he worked away on what was to become his great work in 12 volumes, "The History of Greece" (1856). He was also a Fellow of the Royal Society and Vice-Chancellor of London University. He lived the sort of life most men dream of. His wife adored him and organised the parties at which his wit and humour was much admired. To complete a rewarding life he's buried in Westminster Abbey. Plaque erected 1905. Nearest tube station = Piccadilly.

HAGGARD, Sir Henry Rider (1856-1925) 69, Gunterstone Road, Fulham, W14.
'novelist lived here 1885-1888'
Haggard, born in Bradenham Hall, Norfolk the son of a lawyer and educated at Ipswich Grammar School, only lived here for three years which isn't surprising when you appreciate the years he lived abroad. But it was here where he wrote "King Solomons Mines" (1886) and "Allan Quatermain" (1887). He wrote to relieve the boredom of the Bar to which he had been admitted in 1885. His legal practise started after many years in the Transvaal, working first for the Governor of Natal, before farming ostriches. His books were immediate and great successes and Haggard was pleased to be able to give up the law and just write. He moved to Ditchingham Hall, Norfolk where he lived the life of a country gentleman and wrote on the poor living conditions of the rural population. He was knighted in 1912. Plaque erected 1977. Nearest tube station = West Kensington.

HALDANE, Lord (1856-1928) 28, Queen Anne's Gate, St. James's, SW1.
'statesman, lawyer and philosopher, lived here'
Richard Haldane lived here from 1907 onwards. He was born in Scotland of a famous Scots family and educated at Edinburgh. He became a barrister and entered parliament in 1885 as a Liberal MP. In 1905, as secretary of state for war, he created the Territorial Army. In 1912 he was lord chancellor and remained in that post until 1915. After WW1 he joined the newly emerging Labour party. He was a noted philosopher particularly in the field of education and published several books on the subject. He joined the Webbs in creating The London School of Economics. In 1925, he was created a Peer of the Realm and led the small number of Labour Lords until his death three years later. Plaque erected 1954. Nearest tube station = St. James's Park.

HALL, Radclyffe (1880-1943) 37, Holland Street, Kensington, W8.
'Novelist and Poet lived here 1924-1929'
Margaret Radclyffe Hall was born in Bournemouth. She began as a lyric poet and wrote several volumes of verse, some of which became songs. In 1924 she wrote the first of her several novels, "The Forge" and "The Unlit Lamp", "Adam's Breed" (1926) brought her the Femina Vie Heureuse and the Tait Black Memorial prizes. These novels brought her a modicum of success, however in 1928 she wrote "The Well of Loneliness" a sympathetic story about female homosexuality and this brought her notoriety. The Church in particular caused a furore with the result that the book was banned in Britain for many years. Plaque erected 1992. Nearest tube station = Kensington High Street.

HALLAM, Henry (1777-1859) 67, Wimpole Street, Marylebone, W1.
'historian lived here'
Hallam, born in Windsor and educated at Eton and Christ Church College, Oxford, lived here from 1819 to 1840. Following the death of his father Henry Hallam, he was financially able to retire from the law and devote himself to studying history. The result was the mighty, "Constitutional History of England From the Accession of Henry VII to the Death of George II". Hallam was a weak kindly man who suffered more than most from life's tragedies. His son Arthur died suddenly, whilst travelling on the Continent, aged 22. Arthur was the great friend of Alfred Lord Tennyson who, on learning of his friend's death, was moved to write, "In Memoriam". Hallam was trying to get over his son's death when his daughter, Ellen suddenly died in 1837. Three years later his wife died and he was all alone. Through all his misfortune Hallam won the respect of his friends for the manner in which he continued living and working. Plaque erected 1904. Nearest tube station = Regent's Park.

HAMMOND, J. L. and Barbara, 'Hollycot', Vale of Health, Hampstead, NW3.
'social historians, lived here 1906-1913'
John Lawrence Le Breton Hammond was born in Yorkshire, the son of a Vicar. Educated at Bradford Grammar School and Oxford, he joined the Civil Service. He married Lucy Barbara Bradby in 1901 and on the outbreak of war in 1914 left the civil service for the army. Thereafter, the Hammonds worked together writing and publishing works on the history of working class people. "The Village Labourer, 1760-1832" (1911), "The Town Labourer, 1760-1832" (1917) and "The Skilled Labourer, 1760-1832" (1919). Hammond's best known work is his biography of Gladstone as it appeared in his, "Gladstone and the Irish Nation" published in 1938. Plaque erected 1972. Nearest tube station = Hampstead.

HANDEL, George Frederick (1685-1759) 25, Brook Street, Mayfair, W1.
'musician, lived and died here'
Handel was born in Halle, Germany but became a naturalised Englishman in 1712. Although Handel never married, he had an ongoing relationship with the German speaking matron of Bloomsbury's Foundling Hospital. As a consequence he left, in his will, the score and any royalties that might ensue, of "The Messiah", for ever. He never mastered the English language and claimed music was the language of the civilised world. He had an enormous appetite and when one day he was dining alone, and had ordered enough for three, he was kept waiting. On enquiring why, he was told by the waiter . . . "I am waiting for your company to arrive" to which Handel replied, "Ach, I am the company". He composed "The Water Music" as a sop to the Hanovarian George I; as a result the King awarded Handel a life's pension. In all he wrote 46 operas and 32 oratorios. He is buried in Poet's Corner, Westminster Abbey. Plaque erected 1952. Nearest tube station = Oxford Circus.

HANDLEY, Tommy (1892-1949) 34, Craven Road, Paddington, W2.
'radio comedian lived here'
Tommy Handley was born in Liverpool and lived here during WW2. Following his early years of touring the country in revues, vaudeville and pantomime, Handley settled for radio and during the war became as famous as any general or politician. His radio show "ITMA" (It's That Man Again) was required listening both at home and for the forces overseas. His contribution to the morale of war time Britain is immeasurable. Had he lived longer there is no doubt he would have been awarded an important honour. Plaque erected 1980. Nearest tube station = Paddington.

HANSOM, Joseph Aloysius (1803-1882) 27, Sumner Place, Knightsbridge, SW7.
'architect, founder editor of "The Builder" and inventor of the Hansom Cab, lived here'
Hansom was born in York and educated in Yorkshire. He lived here from 1873 to 1877. He qualified as an architect and designed Birmingham's Town Hall in 1831 and the Catholic cathedral at Plymouth. Through no fault of his, the contractor working on the Birmingham project failed to complete the job and Hansom was held responsible and made bankrupt. In 1836 he designed a cab that was considered safe for public use. He became famous for the 'Hansom Cab' but he didn't make any money out of the project and instead started a magazine for the building trade; "The Builder". Plaque erected 1980. Nearest tube station = South Kensington.

HARDY, Thomas (1840-1928) 172, Trinity Road, Tooting, SW17.
'poet and novelist lived here 1878-1881'
Hardy took this house on a three year lease; but didn't enjoy his stay. He disliked London, it was too big, and he yearned to return to the West Country. He was born in Upper Bockhampton, near Dorchester, the son of a stonemason and educated locally, before training, in London, as an architect. During his stay here he wrote, in November 1878, "The Return of the Native". Also whilst living here Hardy met Mathew Arnold and Tennyson. But Hardy wasn't well in the winter of 1880, he was bedridden for many weeks and it wasn't until the following Spring that he was able to walk on Wandsworth Common. It was with great relief when in 1882 he, and his wife Emma, who he had married in 1874, moved to Dorset. Here, following the death of his wife after a turbulent marriage, Hardy wrote some of the most moving poems in the English language. Later he married again, this time to Florence Dugdale who acted as his secretary in the writing of his autobiography, which eventually appeared under her name. Although Hardy wrote some famous novels, "Tess of the D'Urbervilles", "Far From the Madding Crowd", "The Mayor of Casterbridge" and many more, he once said "I regard poetry as superior to fiction". Plaque erected 1940. Nearest tube station = Balham.

HARMSWORTH, Alfred, Viscount Northcliffe (1865-1922) 31, Pandora Road, West Hampstead, NW6.
'journalist and newspaper proprietor, lived here'
Harmsworth was born in County Dublin and educated locally. He became a journalist for a local paper before coming to London. He lived here, from 1888, for three years. Whilst here he published "Comic Cuts" and "Answers to Correspondents" and planned his future newspaper empire. This would one day include "The Evening News", "The Daily Mail", "The Daily Mirror", "The Times" and "The Observer". The Amalgamated Press and the Harmsworth Brothers were often criticised for their influence in politics on behalf of the Conservatives. After his death the group was run by his younger brother Harold (Lord Rothermere), one of whose blunders, in the thirties, was backing the British fascists under Oswald Mosley. Plaque erected 1979. Nearest tube station = West Hampstead.

HARRISON, John (1693-1776) Summit House, Red Lion Square, WC1.
'inventor of the marine chronometer, lived and died in a house on this site'
Harrison was born in Foulby, near Pontefract in Yorkshire. He became responsible for building a chronometer that accurately determined longtitude. This he only achieved after the intervention of the King, who cut out the red tape the civil servants were creating. During the trials voyage to Jamaica in 1761, he determined the longtitude to within 18 geographical miles, so winning the 1st prize the government had offered. Plaque erected 1954. Nearest tube station = Holborn.

HARTE, Francis Bret (1836-1902) 74, Lancaster Gate, Bayswater, W2.
'American writer lived here'
Harte, the American short story writer, was born in Albany, New York. In 1854 he went to San Francisco and worked on various newspapers. He became secretary of the U. S. Mint (1864-70) and later held other official posts but he was always writing. He first came to London in 1885. Following his retirement as American Consul in Glasgow, Harte lived in this house from 1895 until his death in 1902. Amongst his best known works about gamblers, prostitutes and prospectors was, "The Luck of Roaring Camp" (1870) and "Mrs Scagg's Husbands" (1873). Harte's paternal grandfather was an English Jew, born in London, and originally responsible for the family emigrating to America. Plaque erected 1977. Nearest tube station = Lancaster Gate.

HAWKINS, Sir Anthony Hope (1863-1933) 41, Bedford Square, Holborn, WC1.
'novelist lived here 1903-1917'
Hawkins used his forenames under which he wrote his most famous book "The Prisoner of Zenda" (1894). He was born in Clapton, London the son of a clergyman. Educated at Balliol College, Oxford, he was called to the bar in 1887. Although a successful barrister, his first love was writing. After the success of Zenda he gave up the law and concentrated on writing. "Rupert of Hentzau" followed in 1898. During WW1 he worked for the Ministry of Information disseminating information to mislead the Germans. Plaque erected 1976. Nearest tube station = Tottenham Court Road.

HAWTHORNE, Nathaniel (1804-1864) 4, Pond Road, Blackheath, SE3.
'American author stayed here in 1856'
Hawthorne was born in Salem, Mass. , the son of a sea captain who died when his son was 4 years old. He and his mother then eked out a poor existance in Maine. After a brief education Hawthorne worked at a variety of jobs. He spent all his spare time writing but with no success. In 1841 he joined the Brook Farm community, an early Socialist experiment, rather like the later Kibbutz in Israel. In 1853, anxious to come to Britain where his work was beginning to be appreciated, he was able to secure his appointment as U.S. Consul in Liverpool. Following this post, he and his family came to live here where he was reported to "have been most happy". Hawthorne spent all his spare time writing, in 1850 he published, "The Scarlett Letter" about Puritanism and secret sin. Other works included "Twice Told Tales" (1837), "The House of the Seven Gables" (1851) and "Tanglewood Tales" (1853), a collection of Greek myths reworked for children. Plaque erected 1953. Nearest Station = Blackheath.

HAYDON, Benjamin (1786-1846) 116, Lisson Grove, St. John's Wood, NW8.
'painter, and John Charles Felix ROSSI (1762-1839), sculptor lived here'
Haydon, born in Plymouth, lived here in part of the house that Charles Rossi the sculptor had built. Haydon's health was poor but he managed to establish himself as a painter of historical and religious subjects; but there were few buyers. His main claim to fame (although Greeks wouldn't agree) was his part in the purchase of the Elgin Marbles. He left Lisson Grove in 1820 to live elsewhere. In 1823, whilst painting "The Raising of Lazarus" now at the Tate, he was arrested for debt. George IV purchased Haydon's "Mock Election" which allowed him to pay off his creditors. In 1846 he hired the Egyptian Hall in Piccadilly. There he displayed what he considered to be his masterpiece, the monumental painting, "Christ's Entry in Jerusalem". Everyone came to see it. No-one bought it. In a fit of self pity he scrawled the words, 'God forgive me' in his diary and committed suicide in front of his painting. Plaque erected 1959. Nearest tube station = Marylebone.

HAZLITT, William (1778-1830) 6, Frith Street, Soho, W1.
'essayist died here'
Hazlitt spent the last six months of his life here. He died an embittered man. Separated from his wife, hounded by creditors, he was a broken man. But it hadn't always been this way. He was born in Maidstone, Kent, the son of a Unitarian minister. He spent some time in Paris painting portraits, before returning to London in 1812. Here he turned to writing. He had been influenced by the French Revolution and admired its aims. He wrote an essay criticising Colerdige for turning away from the radical aims of the French. He worked for the "Morning Chronicle", "The Edinburgh Review" and the "London Magazine". His critical works included "Characters of Shakespeare's Plays" (1817), "Lectures on the English Poets" (1818). He had a chequered love life, including a widow who paid for their trip to Italy but refused to pay for the return home. He was a master of invective and withering irony with a style that ranged from whispered gossip to glowing praise. In his latter years he was crippled by ill-health and had money problems. His last words were . . . "Well, I've had a happy life". Plaque erected 1905. Nearest tube station = Leicester Square.

HEATH ROBINSON, W (1872-1944), '75, Moss Lane, Pinner, Middlesex.
'illustrator and comic artist lived here'
A "Heath Robinson Affair" meant a humourous drawing depicting some ludicrous mechanical scene. He was a well known artist and his drawings regularly appeared in English and American magazines. Born in Hornsey Rise, London, he went to Islington School of Art. He lived here from 1913-1918: right through World War One in which he worked for the Ministry of Information. He was also commissioned to create humourous drawings for the U.S. forces in France, who arrived there during 1917. Plaque erected 1976. Nearest tube station = Pinner.

HEINE, Heinrich (1799-1856) 32, Craven Street, Strand, WC2.
'German poet and essayist lived here 1827'
Heine stayed here during his visit to London in 1827. He didn't enjoy his trip and wrote to his friend, Friedrich Merckel, complaining of the weather, the damp and the lack of a fire in his room . . . 'No one speaks German and no-one understands me'. He was born Chaim Harry Heine, of middle class Jewish parents, in Dusseldorf and at 17 was sent to Frankfurt to learn banking. He hated that job and two years later started training as a lawyer. Although he got his degree his heart was now set on writing poetry. He spent from 1831 onwards in Paris and is chiefly recalled for his romantic lyrical poetry, "Book of Songs" (1827). Later, he became critical of Romanticism, perhaps because he was in constant pain from spinal paralysis. Plaque erected 1912. Nearest tube station = Charing Cross.

HENDERSON, Arthur (1863-1935) 13, Rodenhurst Road, Clapham, SW4.
'statesman, lived here'
Henderson, born in Glasgow the son of a coal miner, was brought up in Newcastle by an aunt. He worked as an iron moulder and also became a lay preacher. He was first elected an MP in 1903. Together with Ramsey MacDonald and Keir Hardie, they formed the modern Labour Party. He became foreign secretary (1929-1931) and worked, via the League of Nations, for lasting peace. Following his presidentsy of the World Disarmament Conference (1932), he was awarded the Nobel Peace Prize in 1934. He lived here from 1909 to 1921. Plaque erected 1980. Nearest tube station = Clapham North

HENTY, G. A. (George Alfred) (1832-1902) 33, Lavender Gardens, Clapham, SW11.
'author, lived here'
Henty was born in Trumpington, Cambridge and educated at Westminster and Caius College, Cambridge. He spent such an exciting life as an overseas journalist it isn't surprising that he turned to writing boys' adventure stories when he retired. He lived here from 1894 until his death and churned out his tales; always on the theme, of colonial military history, gleaned from acting as war correspondent for "The Standard", and covering all the major wars, in Europe and the colonies, between 1866 and 1876. His best known works are, "With Clive in India" (1884) and "With Moore at Corunna" (1898). Plaque erected 1953. Nearest tube station = Clapham Junction.

HERBERT, Sir Alan (A. P. H.) (1890-1971) 12, Hammersmith Terrace, Hammersmith, W6.
'author, humorist and reformist MP lived and died here'
Herbert, born in London, qualified as a barrister but fortunately never practised. Not that he wouldn't have made an excellent lawyer, but because we would probably not have had the advantage of enjoying his very witty verses and articles. He wrote much for "Punch" and he was a libretti for many comic operas. His best known work is "Bless the Bride" (1947). He also wrote novels, "The Secret Battle" (1919) and "Holy Deadlock" (1934) amongst many. He campaigned against what he called "officialese" and called for government proclamations to be written in simple English. He became MP for Oxford University in 1935 and served fifteen years in the Commons as an Independent. He was responsible for the introduction of "The Matrimonial Causes Act 1938" which did much to improve divorce conditions. Herbert lived here for many years and was a familiar figure here and in Chiswick. In his later years, when he wasn't watching cricket, he would hold forth in the Black Lion, his favourite watering hole, and close to home. Plaque erected 1990. Nearest tube station = Ravenscourt Park.

HERFORD, Robert Travers (1860-1950) Dr. William's Library, 14, Gordon Square, Holborn, WC1.
'Unitarian minister, scholar and interpreter of Judaism lived and worked here'
The library created by Travers Herford, born in London, is open to the public. A liberal theologian scholar, free from theological prejudices, he strove to present Pharisaic Judaism in an unprejudiced light. Herford saw the difference between Judaism and Christianity as the difference between faith in a divinely revealed law. He claimed that Christianity needed Judaism's pure faith, which rejects any compromise with paganism, because without Judaism, Christianity faces danger of being assimilated by paganism. He wrote much, perhaps his most important books were, "Christianity in Talmud and Midrash" (1903), "The Pharisees" (1924) and "Judaism in the New Testament Period" (1928). Plaque erected 1990. Nearest tube station = Euston Square.

HERZEN, Alexander (1812-1870) 1, Orsett Terrace, Bayswater, W2.
'Russian political thinker lived here 1860-1863'
Herzen was born in Moscow the illegitimate son of a nobleman. Following imprisonment in 1834 for preaching socialism, he was exiled. Following his release from prison in 1847 he left Russia. He was a revolutionary writer and edited, "The Kolokol" (The Bell), from 1857-1867. He was a brilliant thinker and conversationalist, which endeared him to fellow Russian writers, Tolstoy and Dostoyevsky; both of whom came to see him here. He published his memoirs between 1861 and 1867 entitled, "My Past and Thoughts". Plaque erected 1970. Nearest tube station = Royal Oak

HESS, Dame Myra (1890-1965) 48, Wildwood Road, Golders Green, NW11.
'pianist lived here'
Myra Hess was born in London of Jewish parents who encouraged their daughter to persevere with the piano. Myra won a scholarship to the Royal Academy of Music and made her debut in 1907. During the height of the German air blitz in WW2, Myra Hess became an inspiration. Her lunch time concerts at the National Gallery, in bomb scarred London, won her the heart and imagination of the free world. Besides the live audience, her concerts were broadcast on the BBC World Service. They were particularly welcomed in Occupied Europe, much to the chagrin of the Germans who made it clear that when they overran England, Myra Hess would be "disposed of". In recognition of her work in maintaining morale she was created a Dame of the British Empire in 1941. Plaque erected 1987. Nearest tube station = Golders Green.

HILL, Octavia (1838-1912) 2, Garbutt Place, Marylebone, W1.
'housing reformer, co-founder of the National Trust worked here'
Born in London, Octavia Hill became an active worker for the improvement of London's housing conditions. She didn't just talk about it she was positive about what should be done. She went around begging and borrowing from everyone she knew, in order to buy up slums and renovate them, and so house the poor and needy. She was also active in promoting the quality of London life and she campaigned for open spaces in high density areas. She wrote on the subject and sent her pamphlets to MPs, in order they understand the problems. She wrote at length on the subject in , "Homes of the London Poor" (1875) and "Our Common Land" (1878). She later became a co-founder of what is now known as the National Trust. She would have been ashamed to see how it has not fulfilled her ambition for the fund to be for the advantage of the poor to enjoy beautiful things for nothing. Instead the Trust appears to exist for its own elitest purposes. Plaque erected 1991. Nearest tube station = Bond Street.

HILL, Sir Rowland (1795-1879) 1, Orme Square, Bayswater, W2. AND Royal Free Hospital, Pond Street, Hampstead, NW3. (site of original house)
'Postal reformer and originator of the Penny Post. lived here'
Hill lived at Orme Square from 1839 to 1844 and in Hampstead from 1849 to 1879. In 1839 his idea for the Penny Post was included in that year's budget. He was born at Kidderminster, when carpet making was starting by Flemish immigrants. He became a headmaster at a school in Birmingham but his main interest was the start of a cheap and efficient postal service. His pamphlet, "Post Office Reform: Its Importance and Practicability", was the forerunner of this work. He sent a copy to the government, who weren't exactly enthusiastic. Hill persevered and in 1840 the postal service started. In 1867, he publicly advocated the public ownership of the nation's railways. It eventually happened in 1945, but is again in danger of becoming private. He is buried in Westminster Abbey. Plaque erected 1907. Nearest tube stations = Queensway AND Hampstead.

HOBBS, Sir John Berry (Jack) (1882-1963) 17, Englewood Road, Clapham, SW12.
'cricketer, lived here'
Hobbs was born in Cambridge. He became one of England's greatest cricketers and knighted in 1953, for what he achieved for the game, his country and himself. His career in first class cricket began when he played for Cambridgeshire in 1904. He started playing for Surrey the following year and stayed for thirty, (1905-1935). During his career he played in 61 test matches and made 197 centuries. His score at Lords in 1926 of 316 still stands. This was the year he first captained England. He was the first cricketer to be knighted. He retired to run a sports shop. He is regarded, together with Bert Sutcliffe and Frank Woolley, as one of the greatest exponents of classical English batting. In total he scored 61,237 runs, nearly 5,000 more than W. G. Grace. Plaque erected 1986. Nearest tube station = Clapham South.

HODGKIN, Thomas (1798-1866) 35, Bedford Square, Holborn, WC1
'physician, reformer and philanthropist, lived here'
Hodgkin was born in Tottenham and lived here whilst practising at Guys Hospital, London. He specialised in discovering and treating glandular diseases, in particular 'lymphadenoma', a cancerous condition named after him and now known as, Hodgkin's Disease. Up to recent times this disease was usually fatal, however, it is now generally treatable by radio and chemo-therapy. Plaque erected 1985. Nearest tube station = Goodge Street.

HOGG, Quintin (1845-1903) 5, Cavendish Square, Marylebone, W1.
'founder of the Polytechnic, Regent Street, lived here 1885-1898'
Hogg, born in London and educated at Eton, spent 13 years here. The son of a rich man, Hogg hadn't excelled himself in education or profession and wasn't considered the type to interest himself with the problems of educating the poor but, for reasons best known to himself, he bought and equipped premises in Regent Street, the part that lays North of Oxford Circus and created a school for some 2000 pupils. It later became "The Regent Street Polytechnic". It has, over the years, become famous and has spawned the principle of giving many young people the advantage of further education, of a type, that is as beneficial as any university. During a board meeting, at the Polytechnic, Hogg collapsed and died. Plaque erected 1965. Nearest tube station = Oxford Circus.

HOLMAN-HUNT, William, OM. (1827-1910) 18, Melbury Road, Fulham, W14.
'painter lived and died here'
Holman-Hunt, born in London, was a gifted painter of the Pre-Raphaelite school. He gradually became obsessed with the belief that religious teaching, through art, was his role in life. In pursuance of this belief he spent many hours in meditation, before the commencement of any new project. He spent many years in Palestine painting, at their original settings, stories from the bible. He lived at Melbury Road for thirty years and it was here that he finished "The Triumphs of the Innocents". His other known paintings include "The Light of the World" and "The Awakening Conscience". He was awarded the Order of Merit, in recognition of his work and dedication. Plaque erected 1923. Nearest tube station = Kensington (Olympia).

HOOD, Thomas (1799-1845) Devonshire Lodge, 28, Finchley Road, St. John's Wood, NW8.
'poet died here'
Hood, born in London the son of a Scottish bookseller from Errol, spent the last two years here and died aged 45. In his short life he secured himself a place in English literature. He was born a cockney and first saw the light of day in rooms above his father's bookshop in Poultry, City of London. He became a popular writer and edited his own magazine, "Hood's Magazine". His great friend was Charles Dickens, who visited him many times here. Hood's sense of the absurd never deserted him. As he lay sick he sent letters to his many friends headed, "From My Bed". From this bed he wrote his, "Drop of Gin", poem for "Punch" and then "The Song of the Shirt", a protest against sweated labour. This appeared in the Christmas edition of "Punch" and was such an immediate success; it trebled the magazine's circulation. Unfortunately, "Punch", the great satirical magazine, that is probably the most mentioned journal in this book, ceased publication in 1991. Hood's only son Tom, followed in his father's footsteps, by becoming editor of "Fun" in 1865. Plaque erected 1912. Nearest tube station = St. John's Wood.

HOPKINS, Gerald Manley (1844-1889) Gatepost at Manressa House, Holybourne Avenue, Roehampton, SW15.
'poet lived and studied in Manressa House'
Hopkins was born in Stratford, London the son of a prosperous marine insurance agent. Educated at Highgate School and Balliol College, Oxford, he became a Jesuit in 1868 and ordained a priest. At various times he studied and taught at Manressa House. However, despite his religious fervour, he continued writing. His best known poem is probably "The Wreck of the Deutschland" (1876), which he wrote when five nuns died in a shipwreck on the Goodwin Sands. In 1884 he was appointed to the chair of Greek at University College, Dublin. After his death, in 1889, his friend and lover Robert Bridges, published many of his poems. These showed his originality in rhythm and imagery. Plaque erected 1979. Nearest Station = Barnes.

HORE-BELISHA, Lord (1893-1957) 16, Stafford Place, St. James's, SW1.
'statesman lived here'
Leslie Hore-Belisha, born of Jewish parents, was educated at Clifton College and Oxford. His father was Jacob Belisha who died when Leslie was an infant. Leslie's mother later married Sir Adair Hore and Leslie added his surname to his own. At Oxford Hore-Belisha was president of the Union. After graduation he joined the army and during WW1 served with distinction, being mentioned in despatches. After the war he studied law and was called to the Bar (1923). He entered Parliament as a Liberal and later joined the National Government, under Ramsay Macdonald, as parliamentary secretary to the board of trade. When the Liberal party left the coalition he remained in the government as a National Liberal. As Minister of Transport (1934-7) he brought in several measures to reduce road accidents. These included pedestrian crossings which were, and still are, marked by tall black and white beacons. These became known as "Belisha Beacons". In 1937, he was appointed secretary of state for war. At the War Office he introduced reforms to modernise the services, especially amongst the top ranks and democratize the administration. His measures were bitterly resented and attacks on him contained elements of anti-semitism. He resigned from government in 1940 but continued, as an Independent MP, until 1945 when he lost his seat in the post-war election. In 1954 he was created a peer. Plaque erected 1980. Nearest tube station = St. James's Park.

HORNIMAN, John (1803-1893) Coombe Cliff Centre, Coombe Road, Croydon.
'and Frederick John HORNIMAN (1835-1906) tea merchants, collectors and public benefactors lived here'
THE HORNIMAN MUSEUM and GARDENS, The Horniman Museum, London Road, Forest Hill, SE23.
'were given to the people of London in 1901 by Frederick and John HORNIMAN, who lived near this site'
The Hornimans, father and son, were merchants with a public conscience. They had made a fortune from tea plantations in Ceylon and India and created a museum that would enlighten Londoners about the East. Frederick's daughter, Anne Elizabeth HORNIMAN (1860-1937), is the most interesting one of the family. She decided she would become an actress, she studied at the Slade and travelled widely, before appearing, on the London stage, in 1894. Both she and the play failed. Never daunted, she decided to become a producer and base herself in Ireland. She produced the first plays of both Shaw and Yeats and used her share of the family money to sponsor the building of the Abbey Theatre in Dublin. In 1908 she bought the Gaiety Theatre in Manchester and there produced over a 100 new plays, mostly directed by Lewis Casson who later married a member of the company; Sybil Thorndike. Plaque erected 1985 and 1988. Nearest Station = Forest Hill.

HOUSEMAN, A. E. (1859-1936) 17, North Road, Highgate, N6.
'poet and scholar wrote "A Shropshire Lad" while living here'
Houseman was born in Fockbury, Worcestershire and educated at Bromsgrove School and St John's College, Oxford. He came to live here, whilst teaching at University College, London. Whilst here he wrote his most famous lyric poem, "A Shropshire Lad" (1896). In 1911 he was Professor of Latin at Cambridge. He was a homosexual who could only express his love for young men in his poetry. As a result, he was shy and retiring and immersed himself deeply in academia. His last poems were published posthumously. Plaque erected 1969. Nearest tube station = Highgate.

HOWARD, Ebenezer (1850-1928) 50, Durley Road, Stamford Hill, N16.
'pioneer of the Garden City movement lived here'
Howard, born in London, lived here before emigrating to Nebraska in 1872. He returned five years later, lived here and became a parliamentary short hand writer. This work led to his book "Tomorrow" (1898). It described his vision of self contained communities, where people would live and work in rural areas, close to major overcrowded cities. His book led to the Garden City Association. Then came "the lay out plan" that would become Letchworth in Hertfordshire. There followed the outline of Welwyn Garden City. Doubtless, Canada's loss was Britain's gain. He was knighted in 1923. Plaque erected 1991. Nearest tube station = Manor House.

HOWARD, John (1726-1790) 23, Great Ormond Street, Holborn, WC1.
'prison reformer lived here'
Howard lived here from 1777-1790. He was born in Hackney, London and later inherited a large estate in Bedfordshire. He was appointed High Sheriff of the county (1773) and his work brought him into contact with prisons and prison life. He travelled abroad and saw, first hand, what conditions in prisons were like overseas. He published "The State of Prisons in England and Wales", which led to reforms and 2 acts of Parliament (1774) to implement those reforms. He later wrote "An Account of the Principal Lazarettos in Europe" (1789). His work led to the establishment of The Howard League of Penal Reform which to-day, is still trying to bring about humane prison conditions in Britain. Howard died of typhus, caught whilst visiting a British military hospital in the Crimea. Plaque erected 1908. Nearest tube station = Russell Square.

HUDSON, W. H. (William Henry) (1841-1922) 40, St. Luke's Road, Notting Hill, W11.
'plaque placed here by his friends'
Hudson was born of English parents in Argentina, where he grew up roaming the grasslands (Pampas) until 1869, when he came to London. He arrived penniless and struggled to keep himself and his wife by writing whatever local newspapers and wayout magazines wanted. He persevered and, in 1885 he published, "The Purple Land". This gave a romantic insight into South America. Then came a long gap until, in 1903, he published "Hampshire Days", an account of his walks through the New Forest. This was followed the following year, by a romantic novel, "Green Mansions". Whilst these brought some success, his fortunes didn't much improve until his wife inherited 40, Lukes Road. This they created into a boarding house which gave them their long sought after security. In 1925, Sir Jacob Epstein's, "Rima", a sculpture of a bird sanctuary was dedicated to the memory of Hudson. Plaque erected 1938. Nearest tube station = Notting Hill.

HUGHES, Arthur, (1832-1915), Eastside House, 22, Kew Green, Richmond.
'Pre-Raphaelite Painter lived and died here'
Hughes was born in London in 1830 not 1832, as his plaque claims, and educated at the Royal Acadamy Schools. He never joined the Pre-Raphaelite Brotherhood he was just associated with them. He was a very precise painter who enjoyed great success in the middle years of the 19th century but gradually faded. In his latter years whilst living here he became a recluse. Plaque erected 1993. Nearest tube station = Kew

HUGHES, David Edward (1831-1900) 94, Great Portland Street, W1.
'scientist and inventor of the microphone lived and worked here'
Although Hughes was born in London he was taken to Virginia, at a young age and brought up there. He later became professor of music at Bardston College, Kentucky. He invented a telegraphic typewriter (1855) and a microphone (1878). He returned to London in 1890, when he came to live here. He never married, because the woman he loved in America had a sick husband who, she felt in good conscience, she could never leave. In his will he left his considerable fortune to several London hospitals. Plaque erected 1991. Nearest tube station = Oxford circus.

HUGHES, Hugh Price (1847-1902) 8, Taviton Street, Holborn, WC1.
'Methodist preacher lived and died here'
Hughes was born in Carmarthen, but lived most of his life in London and moved here in 1889. He was an evangelist who saw that religion alone was not the answer to the problems of poverty and sickness. In his preachings, he advocated socialism as the answer. His honest and open preaching combined methodism and socialism and turned public opinion against Parnell, depicted as an evil womaniser. Hughes founded the "Methodist Times" in 1885 and, after serving as the original editor, opened the West London Mission in 1889. Plaque erected 1989. Nearest tube station = Euston

HUGHES, Mary (1860-1941) 71, Vallance Road, Hackney, E2.
'friend of all in need, lived and worked here 1926-1941'
Mary Hughes inherited a great deal of money from her father, the author of "Tom Brown's Schooldays". She used it to great effect. In 1926 she bought this property and turned it into a haven for the poor. She organised socialist gatherings and brought in educators. She became a JP and, unlike the majority of JPs of her time, dispensed justice with mercy and pragmatism, rather than avenging punishment. In her later years she was an invalid, having being knocked down and kicked by the police, whilst marching in support of the unemployed. Plaque erected 1961. Nearest tube station = Aldgate East.

HUNT, James Henry, Leigh (1784-1859) 22, Upper Cheyne Row, Chelsea, SW3.
'essayist and poet lived here'
Hunt, born in Southgate, Middlesex and educated at Christ's Hospital, lived an exciting but very poor life. He was a much admired poet, whose better works included "Abou Ben Adhem" (1834) and "Jenny Kissed Me"(1844). His essays and novels e.g. "The Feast of the Poets", "Wit and Humour", "Imagination and Fancy", all brought praise but little money. In his younger days he caroused with Shelley and Byron and visited them in Italy. In 1813, whilst writing in "The Examiner", which he edited for many years, he referred to the Prince Regent in insulting terms and, as a result, was put in prison. Whilst living here, from 1833 to 1840, Hunt was probably at his poorest and how to feed his wife and seven children his most urgent problem. He never solved it and died in abject poverty, but he left a legacy of newspaper writing, that is an example for present day journalists. Plaque erected 1905. Nearest tube station = Sloane Square.

HUNTER, John (1728-1793) 31, Golden Square, Mayfair, W1.
'surgeon lived here'
Hunter was born in Long Calderwood, Scotland. In 1745, he began studying medicine and assisting in his brother William's surgical work. He later came to London and studied at the Chelsea Hospital, as well as at Barts and St. Georges. A lifetime of research and study, was Hunter's contribution to the scientific understanding of curative medicine. In 1760 he was a staff-surgeon in the army and saw active service in Portugal. Later, he became an expert on anatomy and founded the museum at The Royal College of Surgeons, to which he donated over 10,000 specimens from his unique collection. The museum lasted until the German air force bombed it away in WW2. The Hunterian Museum, in Glasgow, is so called because of the pioneering work of John Hunter and his brother William. John married Anne Home in 1771. She is remembered as the author of "My mother bids me bind my hair" which was set to music by Haydn. John Hunter was originally buried in St-Martin-in-the-Field but, in 1859, his body was removed and placed in Westminster Abbey. Plaque erected 1907. Nearest tube station = Piccadilly.

HUNTER, William (1718-1783) Lyric Theatre (rear portion), Great Windmill Street, Soho, W1.
'This was the home and museum of Dr. William Hunter anatomist'
William was the elder brother of John Hunter. He studied divinity for five years, before taking up medicine and training in anatomy at St. George's Hospital, London. From 1748 he concentrated on midwifery and, in 1764, was appointed physician to Queen Charlotte. Here he taught his students what he had learnt about the uterus. At this time he started collecting paintings and object d'art. Unfortunately, the two brothers later quarrelled; over who had made the most important anatomical discoveries. Plaque erected 1952. Nearest tube station = Piccadilly.

HUSKISSON, William (1770-1830) 28, St. James's Place, St. James's, SW1.
'statesman, lived here'
Huskisson's main claim to fame is that he was run over by a railway engine and killed, whilst officiating at the ceremonial opening of the Liverpool and Manchester Railway. He was at the ceremony because, as president of the board of trade in the Conservative government of the day, he had authorised this rail link. He was born in Birts Morton, Worcestershire and lived here from 1804 to 1806. Although of slovenly appearance and constantly showing the effects of dandruff, he was able to persuade the big industrialists of the day to invest in his projects. Plaque erected 1962. Nearest Tube Station = Piccadilly

HUTCHINSON, Sir Jonathan (1828-1913) 15, Cavendish Square, W1.
'surgeon, scientist and teacher lived here'
Hutchinson, born in Selby, Yorkshire, lived here for some forty years, until his death. He left his mark as a surgeon-scientist as well as an enthusiastic teacher. He achieved the highest honours the medical world and a grateful nation could bestow. "Hutchinson's triad", are the three symptoms of congenital syphilis, first described by him, and still taught in medical schools. Plaque erected 1981. Nearest tube station = Goodge Street.

HUXLEY, Thomas Henry (1825-1895) 38, Marlborough Place, St. John's Wood, NW8.
'biologist lived here'
Huxley was born in Ealing, Middlesex. In 1872 his family moved here and stayed until, in his last years, he moved to Eastbourne for the sea air. He studied medicine at Charing Cross Hospital after which he joined the Royal Navy medical branch and served as surgeon on H.M.S. Rattlesnake. His voyages to the South Seas launched his future career. He was a brilliant biologist and a foremost exponent of Darwin's theory of evolution. He spent a lot of time lecturing, at universities all over the country, and these were eagerly attended. He ended his career as secretary, then president, of the Royal Society. In 1877 he published his accumulated research under the impressive title, "Anatomy of Invertebrated Animals and Physiography". In the celebrated debate with Bishop Samuel Wilberforce, on Darwin's theories, in 1860, Huxley declared "... I would rather be descended from an ape than a bishop ... " Plaque erected 1910. Nearest tube station = St. John's Wood.

HYNDMAN, Henry Mayers (1842-1921) 13, Well Walk, Hampstead, NW3.
'socialist leader lived and died here'
Hyndman, born in London the son of a wealthy industrialist, moved here in 1916 (it was previously the home of John Masefield. It's a bit surprising there isn't a commemorative plaque to him also). Hyndman was the man responsible for introducing and getting accepted, Karl Marx's socialist theories into the British labour movement. He founded "The Marxist Social Democratic Federation" in 1884. In spite of his expressed ideals, he was regarded with suspicion. He came from the upper classes and his working class comrades claimed he only paid lip service to the changes he was advocating. They couldn't, for example, reconcile his luxury home in the better part of Hampstead, with their slum dwellings. Plaque erected 1972. Nearest tube station = Hampstead.

INNER LONDON EDUCATION AUTHORITY, Main Entrance, County Hall, SE1.
It isn't clear why this plaque has been erected when the plaque commemorating COUNTY HALL says it all. However it must be acknowledged, that experts claim and the teachers concur, the education standards set down by the LCC 1904-1965, were far superior than the policies advocated in the Education Act 1991. Plaque erected 1986. Nearest tube station = Westminster.

LONDON COUNTY COUNCIL
LORD
HALDANE
1856 - 1928
STATESMAN
LAWYER AND
PHILOSOPHER
LIVED HERE

ENGLISH HERITAGE
JAMES
ROBINSON
1813 - 1862
Pioneer of Anæsthesia
and Dentistry
lived and worked
here

GREATER LONDON COUNCIL
Viscount Grey
of Falloden
SIR
EDWARD GREY
1862–1933
Foreign Secretary
lived here

GREATER LONDON COUNCIL
GENERAL
CHARLES DE GAULLE
President of the
French National Committee
set up
the Headquarters of the
Free French Forces
here in
1940

LONDON COUNTY COUNCIL
ELIZABETH
GARRETT
ANDERSON
1836~1917
The first woman to
qualify as a doctor
in Britain
lived here

GREATER LONDON COUNCIL
LADY
OTTOLINE
MORRELL
1873-1938
Literary Hostess
and
Patron of the Arts
lived here

GREATER LONDON COUNCIL
SIR
RONALD
ROSS
1857-1932
Nobel Laureate
Discoverer of the
mosquito transmission
of malaria
lived here

GREATER LONDON COUNCIL
RAM
MOHUN
ROY
1772-1833
Indian Scholar
and Reformer
lived here

Hector BERLIOZ 1803-1869. COMPOSER stayed here in 1851

KENNETH GRAHAME 1859-1932 Author of THE WIND IN THE WILLOWS lived here 1901-8

QUINTIN HOGG 1845-1903 Founder of the Polytechnic, Regent Street lived here 1885-1898

CHARLES 3RD EARL STANHOPE 1753-1816 REFORMER AND INVENTOR lived here

GEORGE CANNING 1770~1827 Statesman lived here

THOMAS YOUNG 1773-1829 MAN OF SCIENCE lived here

Sir Anthony Hope Hawkins (ANTHONY HOPE) 1863-1933 Novelist lived here 1903-1917

Dame Millicent Garrett FAWCETT 1847-1929 pioneer of women's suffrage lived and died here

WILLIAM
BUTTERFIELD
1814-1900
Architect
lived here

ENGLISH HERITAGE
JOHN BEARD
c 1717 - 1791
Singer
and
WILLIAM EWART
1798 ~ 1869
Promoter of public
libraries
lived here

Alfred
LORD MILNER
1854-1925
STATESMAN
lived here

GEORGE
BENTHAM
1800-1884
Botanist
lived here
1864-1884

Here lived
and died
JOHN LOUGHBOROUGH
PEARSON
1817-1897
and later
SIR EDWIN LANDSEER
LUTYENS
1869-1944
Architects

Field-Marshal
EARL KITCHENER
of Khartoum. K.G.
(1850-1916)
Lived here
1914-15

SIR
JAMES
MACKENZIE F.R.S.
1853-1925
PHYSICIAN
lived and worked
here
1907-1911

BRAM
STOKER
1847-1912
Author of
"DRACULA"
lived here

INNES, John (1829-1904) Manor House, Watery Lane, Wimbledon, SW20.
'founder of the John Innes Horticultural Institute, lived here'
Innes, born in London, made his fortune as a property developer. He bought the Merton Park Estate (1867) and the stately manner in which he lived, contrasted sharply with the mass density estates he built to house the hordes of farm workers, and their large families, who were leaving the countryside to live and work in London. "Instant slums" was how one social worker put it. Innes, in order to ingratiate himself with the establishment, promoted horticultural experiments and research and left much of his fortune for that purpose. Despite his charitable efforts he didn't receive the knighthood he so much wanted and which he thought he deserved. Plaque erected 1978. Nearest Station = Merton Park

IRVING, Edward (1792-1834) 4, Claremont Square, Islington, N1.
'founder of the Catholic Apostolic church lived here'
Irving was born in Annan, Scotland and studied at Edinburgh University before becoming, first a teacher, then a clergyman in the Church of Scotland. In 1822 he came here whilst spending a term preaching at the Caledonian Church in Hatton Garden. From 1825, he spent most of his time warning all who would listen that the second coming was imminent. He frightened the weak minded with his unfounded ravings about supernatural phenomena. It was all too much for his church superiors who, after finding him guilty of heresy, expelled him (1833). He came to London where, in 1834, he founded the Catholic Apostolic Church and his too few members became known as "Irvingites". He died the same year. Plaque erected 1982. Nearest tube station = Angel.

IRVING, Sir Henry (1838-1905) 15a, Grafton Street, Mayfair, W1.
'actor lived here 1872-1899'
Irving born in Keinton-Mandeville, Somerset, lived here for the most important part of his life. He was born John Henry Broadribb but decided this wasn't a name for an actor. He established his reputation in 1874 with his performance of Hamlet. Then followed his triumph as Mathias, in the melodrama "The Bells". He then turned to management and, in 1878, became manager of the Lyceum. But he never gave up acting, especially the great Shakespearean roles, many of which he played with Ellen Terry. In 1895 he became the first actor ever to be knighted. Irving and his company toured the USA eight times, bringing Shakespeare and the classics to the culturally illiterate. In 1893 he turned his hand to writing plays, only "The Drama" survives. His ashes are interred in Westminster Abbey. Plaque erected 1950. Nearest tube station = Bond Street.

IRVING, Washington (1783-1859) 8, Argyll Street, Mayfair, W1.
'American writer, lived here'
Argyll Street is a small street and the home of the London Palladium. Irving, born in New York the son of a wealthy merchant, was a popular writer in Britain. His comic essays e.g. "History of New York" by 'Diedrich Knickerbocker' (1890) as well as "Rip Van Winkle", "Sleepy Hollow" and the lives of "J. J. Astor, Washington", were the type of "Punchlike" stories so beloved by the English. He was US Ambassador to Spain 1842- 46. Plaque erected 1983. Nearest tube station = Oxford Circus.

ISAACS, Rufus, 1st Marquess of Reading (1860-1935) 32, Curzon Street, Mayfair, W1.
'lawyer and statesman, lived and died here'
Isaacs was born in London, the son of a wealthy Jewish fruit merchant. At 16, fed up with school, he ran off to sea as a cabin boy. Two years later he was back working at the London Stock Exchange. He become a broker but in 1884, unable to pay his debts, was hammered. Isaacs decided to sail to Panama and seek his fortune but was persuaded by his mother to stay at home and study law. Three years later he was called to the bar, built up a large commercial practise and in 1898 took silk. As a Q.C. he became one of the greatest advocates of his time. All his work brought wealth and honour and he was urged to enter Parliament. This he did in 1904, as a Liberal, and rose to become Solicitor-General. In 1910 he was appointed Attorney-General, so becoming the first Jew to be a member of the Cabinet. He was also knighted. In 1913 Sir Rufus Isaacs was appointed Lord Chief Justice of England and became Lord Reading. During WW1 he was made responsible for securing large loans from the U.S. government in order to help pay for the war which the Americans didn't enter until 1917. He was the judge at the trial of Sir Roger Casement, in which he demeaned himself by leaning heavily on the side of the prosecution; for political purposes. Between 1920 and 1926 he was Viceroy of India and upon his return was given the title of marquess. He remained a prominent figure in the Liberal party and in 1931, served briefly as foreign secretary in Ramsay MacDonald's national government. His last speech in the House of Lords, shortly before his death, was devoted to awakening the world to Hitler's persecution of the Jews in Germany. Plaque erected 1971. Nearest tube station = Green Park.

JACKSON, John Hughlings (1835-1911) 3, Manchester Square, Marylebone, W1.
'physician, lived here'
Jackson, born in Providence Green, Yorkshire, lived here for forty years and died here. During this time he worked on researching the localities of the brain functions. His greatest discovery, during his work on finding cures for nervous diseases, was proof that certain portions of the brain controlled the voluntary movements of the body and that diseases of this part caused fits and paralysis. Ironically his wife, Elizabeth, died of thrombosis of the cerebral veins, the sort of complaint Jackson was investigating. Plaque erected 1932. Nearest tube station = Baker Street.

JAMES, Henry (1843-1916) 34, De Vere Gardens, Kensington, W8.
'writer, lived here 1886-1902'.
In 1885 James took a 21 year lease of the fourth floor but rarely lived here. He was born in New York but became a naturalised Englishman in 1915. He was awarded the Order of Merit (OM) shortly before his death. He was a prolific writer and published many books that became, and remain, popular. His best known works are "Roderick Hudson" (1876) then at divers dates appeared "Portraits of a Lady", "The Bostonians", "Ivory Tower", "The Asprey Papers", "What Maisie Knew", "Washington Square", "The Golden Bowl", and much more. Several of his books have been made into feature films. The house he lived in, in Rye, East Sussex, is open to the public. Plaque erected 1949. Nearest tube station = Kensington High Street.

JEFFERIES, Richard (1848-1887) 59, Footscray Road, Eltham, SE29.
"naturalist and writer, lived here'
Jefferies' work as a naturalist started in his native Wiltshire. He came to London in connection with his work as a civil servant and lived here. He soon turned to his first love, writing novels. "Bevis: The Story of a Boy" (1882), was an immediate success and this was followed, in 1883, by "The Story of My Heart" describing rural Wiltshire as a personal mysticism. He became ill shortly afterwards and found it difficult to concentrate. He was 39 when he died. Plaque erected 1986. Nearest Station = Eltham.

JELLICOE, Admiral of the Fleet, Earl, OM (1859-1935) 25, Draycott Place, Chelsea, SW3.
'lived here'
Jellicoe, born in Southampton, the son of a sea merchant, only spent two years here, 1906-1908. Because he was a personal friend of the first sea lord, John Fisher, he was, on the outbreak of WW1, appointed Commander-in-Chief of the Fleet. Fisher was repaying the support he had received from Jellicoe over the design and production of the new class of Dreadnought battleships Fisher had set his heart and reputation on. Jellicoe, as C-in-C, was a failure as evidenced by the Battle of Jutland. The losses sustained by the Royal Navy, in the 1916 battle, were out of all proportion to the size of the enemies fleet. Jellicoe's actions were whitewashed and his resignation delayed until 1917. All this however didn't prevent him receiving an Earldom and promotion to Admiral of the Fleet. In 1920 he was taken out, dusted down and appointed Governor-General of New Zealand. He stayed 4 years and returned home claiming he never wanted to see another sheep ever again. Plaque erected 1975. Nearest tube station = Sloane Square.

JEROME, Jerome K (1859-1927) 91-104, Chelsea Gardens, Chelsea Bridge Road, SW1.
'author, wrote "Three Men in a Boat" while living here at Flat 104'
Why it has taken so long to commemorate a writer who has given so many people so much pleasure is a mystery. He was born in Walsall, Staffs but brought up in London. The K stands for Klapka. Before making writing his living he was successively a clerk, schoolmaster, reporter, actor and journalist. In 1892 he started his own twopenny weekly, "To-Day". Although Jerome is known for his light novels such as, "Three Men in a Boat" (1889) and "Idle Thoughts of an Idle Fellow" (1889) there was a serious side to his writings, as evidenced in his modern morality play, "The Passing of the Third Floor Back" (1908). Perhaps his most interesting book was, "Three Men on a Brummel" (1900), this is a story of how three friends have a cycling holiday in Germany. The insight Jerome has of German philosophy, patriotism and morality is amazing, as the world in general wouldn't be aware of it until 1933 and Hitler had come to power. In 1926 he wrote his biography, "My Life and Times". Plaque erected 1989. Nearest tube station = Sloane Square.

JINNAH, Mohammed Ali (Quaid i Azam) (1876-1948) 35, Russell Road, West Kensington, W14.
'founder of Pakistan, stayed here in 1895'
Jinnah was born in Karachi and stayed here whilst studying law in London. He was called to the bar in 1906 and returned to India to practise. He went on to become a politician and, in 1913, was elected as a Muslim representative on the Imperial Legislative Council. He became convinced that Muslims couldn't live together with Hindus in an independent India, as envisaged by Gandhi. In 1940, whilst Britain was trying to save India from Japanese invasion, and ignoring Gandhi's pleas, Jinnah began fermenting the principle of a Muslim country to be called Pakistan. Critics claim Pakistan came about because, upon Indian independence, Jinnah didn't relish becoming number two to Gandhi. Plaque erected 1955. Nearest tube station = Barons Court.

JOHN, Augustus (1878-1961) 28, Mallord Street, Chelsea, SW3.
'This house was built for AUGUSTUS JOHN, painter.'
John was born in Tenby, Wales and studied at the Slade School of Art in London. Influenced by post-impressionism and Rembrandt, he began to show a special gift as a portrait painter. His work included portraits of Shaw, Hardy and fellow Welshman Dylan Thomas. His portraits of women were better than of men, viz "The Smiling Woman" and probably best of all, "Madame Suggia" his painting of the cellist in 1923. He was elected to the Royal Academy in 1928 and was President of the National Portrait Society 1948-53. It is a sad fact that his social portraits in later life failed to live up to his early promise and, as though to compensate, his attitudes towards dress and behaviour defied social convention to border on the ridiculous. Plaque erected 1981. Nearest tube station = Sloane Square.

JOHNSON, Amy (1903-1941) Vernon Court, Hendon Way, Cricklewood, NW2.
'Aviator lived here'
Amy Johnson was born in Hull, the daughter of a fish merchant. She studied economics at Sheffield University before coming to London and living here. She worked as a typist in order to finance her flying lessons. She got her PPL in 1929 and a year later she became the first woman to make a solo flight from England to Australia (May 1930). The hazards of flying a single engine aircraft, over vast tracts of water, cannot be underestimated. There are few pilots to-day, with modern navigational aids and communications, who would attempt it. Her reward was winning the £10,000 prize the Daily Mail had offered. In 1931, she flew to Japan via Moscow and in 1932 she flew solo to Cape Town and back. She married Jim Mollison, a Scottish airman in 1932, and together they created flying records. They divorced in 1938. During WW2, Amy Johnson joined the Air Transport Auxiliary as a pilot. Whilst delivering a new fighter plane to a base, in South East England, the aircraft caught fire. She was lost, after baling out over the Thames estuary. Plaque erected 1987. Nearest tube station = Brent.

JOHNSON, Samuel (1709-1784) 8, Russell Street, Covent Garden, WC2.
'In this house occupied by Thomas DAVIES, bookseller, Dr. Samuel JOHNSON first met James BOSWELL in 1763'
Johnson was born in Lichfield, son of a local bookseller. Educated at the local grammar school and Pembroke College, Oxford, he failed to take his degree. In 1735 he married a rich widow, Elizabeth Porter, whom he fondly called 'Tetty' and together they opened a school at Edial. Amongst his pupils was David Garrick and in 1737 Johnson, his wife and Garrick went to London. There, he wrote "London" an imitation of Juvental's Satires. This brought some financial security and he started on his great work, the "Dictionary of the English Langauge" (1755). In 1759 his mother died. In order to pay for the funeral he wrote the novel, "Rasselas: The Prince of Abyssinia" but it failed and in 1762 Johnson was jailed for debt. Upon his release, George III awarded him a pension of £300 a year. A tour of the Hebrides, together with Boswell, followed and produced "A Journey to the Western Islands of Scotland" (1775). Towards the end of his life, Hester Thrale, his friend's widow who looked after him, went off with an Italian musician. This 'act of betrayal' so wounded Johnson, he died soon after. He is buried in Westminster Abbey. Plaque erected 1984. Nearest tube station = Covent Garden.

JOHNSTON, Edward (1872-1944) 3, Hammersmith Terrace, Hammersmith, W6.
'master calligrapher lived here 1905-1912'
When, in 1905, Johnson and his family moved here the rent was £60 a year. Today it would cost around £60 a day! He was born in Uruguay, where his father was on diplomatic service. He taught himself the art of caligraphy, by studying old manuscripts and learning how to use quills and reeds. From 1899 to 1912 he taught at the Central School of Fine Arts and Crafts. In a room, overlooking the river, Johnston wrote "Writing, Lettering and Illuminating" and, in 1909, published "Manuscript and Inscription Letters", both of which are still used as textbooks. In 1913, Johnson designed the classic sans-serif alphabet typeface, still widely used. Plaque erected 1977. Nearest tube station = Ravenscourt Park.

JONES, Dr Ernest (1879-1958) 19, York Terrace East, Regent's Park, NW1.
'pioneer psychoanalyst, lived here'
Jones was born in Llwchwr, Glamorgan. After studying medicine, at Cardiff University College, he qualified as a physician in London. He was so interested in Freud's new approach to neurosis that he learnt German the better to understand Freud's papers on the subject. In 1908 he introduced psychoanalysis into both Britain and the United States. He was Freud's 'Boswell' and became his lifelong disciple and friend. In 1913 he founded the British Psycho-Analytical Society. Amongst his many writings is a psychoanalytical study of 'Hamlet and Oedipus' and a biography of Freud, (1953-7). Plaque erected 1985. Nearest tube station = Regent's Park.

JORDAN, Mrs Dorothy (nee Bland) (1762-1816) 30, Cadogan Place, Belgravia, SW1.
'actress lived here'
Dorothy Bland, born in Dublin, began acting whilst only a child. Her girlish gaiety was infectious and she never gave herself the airs and graces often affected by other actresses. She was very attractive and a natural comedy actress. It wasn't long before she attracted the attention of young upper class lowlifes, with more money than sense, who hung around the stage doors. She had several affairs, which produced the grand total of fifteen children. Ten of these had the same father, William, Duke of Clarence, son of George III. They lived together for over 20 years until, in 1811, William was forced to break up the arrangement in order to get married and produce a legitimate heir to the throne. She came to live here but the pension a grateful government settled on her was insufficient and William turned his royal back on her. In 1815, shortly after the Battle of Waterloo, she went to France and later died in a lunatic asylum. In 1831 her ex lover, now King William, granted the Earldom of Munster to their eldest son. Plaque erected 1975. Nearest tube station = Sloan Square.

JOYCE, James (1882-1941) 28, Campden Grove, Kensington, W8
'Writer lived here'
Joyce, born in Dublin, was educated by Jesuits before entering University College, Dublin. He lived here briefly. After lengthy correspondence with Ibsen he went to Paris and spent some time there before returning for his mother's funeral. He and his constant companion, Nora Barnacle, spent WW1 in Switzerland before settling in Paris. Joyce was always on the borders of poverty until 1922 and "Ulysses". It was first published in Paris but not in the UK until 1936. Plagued by eye problems Joyce supervised the writing of "Finnegan's Wake" (1939). Joyce is one of the great literary figures of the 20th century. Plaque erected 1994. Nearest tube station = Kensington High Street.

KARSAVINA, Tamara (1885-1978) 108, Frognal, Hampstead, NW3.
'ballerina lived here'
Tamara Platonovna Karsavina was born in St. Petersburg and trained, under Cecchetti, at the Imperial Ballet School. She was one of the original members of Diaghilev's company and danced roles created by Nijinsky. She moved to London in 1918, with her husband, an English diplomat, whose family owned this house. She continued guesting with Ballet Russe and, until 1955, she was vice-president of the Royal Academy of Dancing. She wrote several books on the ballet including, in 1930, her autobiography, "Theatre Street". Plaque erected 1987. Nearest tube station = Finchley Road.

KEATS, John (1795-1821) Keats House, Wentworth Place, Keats Grove, Hampstead, NW3.
'poet, lived in this house'. Open to the public.
Keats was born in London, the son of a stable keeper. He was only 25 when he died from consumption. His brief life has lived on in his glorious poetry. Keats, together with his two brothers, was orphaned at an early age and John began an early apprenticeship to a surgeon at Guys Hospital. He soon discovered he wasn't suited to medicine and preferred literature. He showed some poems to Leigh Hunt, whom he visited at his home in the Vale of Health, Hampstead. Leigh Hunt enthused and encouraged him and introduced Keats to Shelley, Haydon, Wordsworth and many others. In 1817 the brothers settled in Well Walk, at the cottage of Bentley the Hampstead postman, where he wrote "Endymion". Soon after, Keats met Charles Dilke and Charles Brown, who had built a pair of houses at Wentworth Place. Keats moved into one and the other was taken by Mrs Brawne and her two daughters, one of whom Fanny Keats fell in love with. A mark of his great happiness was the lyrical poem, 'Ode to a Nightingale'. In the summer of 1820, Keats was advised, for the sake of his rapidly declining health, to go to live in Italy. In Rome, on February 23rd 1821, he died. Fanny mourned him for 12 years, whilst acting as the curator of the museum opened to honour him; then she retired and at last married. Plaque erected 1896. Nearest tube station = Hampstead.

KELLY, Gerald (1879-1972) 117, Gloucester Place, W1
'Portrait Painter lived here'

Gerald Festus Kelly was born in Paddington, London where his father was the curate of the parish. He was a sickly lad and spoilt by his parents and two sisters. He was encouraged in his love of cricket and this remained a burning passion. His brief sojurn at Eton ended in illness. He spent some time in the sunshine of South Africa and returned to enter Trinity Hall, Cambridge (1897). In 1901 he decided to become a painter and went off to Paris. Visits to the studios of Monet, Degas, Rodin Sickert and others fired his imagination. He developed a particular style of craftmanship. Detail to hands, feet and heads became his speciality. To get over a bad love affair he went off to Burma but returned on the outbreak of WW1 to work at the Admirality as an intelligence officer. After the war he concentrated on portrait painting and became wealthy. His portrait of King George VI and Queen Elizabeth done during WW2 is particularly admired. In 1949 Kelly was elected President of the Royal Acadamy and in 1955 he was knighted. He became well known to millions through his TV programmes on art. Plaque erected 1993. Nearest tube station = Baker Street.

KEYNES, John Maynard (1883-1946) 46, Gordon Square, Bloomsbury, WC1.
'economist, lived here 1916-1946'

Keynes, born in Cambridge and educated at Eton and King's College, Cambridge, represented the Treasury at the Peace Conference of 1919 and made his mark as an imaginative economist. Frustrated by the constraints of the Civil Service, he left and published "Economic Consequences of the Peace", a criticism of the conference; part of which dealt with the stupidity of raping Germany's industrial ability. Following the great depression of 1929, he advocated government spending to stimulate the economy. His book, "The General Theory of Employment, Interest and Money" (1936), profoundly affected capitalist economic attitudes; particularly in the US, where Roosevelt's "New Deal", put many of Keynes' recommendations into practise. In 1943 Keynes took part in the monetary negotiations at Bretton Woods, which would lead to the founding of The International Monetary Fund. In 1945 he negotiated the Anglo-American Loan Agreement, "Lend-Lease". It is interesting to note that many economists in the 1990's are calling for Keynesian methods to alleviate the present depression. Keynes showed an adventurism to his own finances. He often played the market and was cleaned out more than once; but always recovered. He was married to Lydia Lopokova, a Diaghilev ballerina. Her lack of English provided more than one laugh. She once claimed that she disliked the English countryside in summer because she got bitten by barristers. Plaque erected 1975. Nearest tube station = Euston Square.

KINGSLEY, Charles (1819-1875) 56, Old Church Street, Chelsea, SW3.
'writer lived here'
This is the site of St. Luke's Rectory where Kingsley's father was rector. He was born in Holme, Devon. In 1838 he entered Magdalene College, Oxford where, in 1842, he obtained a first in Classics. From 1860 to 1869 he was Professor of Modern History at Cambridge. But before, during and after this period Kingsley was busy writing; "Westward Ho!" (1855), "Hereward the Wake" (1866) and many more novels. Other books, reflected the social conditions of the times and his attitudes to them, as a Christian Socialist appeared; "Hypatia" (1853), "The Water Babies" and "The Heroes" (1863). He wrote many articles, attacking the government and the aristocracy, under the pen name of "Parson Lot". Kingsley became chaplain to Queen Victoria in 1873. Plaque erected 1979. Nearest tube station = Sloane Square.

KINGSLEY, Mary 1862-1900) 22, Southwood Lane, Highgate, N6
'traveller and ethnologist, lived here as a child'
Mary Kingsley was born in Islington, the niece of Charles Kingsley. She had no formal education but spent many hours reading her father's books. She was particularly fond of the scientific variety. Mary had to wait until her parents, who were both long term invalids, died, before she could realise her ambition to travel. In 1893 she went to West Africa and lived amongst the natives. She made no attempt to convert them to European customs, instead she learnt theirs and adapted to their way of life. On her return, she wrote about her journey, "Travels in West Africa" (1899). She was later consulted by British colonial administrators, because of her wide understanding of broad based African culture. During the Boer War she served as a nurse and died of enteric fever. Plaque erected 1975. Nearest tube station = Highgate

KIPLING, Rudyard (1865-1936) 43, Villiers Street, Strand, WC2.
'poet and story writer lived here 1889-1891'
Kipling arrived in London from Bombay, where he was born, with just a few pounds. After India and America he found London cold with 'pea-souper' fogs. Here his three rooms were small with the Strand traffic on one side and the Charing Cross trains on the other. On the plus side was the fact that his rooms were above "Harris the Sausage King" who supplied him with loads of sausage and mash for twopence. He spent many evenings in Gatti's Music Hall. Here he found earthy humour and ribald songs which eventually became the basis for "Barrack Room Ballards" and other poetry, that would become so popular. In 1891 his health broke down, the following year he married Caroline Ballads and they went to live in her home state of Vermont. Here he wrote his famous "Jungle Books" and "Stalky & Co." He returned to England in 1899, following a row with his in-laws, and lived in Sussex. In 1907 he was awarded the Nobel Prize for Literature and in 1937 wrote his autobiography "Something of Myself". Kipling today, in a world void of Empire, is no longer fashionable. Nevertheless, his stories are still enjoyed. Plaque erected 1940. Nearest tube station = Charing Cross.

KITCHENER of Khartoum, Field Marshal Earl, KG (1850-1916), 2, Carlton Gardens, SW1.
'lived here 1914-1915'
Kitchener, born in Balleylongford, Ireland and educated in Switzerland, lived here upon his appointment as Foreign Secretary. He was rewarded with a peerage for winning back the Sudan for Egypt, a British possession following the battle of Khartoum. Then came the Boer war and Kitchener was made a viscount. The first world war was declared in August 1914 and Kitchener devoted all his thinking to raising an army to fight the Germans. We don't know if he ever imagined what a blood bath would follow his call to arms but his pointed finger slogan of "Your Country Needs You" had the desired effect and young men enlisted in their tens of thousands. He let down his 'people's army' by providing them with a weak and often corrupt General Staff, and an inferior officer corps. Kitchener drowned, when H.M.S. Hampshire struck a mine and sank off the Orkneys. Plaque erected 1924. Nearest tube station = Charing Cross

KLEIN, Melanie (1882-1960) 42, Clifton Hill, St. John's Wood, NW8.
'psychoanalyst and pioneer of child analysis, lived here'
Melanie Klein trained in Budapest, where she was born, under Ferenczi, an associate of Freud. She began working with children and adopted the method of Free Association; which meant observing whilst her young patients played with small toys and worked out their fantasies. Although often criticised, she proved the theory of Oedipus and the Superego. The public of her time found it impossible to believe that small children could be capable of evil and great cruelty. In 1926, she moved to England, where she founded the "British Psychological Society". In 1932, she wrote "Psychoanalysis of Children". She later worked with adults , specialising in the theory that paranoid behaviour had its' roots in childhood. She came to live here in 1945 following revelations that most of her family had died in German death camps. Plaque erected 1985. Nearest tube station = Maida Vale.

KNEE, Fred (1868-1914) 24, Sugden Road, Battersea, SW11.
'London Labour Party pioneer and housing reformer lived here'
Fred Knee was born in Frome, Somerset, one of four sickly children. A brother and sister died in childhood and Fred was to suffer all his life from respiratory problems. His parents worked in the spinning mills, his father weaved wool and his mother weaved silk; when there was work available. Fred, who never grew to more than 5 feet, thought when he was 15 that he was destined to become a missionary. He pursued this course for a while but gradually lost his religious faith. His missionary zeal turned towards the cause of Labour. At 13 he left school and took a job in a printer's shop in Frome. The printer printed the local newspaper and Fred became a reporter. He was now 20 and two years later he left Frome and came to London. He enrolled at the Regent Street Polytechnic and continued educating himself. A year later, 1892, he married Anne Francis, a fellow student and they came to live here. Fred joined the Fabian Society and devoted himself in aiding the underprivileged. He wrote many articles for "Justice" as well as keeping diaries that were published towards the end of his life. His best work was as Secretary of the Workmen's National Housing Council. An organisation that sought to provide the working class with basic housing. He wrote many pamphlets on many issues, not least his opposition to the Boer War which he regarded as imperialist. In 1901 he and his family moved to the countryside at Radlet in Hertfordshire. His work continued, despite increasing ill health, as he sought to warn about a possible world war. Plaque erected 1986. Nearest tube station = Clapham Common.

KNIGHT, Dame Laura (1877-1970) 16, Langford Place, St. John's Wood, NW8. 'and Harold KNIGHT (1874-1961), painters lived here'
Laura Knight's maiden name was Johnson and she was born in Long Eaton, Nottinghamshire. She studied art at Nottingham and married a fellow student, the portrait painter Harold Knight. In 1903 they sketched their way around the world. She produced many oil paintings of the ballet world and these were re-produced and sold well. In 1955 they came to live and work here. Plaque erected 1983. Nearest tube station = St. John's Wood.

KOKOSCHKA, Oscar (1886-1980) Eyre Court, Finchley Road, St. John's Wood, NW8.
'painter lived here'
Kokoschka was born in Pochlarn, Austria and left school and home at an early age to travel and paint. The result was one of storm and protest, at some of the violent scenes he painted. However, at his first exhibition in Vienna in 1909, he showed his painting "Children Playing", now in the Duisburg, Kunstmuseum. Here he depicts children, in a wistful and compassionate attitude, in sharp comparison to the formal portraits of Reynolds or Gainsborough. His methods lacked conventional draughtsmanship, instead his line was relaxed and charming. His landscapes showed the harshness of the countryside and the problems of the farmers. From 1919 to 1924 he was Professor of Art at Dresden Academy of Art. As a Jew, he was forced to leave Austria and found refuge in London. Amongst his later work were the series of lithographs he did on the life of David and Saul. In 1953 he went to live in Switzerland. Plaque erected 1986. Nearest tube station = St. John's Wood.

KOSSUTH, Louis (1802-1894) 39, Chepstow Villas, Notting Hill, W11
'Hungarian patriot, stayed here'
Kossuth, born in Monok, Hungary, came to live in London in 1851 as a refugee, following the collapse of the short lived Hungarian Republic he helped form in 1848. The revolution, against the Hapsburg empire, came as a shock to the ruling monarchs of Eastern Europe and Russian Imperialist troops soon helped the Austrians regain control. Kossuth was particularly active in the emancipation of minority groups and during the brief liberalisation of Hungarian life the government granted equality to the Jews, the largest minority and the most active in support of the revolution. For the rest of his days Kossuth was kept busy lecturing, all over Europe and the USA, on the needs of Hungarian freedom. In 1890, whilst living in Italy, he started writing, in three volumes, 'Memories of my Exile', he just managed to finish them before he died. Plaque erected 1959. Nearest tube station = Notting Hill Gate.

KROPOTKIN, Prince Peter (1842-1921) 6, Crescent Road, Bromley.
'theorist of anarchism, lived here'
In 1874, Kropotkin was arrested in Moscow, where he was born, for spreading nihilist propaganda. In 1876 he escaped from prison and came to England where he lived, on and off, for 30 years. In 1881 he was accused of playing a part in the attempted assassination of the Tsar and the authorities wanted Britain to extradite him. This was refused. He went to France where, in Lyon, he was given five years imprisonment for anarchy but released after three. In London, in 1886, he wrote and lectured. In 1900 he published "Memoirs of a Revolutionist" and, in 1902 wrote "Mutual Aid". This attempted to harmonise the attitudes between anarchism and socialism, arguing that co-operation was essential to human survival. Following the Russian revolution of 1917, he returned to Moscow. Plaque erected 1989. Nearest Station = Bromley North.

LABOUR PARTY, Caroone House, Farringdon Street, EC4.
'Site of the Congregational Memorial Hall; The LABOUR PARTY was founded here, 27th February 1900'
In 1900 the first Labour MP was returned to the House of Commons. In 1923, the Labour Party became the official opposition party, in place of the Liberals. In 1924 they formed a government. The party was promoted by the trade unions on the principles advocated by the Fabian Society and devoted to social change by means of evolution. In recent years, in order to capture the middle class vote, the principles of public ownership have been replaced by a form of benevolent capitalism. Plaque erected 1985. Nearest tube station = Farringdon.

LAMB, Charles 'Elia' (1775-1834) 64, Duncan Terrace, Islington, N1.
'essayist lived here'
Lamb was born in London and educated at Christ's Hospital where he met Coleridge and formed an ongoing friendship. He was 48, and about to retire from The East India Company where he worked as a shipping clerk, when he came to live here. Lamb had the responsibility of caring for Mary, who had been placed in his care in 1796, following a fit of inherited insanity, when she killed their mother. He was able to buy this house from the proceeds of his literary output. "Specimens of English Dramatic Poets" (1808), "Tales From Shakespeare" (1809), "Beauty and the Beast" (1811) and "Essays of Elia" (1823). Mary began showing signs of increasing mental ill-health. This depressed Charles and when, in 1834, Coleridge died, he felt he had little to live for and died a few months later. He is buried in Edmonton churchyard. Mary, with the help of kind neighbours, continued living on her own for thirteen years. When she died she was buried alongside her brother. Plaque erected 1907. Nearest tube station = The Angel.

LANG, Andrew (1844-1912) 1, Marloes Road, Kensington, W8.
'man of letters lived here in 1876-1912'
Lang was born in Selkirk and educated in Scotland before going on to Balliol College, Oxford. He came to London to work, with S. H. Butcher, on the 'Odyssey' in 1879. He then specialised in works relating to Scotland and on Mary, Queen of Scotland and the rising of 1745. He also worked on a series of 'Fairy Books' which were multi-coloured and popular. But Lang is mainly known as a poet, whose works included, "Ballards of Blue China" (1880) and "Grass of Parnassus"(1888). He also found time to write on anthropology and published "The Making of Religion" in 1898. Plaque erected 1959. Nearest tube station = Kensington High Street.

LANGTRY, Lillie (1852-1929) Cadogan Hotel, 21, Pont Street, SW1.
'actress lived here'
Lillie Langtry lived at the Cadogan Hotel from 1892-1897 and the bill was picked up by the Prince of Wales. He had an ongoing love affair with her from 1877, unconcerned that she was married. Her real name was Emilie Charlotte Le Breton, but she was called Jersey Lillie, by an American rancher who had gone to the island of Jersey, where she was born, to buy a herd of cows. Lily was his mother's name and he declared that ". . . Miss Langtry was prettier than my Mom or any cow! She's my Jersey Lillie". It stuck. Two marriages to rich men, the first was Edward Langtry in 1874, and two widowhoods, allowed her to indulge her passion as a racehorse owner. But she wasn't very successful. She died in Monte Carlo after an evening gambling away more than she could afford. In 1925 she wrote her biography, "The Days I Knew". Plaque erected 1980. Nearest tube station = Sloane Square.

LASKI, Harold (1893-1950) 5, Addison Bridge Place, Fulham, W14.
'teacher and political philosopher, lived here 1926-1950'
Laski was born in Manchester into a middle class Jewish family. He was educated at Manchester Grammar School and New College, Oxford; graduating in political science. He lectured at McGill University in Montreal from 1914-1916 then onto Harvard, where he met Oliver Wedell Holmes, the great American jurist. In 1920 Laski returned to England and the London School of Economics, first as a lecturer then, in 1926, as Professor of Political Science. He was a leading light in the Labour Party and sat on the National Executive from 1936, becoming Chairman of the party in 1945, when Labour won its great majority in the post war election. He continued to have a strong influence in the Fabian Society and wrote a number of political works. During the Palestine troubles, leading to Israeli statehood, he frequently clashed with Ernest Bevin, who hadn't the intellectual ability to cope with his office as foreign secretary, let alone with an intellect that Laski possessed. He wrote several political books both on Britain and America. Plaque erected 1974. Nearest tube station = West Kensington.

LAUDER, Sir Harry (1870-1950) 46, Longley Road, Tooting, SW17.
'music hall artist lived here 1903-1911'
Lauder exploited his Scottish background, he was born in Portobello, and made it the backbone of his music hall act. He wore a kilt and carried a walking stick that was similar to a Highland crook. His great ability was to have an audience eating out of his hand by a mixture of comedy and sentimental songs. These songs became world famous, he wrote them himself and they made him a fortune. They included "Keep Right on to the End of the Road", "Roamin in the Gloamin", 'and "I Love a Lassie". They are still popular at any Scottish sing along. In 1919, as a reward for organising entertainment for the army, Lauder was one of the first music hall artists to be knighted. Plaque erected 1969. Nearest tube station = Tooting Broadway.

LAUGHTON, Charles (1899-1962) 15, Percy Street, Soho, W1.
'actor lived here, 1928-1931'
Laughton was born in Scarborough, where his father ran a hotel. Charles worked in the family business, before deciding to become a full time actor. He appeared, for the first time in London, in 1926. He was a member of The Old Vic and appeared in several of Shaw's plays, before playing Shakespeare and receiving rave notices for his Macbeth and Lear. In the thirties, he switched to films and his roles have become legendary. He received the Academy Award for his part as Henry VIII in, "The Private Life of Henry VIII" (1932). However, his private life was unhappy. Although married to Elsa Lanchester, Laughton was a secret homosexual at a time when it was both illegal and socially unacceptable. He became an American citizen in 1950. Plaque erected 1992. Nearest tube station = Tottenham Court Road.

LAVERY, Sir John (1856-1941) 5, Cromwell Place, South Kensington, SW7.
'painter lived here 1899-1940'
Lavery was born in Belfast the son of a publican. After studying at Glasgow, Paris and London, he became a popular portrait painter. His most famous picture was "The Tennis Party", hung at the 1886 Royal Academy exhibition. Lavery was a Scot who, when Queen Victoria opened the Glasgow Exhibition in 1888, was commissioned to paint a painting of the grand event. He specialised in conversation pieces and paintings of women. In his early days he was "a bit of a lad" with women, but advancing age, a watchful wife and a knighthood, cured him. Plaque erected 1966. Nearest Tube Station = South Kensington.

LAWRENCE, David Herbert (1885-1930) 1, Byron Villas, Vale of Health, Hampstead, NW3.
'novelist and poet lived here in 1915'
Lawrence and his wife Frieda spent only a few months here. Why a plaque should be erected here, when they lived four years at Colworth Road, Croydon, where Lawrence taught at the Davidson Road school, is difficult to understand. The assumption must be one of snobbishness. At the Hampstead address Lawrence met those who would later help him get published. He was born in Eastwood, Nottinghamshire, the son of a coal miner and became a teacher. At the outbreak of WW1 he married Frieda von Richtofen, a cousin of the airman who would soon be shooting down RFC pilots. It wasn't very good timing, especially as they had been living together since 1912, when he took her away from her husband. The Lawrences were regarded with much suspicion and some hostility. Following publication, in 1915, of "The Rainbow", Lawrence was charged with obscenity. He left England in 1919 never to return. His novel "Lady Chatterley's Lover" published in Florence in 1928 didn't appear in the UK until 1961; and that was only after a famous obscenity trial. After living for some years in America and Mexico, he finally made his home in Italy, where he died of TB. Plaque erected 1969. Nearest tube station = Hampstead.

LAWRENCE, Susan (1871-1947) 44, Westbourne Terrace, Bayswater, W2.
'social reformer lived here'
Susan Lawrence was born in London and educated at Newnham College, Cambridge. She worked for various organisations that dealt with the relief of suffering, experienced by the slum dwellers of London. In 1923, she became Labour MP for East Ham North losing her seat in the following year. In the 1926 General Election she returned, regained the seat for Labour and held it until 1931. In 1930, she became the first woman chairperson of the Labour Party. She wrote much, particularly articles on her continuing interest in all aspects of social reform that would benefit the unemployed and lower paid. She lived here, towards the end of her life and held open house to a multitude, especially during the second world war. Plaque erected 1987. Nearest tube station = Paddington.

LAWRENCE, T. E. (1888-1935) 14, Barton Street, Belgravia, SW1.
' "Lawrence of Arabia" lived here'
Lawrence who was born in Tremadoc, Caernarvonshire and educated at Jesus College, Oxford, came to live here following his Middle East adventures during WW1. Encounters in "The Times" of his exploits against the Turks, made Lawrence a popular hero. Following the publication of "Seven Pillars of Wisdom", the publicity became too much. Lawrence was still suffering from mental problems of a sexual nature that had probably begun during adolescence and surfaced during the war. To escape his fame and publicity, Lawrence joined the RAF and became AC2 Ross. Here he met other homosexuals but no breath of scandal emerged; instead he was recognised as the great Lawrence of Arabia and discharged. Then followed a short period in the army, before returning, in 1925, to the RAF. He was discharged in 1935 and for a few months he found seclusion in the Dorset countryside, before dying in a motor cycle accident. He wrote several books, "The Mint" was published posthumously. Plaque erected 1966. Nearest tube station = Westminster.

LEAR, Edward (1812-1888) 30, Seymour Street, Marylebone, W1.
'artist and writer lived here'
Lear, born in London, spent only a short time here and then only because he had been commissioned, by Regent's Park Zoo, to do some drawings of parrots and Seymour Street was convenient. The portfolio was a financial success and provided Lear with the money he needed to launch him as a writer. He travelled widely throughout Europe and constantly wrote his nonsense poems which are beloved by all who read them. He spent most of his later years in Italy. Plaque erected 1960. Nearest tube station = Baker Street.

LECKY, W. E. H. (William Edward Hartpole) (1838-1903), 38, Onslow Gardens, SW7.
'historian and essayist lived and died here'
Lecky, born near Dublin and educated at Trinity College, Dublin, lived here for thirty years, during which time he was member of parliament for Dublin University and an even handed orator on Irish problems. He was a writer of history who created controversy, with his eight volume work "A History of England in the 18th Century". He was appointed a privy councillor in 1897. Plaque erected 1955. Nearest tube station = South Kensington.

LEIGHTON, Frederick, Lord (1830-1896) Leighton House, 12, Holland Park Road, Holland Park, W14.
'painter lived and died here'
Leighton was born in Scarborough, the son of a doctor. He became a successful Victorian painter and President of The Royal Academy in 1878. He inherited a considerable fortune and decided to build a magnificent house that would be devoted to art. The main feature was the Arab Hall, the dome of which was decorated with old tiles Leighton had collected during his Middle Eastern travels. Here gathered the luminaries of his day; Disraeli, Macauley, Gladstone, Thackeray and others. The house became the focal point of the pre-Raphaelites, who regarded Leighton as their leader. This unusual house is now a museum and often used as an art gallery. His painting, "Wedded", was one of the first to be reproduced by photogravure methods. It sold widely. He never married and left his fortune to various charities. Plaque erected 1958. Nearest tube station = Holland Park.

LENO, Dan (1860-1904) 56, Akerman Road, Brixton, SW9.
'music hall comedian lived here 1898-1901'
Leno's real name was George Galvin. He was born in Holborn of theatrical parents who, before he could talk, put him on the stage as part of their act. He made his reputation in pantomime and was "The Dame" for many years in the roles of "Widow Twankey and Mother Goose". He was only 44 when he died, following the death of his friend and colleague, Herbert Campbell for whom he pined. He achieved the honour of having been the first music hall artist to play a Command Performance; Edward VII. Plaque erected 1962. Nearest tube station = Brixton.

LETHABY, William Richard (1857-1931) 20, Calthorpe Street, WC1.
'architect lived here 1880-1891'
AND
LETHABY, William Richard (1857-1931) Central School of Arts and Crafts, Southampton Row, Holborn, WC1.
'architect and first principal of this school in 1896 to 1911'
Lethaby, born in Barnstaple, Devon, was the chief assistant to Norman Shaw, a popular architect in the latter part of the 19th century. Shaw built large, unimaginative and solid looking houses. Lethaby decided against this trend, when he left Shaw and started on his own. He concentrated on design and decided to impart his knowledge and enthusiasm for his work to the young. He joined those who started the Central School in Holborn and became Principal in 1902, overseeing the expansion that followed. The fact that the school has continued to expand and survive is directly due to the foundations he imposed. Plaques erected 1957 and 1979. Nearest Tube Stations = Russell Square and Holborn.

LEWIS. Percy Wyndham (1882-1957) 61, Palace Gardens Terrace, Kensington, W8.
'painter lived here'
Lewis was born in Amehurst, Nova Scotia educated at Rugby School and the Slade School of Art. He became a painter and author. His paintings reflect his work with the Vorticist movement of which he was the acknowledged leader. Their theory was that modern art should be based on the principles of an industrial civilisation. Their journal was "Blast" and contributors included Ezra Pound and T. S. Eliot. From 1916, Lewis served in the army in France as a bombardier, before being appointed a war artist. Lewis wrote novels which included, "The Childermass" (1928) and "Apes of God" (1930) which attacked cultural fashions of the 1920s. As a writer, he has been ranked alongside James Joyce and as a painter, he is considered a portraitist of the highest order. In the thirties he, in common with Pound and Eliot, supported fascism. At the outbreak of WW2, rather than stay in Britain, he went to Canada. He returned in 1945. Although blind from 1951 he wrote two biographical type books, "Self Condemned" (1954) and in 1955, "The Human Age". Plaque erected 1983. Nearest tube station = Notting Hill Gate.

LEYBOURNE, George (1842-1884) 136, Englefield Road, Islington, N1.
'music hall comedian "Champagne Charlie", lived and died here'
Leybourne was born in Gateshead, where his father worked for the local Council. George left school at 12 and went to train as a mechanic. He joined a local church choir and supplemented his earnings by singing in local clubs. At 18 he left to make his fame and fortune in London. He found both in the character of "Champagne Charlie". He would come on stage, dressed immaculately in evening wear and sporting a monocle. In a tipsy manner, he sang about being a man about town. The truth was he wasn't acting. He drank his way to a lonely short life in Islington. This was close to Collin's Music Hall, where he often appeared. Plaque erected 1970. Nearest tube station = Highbury and Islington.

LIND, Jenny (Madame Goldschmidt) (1820-1887) 189, Brompton Road, SW7.
'singer lived here'
Jenny Lind was born in Stockholm. Although her parents were very poor they managed to help their talented daughter by providing her with singing lessons from the age of nine. She then won a scholarship to a conservatoire in Paris. She soon attained great international popularity and became known as "The Swedish Nightingale". She gave up a career as an operatic star, in favour of the concert platform. She toured all over the world, before settling down in London where she married a Frenchman, Pierre Goldschmidt, and came to live here. In 1883 she became a teacher at the Royal College of Music. She endowed many musical scholarships in England and Sweden and gave much to musical charities. Plaque erected 1989. Nearest tube station = Knightsbridge.

LINNELL, John (1792-1882) 'Old Wyldes', North End, Hampstead, NW3.
'painter lived here. BLAKE, William (1757-1827), poet and artist stayed here as his guest'
This area is now one of the most select in Hampstead; in Linnel's day it was isolated and belonged to Eton College. Linnel, an average painter who made a fair living from portrait and landscape painting, was sufficiently well off to give William Blake money, and when he needed it, room and board. He also gave Blake the opportunity of engraving one his more important works "The Book of Job" (1826). Although born in London, for some unaccountable reason he only painted scenes of Surrey. Plaque erected 1975. Nearest tube station = Golders Green.

LISTER, Joseph, Lord (1827-1912) 12, Park Crescent, Mayfair, W1.
'surgeon lived here'
Lister, born in Upton, Essex and educated at London University, made outstanding contributions to modern surgery, much of it whilst living and working here. For nearly thirty years, Lister, ably assisted by his wife, the daughter of a surgeon, concentrated on the reasons why there was such a great mortality rate connected with surgical operations. The conclusions were that insufficient care was given to the treatment of wounds during and immediately after operations. He advanced the principles of antiseptic treatments and became a pioneer in bacteriology. He became President of the Royal Society and was later awarded the Order of Merit. His efforts revolutionized modern surgery methods and dramatically lowered post operative deaths. Plaque erected 1915, (only three years after his death instead of the usual 20). Nearest tube station = Regent's Park.

LLOYD GEORGE, David (1865-1945) 3, Routh Road, SW18
'Prime Minister, lived here'
Lloyd George lived here from 1904 to 1908. During this time he was President of the Board of Trade, in the liberal government of the time and established himself as a great parliamentary orator. Born in Manchester, he was two when his father died and he was taken to Llanystumdwy, Wales to live with his uncle, Richard Lloyd. It was to this uncle that David owed all he was to achieve. For it was from him that David acquired his knowledge of religion, oratory, radical views and Welsh nationalism. Later he spent his holidays at the home he kept at Criccieth. There he would charge his batteries and return to the political fray, full of fire. In 1908 he became Chancellor. His 1909 budget, which sought to introduce old age pensions, was thwarted by the House of Lords. This led to his promotion of the Parliament Act of 1911, which curtailed the power of the Upper Chamber. During the middle of WW1, he was asked to succeed Asquith, as prime minister and continued until the general election of 1922. He had several claims to fame. He was responsible for introducing health and unemployment insurance; helping to draw up the Versailles Treaty, for promoting the establishment of the Irish Free State in 1921 and for being one of the very few people who served in parliament throughout two world wars. He was created an Earl in 1945 and died soon after. Plaque erected 1992. Nearest tube station = Wandsworth Common.

LLOYD, Marie (1870-1922) 55, Graham Road, Hackney, E8.
'music hall artiste lived here'
Marie Lloyd was born Matilda Alice Victoria Wood, the daughter of a London waiter and the eldest of 11 children. She was only 15 when she made her first stage appearance and became an overnight success. She specialised in risque songs and was sometimes accused of being coarse. However, many of her songs became household tunes, "The Boy I Love Sits up in the Gallery", "Oh Mr. Porter", and probably the most famous of all music hall songs, "My Old Man Said Follow the Van". She appeared at music halls all over the country and toured America, Canada and South Africa. She died after a theatrical fall at the Edmonton Empire. At that time she was living in a large house in Golders Green, a far cry from the poverty of Hackney. During WW2, German bombs destroyed the Golders Green house, killing several people. What would she have said? Plaque erected 1977. Nearest tube station = Hackney Down.

LOUDON, John Claudius, 3, Porchester Terrace, Bayswater, W2.
'Here lived John and Jane Loudon (1783-1843) and, (1807-1858). Their horticultural work gave new beauty to London Squares'
Loudon, born in Cambuslang, Scotland, was already a well known figure in the world of horticultural design and responsible for the establishment of conservatories in suburban London, when he met, and married, Jane Webb. Together they went on to design many of London's garden squares. They wrote on their subject and built on the popularity John had received with his "Encyclopedia of Gardening" (1823). Together they wrote "The Ladies Companion to the Flower Garden" (1841). After John's death, Jane wrote "How to Enjoy a Country Life Rationally" (1845). In 1818, in Porchester Terrace, Bayswater, John Loudon exhibited, for the first time, his design for the semi-detached house. Plaque erected 1953. Nearest tube station = Queensway.

LOVELACE, Countess Ada (1815-1852) 12, St. James's Square, SW1.
'Pioneer of Computing lived here'
Augusta Ada was the daughter of Lord Byron. Her mother, the former Anna Isabella Milbanke, left her husband soon after giving birth because of her husband's incest with his half sister. Following a brief and shallow education, Ada taught herself mathematics and astronomy with the result she attracted the attention of Charles Babbage, the computer pioneer. She was responsible for interpreting the source of Babbage's work under the title, "Sketch of the Analytical Engine" (1843). The present universal, high-level computer programming language, ADA is so named in her honour. A little compensation perhaps for her short life compounded by a bad marriage. Plaque erected 1992. Nearest tube station = St. James's Park.

LOW, Sir David (1891-1963) Melbury Court, Kensington High Street, W8.
'cartoonist lived here at No. 33. '
Low was born in Dunedin, New Zealand. He came to London in 1919 and joined "The Star", a popular London evening paper. In 1927 he crossed over to a rival paper, and the only London evening paper that still survives; "The Evening Standard". There he achieved fame. He ridiculed all establishment figures particularly politicians and created "Colonel Blimp", an ongoing euphemism for pompous stupidity often, but not always, directed to retired figures critical of the young. In 1950 he went to work for the "Daily Herald", then in 1953, "The Guardian". He wrote several books, including "Low's Autobiography" (1956). Plaque erected 1991. Nearest tube station = Kensington High Street.

LUCAN, Arthur (Arthur Towle) (1887-1954) 11, Forty Lane, Wembley.
'entertainer and creator of Old Mother Riley lived here'
Why this plaque, which stands on a large house near Wembley Stadium, doesn't mention his wife and long suffering partner, Kitty McShane, is hard to understand. Lucan, who came from Dublin, created the character of "Old Mother Riley" and dressed up as an Irish washerwoman. His wife, was his stage daughter and their act consisted of gossipy tales they told on stage and the Irish songs they sung. In reality, Lucan was a drunk who treated his wife badly. The films they made in the thirties can sometimes be seen on TV. Plaque erected 1978. Nearest tube station = Wembley Park

LUGARD, LORD (1858-1945) 51, Rutland Gate, Hyde Park, SW7.
'colonial administrator, lived here 1912-1919'
Located opposite the park, this is a very pleasant part of London in which to live and where the Household Cavalry presently reside. Lugard, born in Fort St. George, Madras, the son of a missionary, was responsible for the formation of The West African Frontier Force (1897-9), before going on to become commissioner of Northern Nigeria (1900-6) and then Governor of all Nigeria (1914-19). He was a forward thinking man who advocated self determination long before it was fashionable. Plaque erected 1972. Nearest tube station = South Kensington.

LUTYENS, Sir Edwin Landseer (1869-1944) 13, Mansfield Street, Marylebone, W1.
'John Loughborough Pearson (1817-1897) and later Sir Edwin Landseer Lutyens, architects lived and died here'
It must be pure coincidence that this house, in a quiet part of Central London, should have housed two architects although they could not have been more dissimilar in style. Pearson was solid and Gothic, whilst Lutyens was imaginative and light. Lutyens, born in London, built many a house for the emerging affluent middle classes and was responsible for a lot of early neo Georgian designs that adorned Mayfair in the early part of this century. His father-in-law was Lord Lytton, Viceroy of India; this was indeed an advantage and led to Lutyens becoming the chief architect who built New Delhi, as India's capital. Lutyens's crowning achievement, and for which he was knighted, was his design for the Cenotaph in Whitehall, built to commemorate those who died in WW1. However, he was most proud of his designs for Liverpool's Catholic Cathedral and the British Embassy in Washington. Plaque erected 1962. Nearest tube station = Oxford Circus.

MACAULAY, Thomas Babington, Lord (1800-1859) Holly Lodge, (now Atkins Buildings), Queen Elizabeth College, Campden Hill, Kensington, W8.
'historian and man of letters, lived here'
Macaulay was a very early starter. He was reading at three and could recount stories far above his years. His understanding of language and meaning was considered remarkable. Born in Rothley Temple, Leicestershire he was schooled at home and later privately, before going on to Trinity College, Cambridge when just 17. He was called to the bar in 1826, but disliked the work preferring politics and writing. He became Liberal MP for Edinburgh (1839). By extreme hard work, which would later take its toll on his health, he combined an intense political life, he was Secretary for War, with his writing and researching for what would eventually appear as his, "History of England from the Accession of James II". Nor did he concentrate only on this work. In 1842 he published, "Lays of Ancient Rome" which became a bestseller. He resigned from parliament in 1856 and received a peerage. He came to live here, and died, whilst working in his library. He is buried in Westminster Abbey. Plaque erected 1903. Nearest tube station = Kensington High Street.

MACAULAY, Zachary (1768-1838) 5, The Pavement, Clapham Common, SW4.
'philanthropist and his son, Thomas Babbington, afterwards Lord Macaulay (1800-1859) historian and man of letters lived here'
This is the father who made it financially possible for son Thomas Babbington's success. Zachary was part owner of a company that dealt in transporting slaves from Africa to Jamaica. Whilst working in Sierra Leone he suddenly had a change of heart about the morality of slave trading. He returned to England and Clapham and formed a Christian sect known as the Clapham Sect; devoted to the abolition of slaves and adherence to Christ's message. However, all this new founded Christian zeal didn't prevent him living well on the proceeds of his slave trading days. Plaque erected 1930. Nearest tube station = Clapham Common.

MACDONALD, Ramsay (1866-1937) 9, Howitt Road, Hampstead, NW3.
'Prime Minister, lived here 1916-1925'
MacDonald was born in Lossiemouth, Scotland and joined the newly formed Independent Labour Party in 1894. This was the forerunner to the Labour Party of 1900. He had a varied political career and became the first Labour prime minister (Jan-Nov 1924). Then he served a full term as prime minister (1929-1935), although for part of the time it was a coalition. MacDonald could and should have been a great politician but he allowed himself to be seduced by people wealthier, better educated and more personable, than himself. Most of all, he often forgot his socialist principles in favour of the moment. Plaque erected 1963. Nearest tube station = Hampstead.

McGILL, Donald (1875-1962) 5, Bennett Park, Blackheath, SE3.
'postcard cartoonist lived here'
McGill was the man who made the holiday postcard fun to buy and receive. His fat lady, seeing her henpecked husband looking longingly at the leggy buxom blonde wearing a brief swimming costume, and her subsequent angry reaction caused the postcard business, between the wars, to boom. McGill, originally Fraser Gould, born in Blackheath, London, became an architect's draughtsman. Then, at the beginning of the century, he offered a selection of his drawings to a postcard publisher who promptly saw McGill's talent and did a deal; to buy one card per day, excluding Sundays. All in all, he produced nearly 20,000 designs on all subjects, until his retirement in 1945, when he moved away to the countryside. In 1941 he received critical attention, following an article by George Orwell entitled, "Horizon". Plaque erected 1977. Nearest Station = Blackheath.

The Rachel McMILLAN College (1930-1977) Creek Road, Deptford, SE8.
'Margaret McMILLAN, CH (1860-1931), pioneer of nursery education, lived here'
Margaret McMillan was born in New York but brought up in Inverness. She agitated for medical inspections on workers in factories and the introduction of school clinics. In 1902 she joined her sister Rachel in London and lived in Creek Road for several years. They opened their first clinic in 1908. After her sister's death, Margaret raised the money to open, as a memorial, the Rachel McMillan Training College for nursery and infant teachers. Plaque erected 1985. Nearest Station = Greenwich

MALLARME, Stephane (1842-1898) 6, Brompton Square, South Kensington, SW3.
'poet stayed here in 1863'
Born in Paris, Mallarme came to London, aged 20, to learn English. The result was that 2 years later he married a German governess and came to live here. He worked at being a poet and survived on the proceeds. He formulated theories of Symbolists and, together with Rimbaud and Verlaine, reacted against realism in literature, feeling that poetry should evoke inexpressible states. His work included, "L'apres-midi d'un faune" (1876), illustrated by Manet and later set to music by Debussy, and "Herodiade" (1869). A literary group known as the "Decadents" promoted his work, praising his use of allegory, obscurity and often strange construction. Plaque erected 1959. Nearest Tube Station = South Kensington.

MALLON, Dr. Jimmy, CH (1874-1961) Toynbee Hall, Commecial Street, Whitechapel, E1.
'warden of Toynbee Hall, champion of social reform lived here'
Jimmy Mallon, born in Manchester of Irish parents, became known as the Father O'Flynn of the Labour movement. He was educated at Owen's College, Manchester. In 1906. he was secretary of the National League that worked to establish a minimum wage. After WW1, he applied to become Warden of Toynbee Hall. Much to his surprise, he was selected and stayed until 1954. During this time he served as a Governor of the BBC (1937). He was a leading advocate in the fight to raise the school leaving age and for all his good works he was awarded a CH. For his work at Toynbee Hall, a garden was created facing Commercial Street. It is known as Mallon Garden. In the dining hall is a bronze bust of Jimmy Mallon by his friend, Jacob Epstein. When he died "The Times", in an obituary wrote ". . . the most popular man East of Aldgate Pump'. Plaque erected 1984. Nearest tube station = Aldgate East.

MALONE, Edmond (1741-1812) 40, Langham Street, St. Marylebone, W1.
'Shakesperian scholar lived here 1779-1812'
Although Malone, born in Dublin, was called to the bar in 1767, he practised little law and spent the best part of his life writing and researching on and about William Shakespeare. He failed to shed any light on the question "Did Shakespeare write it all by himself or did he have help". This question has been repeatedly asked and never resolved, the general attitude being "does it really matter?" after all they were written and probably by Shakespeare. In 1907, the Malone Society was established in his honour. Plaque erected 1962. Nearest tube station = Oxford Circus.

MANBY, Charles (1804-1884) 60, Westbourne Terrace, Paddington, W2.
'civil engineer, lived here'
In 1822, the vessel "Aaron Munby" was the first iron steamship to go to sea. It was the result of Manby's work in supervising its construction at London's Surrey docks. Later Manby, born in London, turned his hand to the problem of heating large buildings. That accomplished, he helped design and plan the Suez Canal. Then he had a complete change of interest, (following his attachment to an actress) he became involved with theatre management and took over the running of the Adelphi Theatre. It must have been good for his health, he died aged 80, after a lifetime free from illness. Plaque erected 1961. Nearest tube station = Paddington

MANNING, Cardinal Henry Edward (1808-1892) 22, Carlisle Place, Westminster, SW1.
'lived here'
Manning, born in Totteridge, Hertfordshire and educated at Harrow and Balliol College, Oxford, was converted, in 1851, to the Roman Catholic faith via the Oxford Movement. He became the Archbishop of Westminster, from 1865 and created a cardinal in 1875. Unusual, for a senior catholic of that time, was his deep interest in the social conditions that disadvantaged the poor. He assisted in their education and supported the trade union movement. In 1889, he brought his influence to settling the dock strike. Plaque erected 1914. Nearest tube station = Victoria.

MANSBRIDGE, Albert (1876-1952) 198, Windsor Road, Ilford, Essex.
'founder of the Worker's Educational Association, lived here'
Mansbridge is a typical example why Britain's honours system should be abolished. The Establishment creates peerages and knighthoods, often because the person concerned has bought it; via well defined paths. Mansbridge received nothing, other than the heart felt thanks from the thousands who have profited by the educational advantages the WEA has provided and continues to provide. Mansbridge was born in Gloucester and left school at 14 to become an office clerk. Gradually, through extension classes at King's College, London he qualified as a teacher. In addition to founding the WEA, he founded the National Central Library (1916). Plaque erected 1967. Nearest Station = Ilford.

MANSFIELD, Katherine (1888-1923) 17, East Heath Road, Hampstead, NW3.
'writer, and her husband, John Middleton MURRY (1889-1957) critic, lived here'
Katherine Mansfield was born in Wellington, New Zealand and her full name was Katherine Mansfield Beauchamp. Many of her short stories had a New Zealand setting, e.g. "Bliss" (1920), and "The Garden Party" (1922). In 1918, Katherine married John Murry, having lived with him since 1912, and they moved to Hampstead. The onset of Katherine's tuberculosis set them off to the sunnier parts of Europe but it was too late and she died aged only 35. D. H. Lawrence portrayed them as Gudron and Gerald in "Women in Love". Her husband published her collected works in 1945. Plaque erected 1969. Nearest tube station = Hampstead.

MANSON, Sir Patrick (1844-1922) 50, Welbeck Street, Marylebone, W1.
'father of modern tropical medicine lived here'
Manson, born in Aberdeenshire, became known as "Mosquito Manson". He pioneered the research into malaria and worked as a doctor in East China and Hong Kong. In 1883 he founded a school of medicine that went on to become Hong Kong University. He returned to London and became advisor to the Colonial Office. In 1897 he moved here and in 1889 he founded the London School of Tropical Medicine. He was the first scientist to formulate the policy that the mosquito inhabited the malaria parasite. Shortly before his death he was knighted for medical research. Plaque erected 1985. Nearest tube station = Baker Street.

MARCONI, Guglielmo (1874-1937) 71, Hereford Road, Bayswater, W2.
'the pioneer of wireless communication lived here in 1896-1897'
Marconi, was born in Bolognia, Italy, of an Italian father and an Irish mother. He failed to get financial support, for his research into radio telegraphy, from the Italian Science Board. He came to London and on June 2nd 1896 took out a patent. In 1901, Marconi succeeded in transmitting and receiving signals, between Newfoundland and Cornwall. In 1914, he began experiments in short wave, which led to the beam system of long distance and directed wireless transmission. He had already been awarded the Nobel Prize for Physics in 1909 and this, together with his on-going experiments, prompted him to form "Marconi's Wireless Telegraph Company". His regular radio programmes from Writtle, in Chelmsford, helped encourage the sale of radio receivers. With the establishment of the BBC, these were coming onto the market and radio listening began to take off. From 1921 he lived mostly aboard his yacht, the "Elettra". Later, in the thirties, he became a strong supporter of the fascist leader, Mussolini. Plaque erected 1954. Nearest tube station = Bayswater.

MARRYAT, Captain Frederick (1792-1848) 3, Spanish Place, St. Marylebone, W1.
'novelist lived here'
Marryat, born in London the son of an MP, started his naval career as a midshipman and ended it as a captain. He saw action in the West Indies and later commanded a sloop stationed off St. Helena in case Napoleon tried to escape. After adventures fighting off bandits and pirating river craft in Burma, he dealt with smugglers in the Channel, where he commanded the frigate "Ariadne". In 1830 he resigned and came ashore. Had he remained in the navy he would probably have become an admiral and the literary world would have lost "Mr Midshipman Easy" (1836), "Masterman Ready" (1841) and "Children of the New Forest" (1847) and much more. After some bad luck in money matters, he left London in 1843, for the calm of the Norfolk countryside. When he wasn't working at being a farmer he worked at his writing. Plaque erected 1953. Nearest tube station = Baker Street.

MARSDEN, William (1796-1867) 65, Lincoln's Inn Fields, Holborn WC2.
'surgeon founder of the Royal Free and Royal Marsden Hospitals, lived here'
Born in Sheffield, the son of a doctor, William Marsden trained as a surgeon at St. Bartholomews Hospital, London and was then apprenticed to Mr. Dale of Holborn Hill. He was admitted to the Royal College of Surgeons in 1827. He was most concerned that the very poor couldn't receive hospital treatment and in 1828 he established, in Greville Street, close to Hatton Garden, a small dispensary, where the poor could go for basic medical care. At first, his experiments in welfare medicine, caused protest amongst his colleagues but gradually he won them over, with the result that in 1832, several small dispensaries were established in the poorer parts of London. In 1851, Marsden opened a small house in Cannon Row for cancer sufferers and in 1861 they moved to Brompton Road, where he had room for 120 patients and where he was senior surgeon. In 1834, he had written his book on cancer, "Asiatic or Malignant Cholera". He died of bronchitis whilst living here. In 1994, the fight has been won to save the hospital Marsden founded, as it was scheduled to close in a reappraisal of London's hospital needs. Plaque Erected 1986. Nearest tube station = Holborn

MARX, Karl (1818-1883) 28, Dean Street, Soho, W1.
'lived here 1851-1856'
Alongside Jesus Christ, Marx was probably the greatest and best known philosopher the world has ever known. Marx was born in Trier, Prussia of Jewish parents. His father was a lawyer and when in 1817, an edict prohibiting Jews from practising law came about, Marx Snr. had a simple choice; starve or convert to Protestantism, he converted. Marx's radical ideas caused his expulsion from Germany, he went first to Paris, then, when he was asked to leave, to London via Brussels. He was financed by his lifelong friend, Friedrich Engels. Marx published many articles in divers newspapers and magazines and, from 1852 to 1861, partly supported himself by being London correspondent for the "New York Daily Tribune", commenting on world affairs. Previously, in 1847, he published his "Communist Manifesto" and in 1863 the first part of "Das Kapital". This followed years of study at the British Museum, where Marx, at one time was a daily visitor. In 1874, he sought British citizenship, but was refused by the Home Office who claimed . . . "he had not been loyal to his king". Marx, who produced "Dialectical Materialism", whilst living here, was always on the verge of poverty. He and his family lived for the most part in two rooms and it wasn't until they moved to 9, Grafton Terrace, St. Pancras, that, thanks again to Engels, their living conditions improved. Marx is buried at Highgate cemetary, a shrine for visiting Communists the world over. His "Communist Manifesto" ends with the greatest political rallying cry ever, "The workers have nothing to lose but their chains. They have a world to win. Workers of all lands, unite". Plaque erected 1967. Nearest tube station = Tottenham Court Road.

MATTHAY, Tobias (1858-1945) 21, Arkwright Road, Hampstead, NW3.
'teacher and pianist lived here'
Matthay, born in London, was a radical teacher of the piano who spent only a short time here before moving to the peaceful climes of Dorset. Whilst here he continued giving music lessons on the piano, using his special method of touch, controlled by weight and relaxation. His pupils included Myra Hess (later created a Dame) and Harriet Cohen, who had an on-going 30 year romance with Sir Arnold Bax. Plaque erected 1979. Nearest tube station = Hampstead.

MAUGHAM, William Somerset (1874-1965) 6, Chesterfield Street, Mayfair, W1.
'novelist and playwright, lived here 1911-1919'
Maugham was born in Paris of Irish descent and educated at King's School, Canterbury, before qualifying as a surgeon at St. Thomas's Hospital, London. Maugham senior became most annoyed when his son told him his ambition was to make his living as an author. Maugham had only qualified as a doctor to satisfy his father and never practised. His first novel, "Liza of Lambeth" (1897), met only qualified success but his play "Lady Frederick", (1907) did. In 1908, Maugham had 4 plays running in the West End. However, it wasn't until he wrote, "Of Human Bondage"(1915) and "The Moon and Sixpence" (1919) did he achieve the sort of fame writers dream about. There followed numerous short stories until WW1. During that war he served with a Red Cross unit in France, before joining the British secret service and becoming their agent in Geneva and Petrograd. His novel "Ashendon" (1928) is based on these experiences. He moved to the South of France in 1930 and remained there, serving as a spare time secret agent until, in 1940 he fled, one step ahead of the Germans, with just a small suitcase. He spent the war years in the US, still a secret agent. However, whatever else he was doing, he was always writing, "Razor's Edge" (1945), "Catalina" (1948), "A Writer's Notebook" In 1958 he wrote "Points of View", essays on many famous writers. Plaque erected 1975. Nearest tube station = Green Park.

MAURICE, Frederick Denison (1805-1872) 2, Upper Harley Street, Marylebone, W1.
'Christian philosopher and educationalist, lived here (1862-1866)'
Maurice, born in Normanston, Suffolk, was of those early figures who combined Christian values with advancing Socialism. Educated at Trinity College, Cambridge he became a Dissenter and left without a degree. He felt that working people were disadvantaged, because the rich paid to educate their children and so perpetuate the class system and preserve their wealth. This is still the system but, thanks to people like Maurice who founded places of learning, such as Queen's College for Women and The Working Men's College, there has developed some basis for alternative learning but only at the higher level. Maurice suffered for his radical views. He supported Karl Marx and was forced to resign from King's College until, a more liberal Cambridge, in 1866, gave him the chair of moral philosophy. His son, Sir John Frederick Maurice, a professor of military history, wrote his father's biography, "Life of Frederick Denison Maurice" (1884). Plaque erected 1977. Nearest tube station = Regent's Park.

MAXIM, Sir Hiram. (1840-1896) 57d, Hatton Garden, Holborn, EC1.
'inventor and engineer, designed and manufactured THE MAXIM GUN in a workshop on these premises'
Maxim, born in Sangersville, USA, came to London following the 1881 Paris Exhibition, where he received an award for inventing the electrical current regulator. He rented these premises, (now the centre of the diamond trade) and set to work realising, what he had thought out in the States, namely a gun that would automatically fire hundreds of bullets a minute. It became known as "The killing machine" and earnt its inventor millions of dollars and killed hundreds of thousands of men, women and children before, during and after WW1. Maxim became naturalised in 1900 and a year later, a thankful British government awarded him with a knighthood. Plaque erected 1966. Nearest tube station = Chancery Lane.

MAXWELL, James Clerk (1831-1979) 16, Palace Gardens Terrace, Kensington, W8.
'physicist lived here'
It was here, in the garret, that Maxwell, born in Edinburgh, carried out some of the experiments that have made him famous in the world of physics. As great as Newton and Faraday his admirers claim. His 4 equations, concerning electric and magnetic fields, described interaction between electricity and magnetism and removed the mystery surrounding these two phenomena. Further, he deduced that light is electro magnetic and he predicted the existence of electromagnetic waves (radio). He was appointed to the chair of chemistry at Cambridge (1871) and founded the Cavendish Physical Laboratory in 1874. It is now recognised that his work paved the way for Albert Einstein and Max Planck. Plaque erected 1923. Nearest tube station = Kensington High Street.

MAY, Phil (1864-1903) 20, Holland Park Road, Notting Hill, W14.
'artist lived and worked here'
Although officially dubbed an artist, Phil May was a popular cartoonist and a genius at caricaturing the people and events of his day. Philip William May was born in Wortley, near Leeds. He was orphaned when he was 9 years old and endured many years of poverty, before he became a poster artist. In 1886, he went to Australia and, on his return in 1890, came to live here. He contributed to "Punch" and he published "Annual", which he gave up in 1902, due to ill health. A lot of his work showed East Londoners, an area usually forgotten about in his time. May pioneered a simple and relaxed manner in cartooning that led the way for later artists. Plaque erected 1982. Nearest tube station = Holland Park.

MAYHEW, Henry (1812-1887) 55, Albany Street, Regent's Park, NW1.
'founder of "Punch" and author of "London Labour and the London Poor",
lived here'

Alas, "Punch", that wonderful magazine that lulled those waiting, in doctors' and dentists' surgeries, into a false sense of security, is no more. It closed in 1992, victim of the recession and changing tastes. However, Mayhew had other interests especially the poor, and they are still with us, even if 'Punch' isn't. He wrote tracts on his observations and published these between 1849 and 1862 as "London Labour and the London Poor". He was born in London and educated at Westminster School, from which he ran away. The son of a lawyer, he disappointed his father, by turning his back on the law in favour of becoming a playwright. He was moderately successful with "The Wandering Minstrel", his best known work, although novels, written in collaboration with his brother Augustus, were most popular, "The Good Genius that turns everything to Gold" (1847), "Whom to Marry" (1848) are just two. Plaque erected 1953. Nearest tube station = Regent's Park.

MAZZINI, Giuseppe (1805-1872) 183, Gower Street, Camden, NW1.
'Italian patriot lived here'

Mazzini, born in Genoa, Italy, vigorously campaigned for Italian unity and independence until, in 1830, he was exiled and came to London. Here he continued the fight, whilst living a hand to mouth existence. He helped to raise the standards for Italian workers in London and started a school for them and their children in the North Holborn area that was to become known as 'Little Italy'. In 1844 he proved his charge, that the British government were opening his letters and informing his enemies in Italy of their contents. In 1849 he returned to Rome and headed the short lived republic, until royalist forces once again forced him to flee. Garibaldi entered the scene in 1860, and raised an international force, known as the "Red Shirts", that captured Sicily and Naples. Much to Mazzini's regret, Garibaldi, who harvested Mazzini's work, compromised the revolution and agreed to Victor Emmanuel as king. Mazzini's dream was a united Italy under a republic, but this didn't come about until 1945. Plaque erected 1950. Nearest tube station = Euston Square.

MEE, Arthur (1875-1943) 27, Lanercost Road, Tulse Hill, SW2.
'journalist, author and topographer lived here'

Mee was born in Stapleford, Nottingham. He is most widely known for his "Children's Encyclopedia" (1908) but he also founded the "Children's Newspaper" which, although subsequently copied, has never been equalled. From 1936 onwards, he produced a series entitled "The King's England", in which are described all the English counties. He lived here for many years until his retirement, just prior to the commencement of WW2. Plaque erected 1991. Nearest Station = Tulse Hill.

MEREDITH, George, OM (1828-1909) 7, Hobury Street, Chelsea, SW10.
'poet and novelist lived here'
Meredith was born in Portsmouth and educated in Germany. In London he became a solicitor before turning his hand to writing. This did not bring about much financial reward and he had to rely on his wife's money to aid the housekeeping. He had married, in 1849, a rich widow, who decided they were no match for one another and so parted. In 1885 "Diana of the Crossways" was published, and he was on his way to becoming a popular novelist. But it didn't last. His books became fewer, his style pedantic and less readable. Plaque erected 1976. Nearest tube station = Gloucester Road.

METTERNICH, Prince (1773-1859) 44, Eaton Square, Belgravia, SW1.
'Austrian statesman lived here in 1848'
Metternich was an Austrian born in Germany. He was the epitome of a manipulating diplomat. A wheeler dealer in international affairs, a master of negotiation, deception and intrigue. An asset to any thrusting government, then and now. He negotiated Napoleon's marriage to Marie-Louise of Austria (1810), had the foresight to keep Austria out of the Franco-Prussia war (1812- 3), thereby making Austria rich from supplying both sides, and then forming an alliance with Russia and Prussia against France. His was the voice that advocated the "balance of power" theory, expounded at the Congress of Vienna (1814-15). He was sympathetic to Jews who were constantly being persecuted, not only in Austria but in the German states and France, where he was instrumental in having the "Damascus blood libel" exposed. It was partially this support for Jewish problems that led to his downfall, during the revolution of Vienna in 1848. Following his escape from Austria, he came to live here. He disliked England and the English and in 1851 moved to his castle on the Rhine. He was a clever diplomat, had a keen sense of humour and took each day as it came. Plaque erected 1970. Nearest tube station = Sloane Square.

MEYNELL, Alice (1847-1922) 47, Palace Court, Bayswater, W2.
'poet and essayist lived here'
Alice Meynell, nee Thompson, born in Barnes, London was a minor poet of her day who basked in the reflected glory of her more famous contemporaries. She had a mystical experience in her twenties which left her turning to the Roman Catholic church for guidance. This resulted in her first book of verse "Preludes" (1875), received with mixed reviews. Following her marriage to Wilfred Meynell in 1877, she started a rehabilitation scheme for poets and writers suffering from alcohol and drug abuse. Amongst these was the poet Francis Thompson, her cousin. Plaque erected 1948. Nearest tube station = Queensway.

MILL, John Stuart (1806-1873) 18, Kensington Square, Kensington, W8.
'philosopher lived here'
Mill, born in London, lived in the shadow of his father, James Mill, who co-founded the Utilitarian philosophy. Mill senior dominated his son, he made himself responsible for his education and by the age of 3 John was being taught Greek. By the time he was thirteen he was able in Latin, arithmetic, logic and political history. He wasn't allowed the company of other children and his only exercise was a daily walk with his father, who continued educating him orally, as they walked. When he worked at the India Office, it was under his father. No wonder John carried on where his father left off. However, after some years he adjusted his views on more altruistic lines. He favoured democracy and universal suffrage. He wrote and spoke on social reform and emphasized the importance of quality and quantity of pleasure, as a motivating force in life. His books included, "Essay on Liberty" (1849), "Utilitarianism" (1863), and, "Autobiography" (1873). In 1824, he was arrested for distributing pamphlets, amongst the poor of London, urging them to use birth control methods. In 1865 he was elected to Parliament where he argued in favour of women's suffrage. He spent the last years of his life in France and died in Avignon. In 1872 he became the non religious godfather to Bertrand Russell. Plaque erected 1907. Nearest tube station = Kensington High Street.

MILLAIS, Sir John Everett, Bt PRA (1829-1896) 2, Palace Gate, Bayswater, W2.
'painter lived and died here'
Millais was born in Southampton and in 1840 became the youngest ever student at the Royal Academy. He went on to become a leading light in the Pre-Raphaelite Brotherhood and one of the foremost artists of his day. During his working life he averaged a yearly income, from his portraits of society figures and their children, of around £30,000 a year; and that was mid 19th century! No wonder his house was considered one of the most magnificent. It was in fact a mansion that started in 1873 and took five years to complete. Millais was an astute man who jettisoned his pre-Raphaelite friends as soon as he realised that high minded purism wasn't nearly as rewarding as commercialism. Within his mansion was incorporated his studio. It was larger even than many of his friend's houses, with extra wide doors to accommodate the very large canvases he often worked upon. His fame and efforts were rewarded by a baronetcy and burial in St. Paul's Cathedral. Plaque erected 1926. Nearest tube station = Gloucester Road.

MILLBANK PRISON, Millbank, Whitehall, SW1.
'near this site stood Millbank's Prison, which was opened in 1816 and closed in 1890. This buttress stood at the head of the river steps from which until 1867 prisoners sentenced to transportation embarked on their journey to Australia'

MILNE, A. A. (1882-1956) 13, Mallord Street, Chelsea, SW3.
'author lived here'
To keep his son, Christopher Robin, happy, Alan Alexander Milne, born in St. John's Wood, London and educated at Westminster School and Trinity College, Cambridge, wrote him stories. Wonderful and imaginative stories that have filled generations with happiness. He gained a mathematics degree, whilst at Cambridge, with the idea of becoming a teacher, instead, he took to journalism and in 1906, became assistant editor of 'Punch', where his regular features were eagerly read. After WW1, he wrote a couple of plays with mixed success. He had just moved in to Mallard Street, where he was to remain until the outbreak of WW2. Here, he wrote most of the books that made him famous and loved "Winnie the Pooh" (1926), "When We Were Very Young" (1924), and the detective story, "The Red House Mystery" (1922). In 1939, he wrote his autobiography, "It's Too Late Now". It wasn't, he spent many more happy years writing and lecturing. Plaque erected 1979. Nearest tube station = Sloane Square.

MILNER, Alfred, Lord (1854-1925) 14, Manchester Square, Marylebone, W1.
'statesman lived here'
Milner was born in Bonn, Germany, where his father was lecturer in English at Tubingen. Alfred was a brilliant scholar and won a fellowship to New College, Oxford. For a short time he was a journalist on the "Pall Mall Gazette" but he was a natural administrator and he went into the Civil Service. He was chairman of the board of the Inland Revenue (1897-1901), governor of Cape Colony (1901-3) and high commissioner for South Africa, for which he received a barony in 1901 and made viscount in 1902. During WW1, he served in the cabinet from 1916 with special reference to overseas territories. He was a keen Zionist and supported, in cabinet, Arthur Balfour's plan for a post war Jewish National Home in Palestine. In 1919 he became Colonial Secretary and advised independence for Egypt. Plaque erected 1967. Nearest tube station = Marble Arch.

MONDRIAN, Piet Cornelis (1872-1944) 60, Parkhill Road, Hampstead, NW3.
'painter lived here'
Dutch born Mondrian had, for many years, his studio in Paris. There he became the chief exponent of neo-plasticism, a strict form of geometric abstraction. Pictures that were built up from the simplest elements; straight lines and pure colours. This is well demonstrated by his painting "Composition with red, black, blue, yellow and grey" (1920), which survived nazi hatred and hangs in the Municipal Museum, Amsterdam. He sought an art form of clarity and discipline that would reflect the laws of the universe. He was visited, in Paris, by many eager young painters, particularly from the United States. He gave freely of his time and advice. In 1938, following the threat of war, Mondrian came to Britain and Hampstead. However, in 1940, he once again packed his brushes and went off to live, and later die, in New York. Plaque erected 1975. Nearest tube station = Chalk Farm

MONTEFIORE, Sir Moses (1784-1885) 99, Park Lane, Mayfair, W1.
'philanthropist and Jewish leader lived here for sixty years'
Montefiore was born in Leghorn, Italy, whilst his parents were on holiday from London. Educated in London, he was not academically inclined and his father had him apprenticed to a firm of wholesale grocers and tea merchants. He left to become a broker in the City. There, together with his brother Abraham, they started their own brokerage firm. With patronage from the Rothschilds, to whom they were related by marriage, the Montefiores prospered. Moses had an estate at Ramsgate, which included his own synagogue. He was a Conservative who disliked reform in religion as well as in politics. Unlike many rich Jews in England he didn't try to become "more English than the English". He worked for the Jewish community in Britain and anywhere in the world where there was Jewish persecution. He didn't turn his back on civic life and in 1837 he became sheriff of London and knighted by Queen Victoria. At 6'3" he was a presence that couldn't be ignored and when he travelled to harangue a country's leader, for not protecting its Jewish citizenry, he was listened to. He lived for over a hundred years and created a dynasty that continues. Plaque erected 1984. Nearest tube station = Marble Arch

MONTGOMERY, Field Marshal, Viscount of Alamein (1887-1976) Oval House, 52-4, Kennington Oval, Vauxhall, SE11.
'was born here'
History doesn't record how long the Montgomery family lived here. They have some ties with Ireland but Bernard went to school at St. Pauls School, Hammersmith. He left school for Sandhurst military academy. He became an officer in time to serve in WW1. In WW2, at the time of the Dunkirk evacuation, following the collapse of French forces, Montgomery was a Major-General. In 1942 he was given command of the 8th Army (The Desert Rats) and sent to North Africa. Known throughout the army as Monty, but not to his face, he set about restoring confidence, following German successes. It wasn't long before the battle of El Alamein scuppered German hopes in Africa. Unfortunately, Monty was an egotist who constantly had clashes with those who got the limelight. As a result he was constantly at loggerheads with Eisenhower, the Allied Supreme Commander, over tactics that should be used prior to, during and after D-Day, June 6th 1944. His antagonism towards General Patton is typical of what went on. Patton was known as "blood and guts", because of the way he blasted all obstacles in getting to his objective. Monty once commented to reporters, about casualties amongst Patton's troops, saying ". . . their blood, their guts". After the war, he was appointed Chief of the Imperial General Staff. When he was created a Viscount, he chose to take the title of Alamein to commemorate the great battle that helped turn the tide of the war. He wrote several books including his controversial, "Memoirs" (1958) Plaque erected 1987. Nearest tube station = Oval.

MOORE, George (1852-1933) 121, Ebury Street, Belgravia, SW1.
'author lived here'
Moore was born in Ballyglass, Ireland, the son of an MP and wealthy racehorse owner. After some education, at Oscott College, Birmingham, George was destined for the army but came to London instead. Here he became an agnostic, abandoned all thoughts of a career and became a Bohemian. When his father died in 1870 he was left enough money to really indulge himself. He went off to Paris and did the usual things young rich men did in Paris. After some ten years he had little money left and he became bored. He read Zola and reckoned he would become a writer. At first he met with little success. During the Boer wars, and hating England for fighting the Boer he went to live in Ireland. He served as Sheriff of County Mayo and began a friendship with W. B. Yeats that lasted all his life. Moore's best novel is thought to be, "Esther Waters" (1894), which reflected the influence of French naturalism. He also wrote art criticisms that championed impressionism. These reflected his stay in Paris in 1872, when he decided he wanted to be a painter, but came to realise his talent was less than was required. He came to live in Ebury Street in 1911 and stayed until he died. The two novels he wrote whilst living here brought him fame and some fortune. "The Brook Kerith" (1916) and "Heloise and Abelard" (1921). He is now regarded as an important figure in the literary world. His "Hail and Farewell", written in three parts between 1911 and 1914, is a masterpiece. He was a hospitable man, who held open house to all men of letters. Walter de la Mare and Edmund Gosse were amongst many who came. Plaque erected 1936. Nearest tube station = Victoria.

MOORE, Tom (1779-1852) 85, George Street, Marylebone, W1.
'Irish poet lived here'
Moore was born in Dublin, the son of a Catholic grocer. He was educated at Hyhte's School, Trinity College, Dublin and studied law at the Middle Temple. He came here to lodge whilst studying. The area in which he lived was the haunt of French emigres who welcomed Moore to their poor homes. Especially the parents of unmarried daughters. Moore was handsome and witty and far too clever to fall for any girl who didn't have a large dowry. He didn't have to worry overmuch on that score. The wealthy fawned over the witty young man, who sung his cheeky ballads whilst accompanying himself on the piano. He had published some early poems under the pen name "Thomas Little", now he used his real name and a book of verse published in 1806 was savagely attacked in the "Edinburgh Review" by a young critic, Francis Jeffrey, later Lord Jeffrey, High Court judge. Moore challenged Jeffrey to a duel. This was arranged to take place at Chalk Farm Fields, near Hampstead. In the event the duel was foiled by the police, alerted by friends of both men. In 1807, Moore wrote "Irish Melodies", further revised editions continued until 1834. In 1822 he went to live in Wiltshire for the rest of his life. In 1835 he received a pension of £300 a year, handsome for that time, but his last days were saddened by the untimely death of both his sons. Plaque Erected 1963. Nearest tube station = Baker Street.

MORGAN, Charles (1894-1958) 16, Campden Hill Square, Kensington, W8. 'novelist and critic lived and died here'

Morgan was born in Kent, the son of an engineer. He entered the Royal Navy in 1911 as a midshipman, served in China and resigned his commission in 1913. In 1914, at the outbreak of WW1, he rejoined the navy but spent most of the war in an internment camp in Holland. Upon his release in 1917 he went to Oxford University where he became known as a wit. In 1921 he joined 'The Times' and, in 1926, was appointed their principal drama critic until 1939. He wrote several novels, many of which won prizes. The most notable being, "The Voyage" (1940), which won the James Black Memorial Prize. His plays included, "The Burning Glass" (1953). His writings however, were rarely as good as those he reviewed. Plaque erected 1992. Nearest tube station = Notting Hill.

MORRELL, Lady Ottoline (1873-1938) 10, Gower Street, Bloomsbury, WC1. 'literary hostess and patron of the Arts lived here'

Ottoline Morrell was born, Lady Ottoline Violet Anne Cavendish-Bentinck in London, complete with the proverbial silver spoon. After a private education and a certain amount of travelling, she married Philip Morrell in 1902 and started writing poetry. Not very successful, she sought the company of established writers and so began her unique stable of authors and artists whom she entertained at Garsington Manor in Oxfordshire. The names read like an intellectual "Whos Who", Bertrand Russell, D. H. Lawrence, Aldious Huxley, Augustus John, Virginia Woolf, T. S. Eliot, Siegfried Sassoon and many others. She enjoyed their company, they enjoyed her lavish hospitality and they argued, agreed and disagreed with each other. Ottoline was the Grande Dame of her time. She wrote and received letters and many she kept, from luminaries all over the world. She was photographed by Cecil Beaton, painted by Augustus John and dressed by the best designers. Plaque erected 1984. Nearest tube station = Euston Square.

MORRISON, Herbert, Lord Morrison of Lambeth (1888-1965), 55, Archery Road, Eltham, SE9.
'Cabinet Minister and leader of the London County Council lived here 1929-1960'
Herbert Morrison was born in Lambeth, London and never strayed far from home. Educated briefly at the local elementary school, he improved himself by extensive reading. Before becoming a Labour MP in 1923, Morrison led the Labour group on the London County Council. Despite serving as a cabinet minister in several Labour administrations, his heart was always on London's affairs. He was known as "Mr London". Had he lived to see the GLC, which succeeded the LCC, disbanded; it would have broken his heart. It was due entirely to his efforts, that the "Green Belt" around London was created and, despite many threats, has survived largely intact. During WW2, Morrison was deeply involved with the defence of London from German bombs, missiles and rockets. His energy and imagination did much to save London. He was also involved in war production and launched great posters showing servicemen saying to defence workers . . . "give us the tools and we'll finish the job". In 1955 he was defeated by Hugh Gaitskell in a vote for the party leadership. He was created a life peer in 1959 and in 1960 he published "Autobiography". Plaque erected 1977. Nearest Station = Eltham.

MORSE, Samuel (1791-1872) 141, Cleveland Street, Marylebone, W1.
'American painter and inventor of the Morse Code, lived here 1812-1815'
Morse, born in Charlestown, Massachusetts, came to Britain when he was 20 to seek his fame as a painter. For a while he was successful, but London was more concerned about the antics of Napoleon than fine art. Realising he had reached the zenith of his artistic abilities, Morse returned to America. There he studied chemistry and electricity and conceived the idea of the magnetic telegraph. With the aid of a $30,000 advance, from the goverment, he had an experimental line built from Baltimore to Washington and, on the 24th May 1844, the famous message, "What hath God wrought?" was sent and received. The "dots and dashes" system is still used the world over. Ask any Boy Scout or pilot. Plaque erected 1962. Nearest tube station = Goodge Street.

MOZART, Wolfgang Amadeus (1756-1791) 180, Ebury Street, Belgravia, SW1.
'composed his first symphony here in 1764'
Mozart, born in Salzburg, Austria, was eight years old when he composed his first symphony, during a grand tour of Europe his father organised. The family first went to stay with friends, the Williamsons, at 20, Frith Street, Soho, from where a concert was promoted with Wolfgang playing piano and tickets at 5 shillings each. The grand tour lasted nearly three years and took in most of Europe's important cities. The family stayed in London for a year, the majority of the time here at Ebury Street, and enjoyed the patronage of George III in particular, and the Royal Court in general. All enthused over the "little boy's virtuosity", they didn't know how well he played billiards either. Plaque erected 1939. Nearest tube station = Sloane Square.

MUIRHEAD, Alexander (1848-1920) 20, Church Road, Shortlands, Bromley
'electrical engineer lived here'
Muirhead, born in London, invented what was to become the basis of the telephone industry; the duplex cable which allowed the sending of more than one message in different directions simultaneously along the same cable. This was in 1875. Thereafter he established a factory, close to where he lived, for the manufacture of scientific and electrical instruments. In 1904 he was made a Fellow of the Royal Society and continued to live here until his death. Plaque erected 1981. Nearest Station = Shortlands.

NAPOLEON III (1808-1873) 1c, King Street, St. James's, SW1.
'Emperor of the French lived here 1848'
Napoleon, born in Paris the nephew of Napoleon I, lived here, appropriately, for two years, whiling away the time as he anxiously awaited news of Louis Philippe's expected defeat in France. It was a time of upheaval in Europe, with the aristocracy scared witless that mobs would take away their wealth, in an effort of redistribution. Napoleon was on very good terms with Queen Victoria and even enlisted as a Special Constable, in the force raised to defy London's mobs, protesting against social conditions. Napoleon spent his time collecting old masters, antiques and ladies. One in particular, a lady for whom he bought a house in Berkeley Street and later made Comtesse de Beauregard. In 1848, he returned to France as president of the Second Republic, later he claimed the throne as Emperor Napoleon III. In 1870, after the fall of his empire following the war with Prussia, back he came to England. This time to live in Chislehurst, Kent, where three years later, he died. Plaque erected 1875. Nearest tube station = St. James Park.

NASH, Paul (1889-1946) Queen Alexandria Mansions, Bidborough Street, King's Cross, WC1.
'artist lived in Flat 176 1914-1936'
Nash was born in London and educated at St. Pauls and the Slade School of Art. During WW1, (1917) he became an official war artist and in 1919 produced his famous "Menin Road" picture. He became renowned for painting bare essentials which did nothing to reduce the subject. For a while he taught at the Royal College of Art but he fell out with the older members of staff and left, to pursue experiments in painting, which resulted in a spell of Surrealism, interrupted by the start of WW2. Nash again became a war artist. For the RAF and Ministry of Information he produced such pictures as "Battle of Britain" and 'Totes Meer'. Shortly before his untimely death, he commenced on a radical form of flower painting. In 1949 his autobiography, "Outline", completed just before he died, was published by his friends. Plaque erected 1991. Nearest tube station = King's Cross

NEHRU, Jawaharlal (1889-1964) 60, Elgin Crescent, Notting Hill, W11.
'first Prime Minister of India lived here in 1910 and 1912'
Nehru, born in Allahabad was educated at Harrow School and Trinity College, Cambridge. He read for the bar and was called to the Inner Temple in 1912. He returned home and served in the high court. He inherited his fiercely independent stance from his father, Motilal. Nehru senior founded "The Independent", an aggressively nationalist paper that supported Gandhi. Jawaharlal, often in prison during the turbulent thirties, became President of the Congress Party four times and Prime Minister, when independence was achieved in 1947. He adopted an influential neutral stand in foreign affairs which was much admired. In 1966, only two years after his death, his daughter, Mrs Indria Gandhi, became Prime Minister. Later, after her assassination whilst in office, her son succeeded her until, he too was murdered. India, it would appear, owes a lot to the Nehru family. Plaque erected 1989. Nearest tube station = Ladbroke Grove.

NELSON, Horatio, Lord (1758-1805) 103, New Bond Street, Mayfair, W1.
'lived here in 1798'
AND AT, 147, New Bond Street, (site), Mayfair, W1.
'lived here in 1797. Born 1758, fell at Trafalgar 1805'
Nelson was born at Burnham Thorpe, Norfolk and entered the navy when he was 12 years old. He lost his right eye at Calvi, in 1793, his right arm at Santa Cruz, in 1798 and his heart to Lady Hamilton in 1799. When he died, killed by a sniper in the Battle of Trafalgar, he was a Viscount, Admiral of the Fleet and the Commander in Chief. The battle ensured the end of any threat from French or Spanish fleets and a grateful country generously contributed to a commemorative column in a London square that would become Trafalgar Square. He is buried in St. Paul's Cathedral. Had he lived he would have been contemporaneous with Wellington. How London could have existed with two such super egotists is anyone's guess. Plaques erected 1876 and 1958. Nearest tube station = Bond Street.

NEWMAN, John Henry, Grey Court, Ham Street, Ham, Richmond.
'in this house John Henry NEWMAN (1801-1890), later Cardinal Newman spent some of his early years'
Following his years at Trinity College, Oxford, Newman, born in London the son of a banker, became one of the leading figures in the Oxford Tractarian movement. In 1833 he began writing "Tracts for The Times" which is said to have inspired the Oxford Movement, an elitist group of religious academics. Newman converted to Catholicism in 1845. In 1865, in defence of attacks against religion, by Charles Kingsley in his crusade against poverty, Kingsley wrote in "Macmillan's Magazine" about the indifference of the Roman Church to the virtue of truthfulness, which Kingsley claimed, Newman approved. By way of reply, Newman wrote "Apolologia pro Vita Sua". In 1879 he was created a cardinal but did little to alleviate the suffering of the poor. He is particularly remembered for his poem, "The Dream of Gerontius". He died in Edgbaston. Plaque erected 1981. Nearest Station = Richmond.

NEWTON, Sir Isaac (1642-1727) 87, Jermyn Street, St. James's, SW1.
'natural philosopher lived here'
Newton, born in Woolsthorpe, Lincolnshire and educated at Grantham Grammer School and Trinity College, Cambridge, came to live in fashionable Jermyn Street following publication, in 1687, of his "Philosophiae naturalis principia mathematica". After which Newton was fairly well off. In addition to his royalties, he was in receipt of £1,500 a year as Master of the Mint. All this came about because of his discoveries, relating to physics and assertions, concerning planetary motion. He was also able to discover facts about optics, in particular the fact that white light is composed of colours of the spectrum, and as a result he invented the reflecting telescope. In 1697 he moved to Chelsea claiming that the foxes in the fields, opposite his house in Jermyn Street, were constantly attacking his domestic animals. That situation no longer exists. Wolves are often seen but they are of the two legged variety. Plaque erected 1908. Nearest tube station = Piccadilly.

NICOLSON, Harold (1886-1968) and SACKVILLE-WEST, Vita (1892-1962), 182, Ebury Street, SW1.
'Writers and Gardeners lived here'
Nicolson was born in Teheran where his father was British charge d'affaires. He was educated at Wellington College and Balliol College, Oxford. Through his father's connections he entered the diplomatic service in 1909 and saw service in many countries without ever becoming an ambassador. He resigned in 1929 and turned to journalism and writing biographies including the official one on King George V. He was a National Liberal MP for ten years from 1935 during which time, as a close friend of Oswald Mosely, he flirted with fascism. In 1913 he married Victoria Sackville-West who shares this plaque. She was born in Knole House, Kent and started writing plays and novels whilst a child. She continued writing all through her life and for many years had a gardening column in the "Observor". The strange thing is that despite his homosexuality and her lesbian relationships they remained happily married. Plaque erected 1993. Nearest tube station = Sloan Square

NIGHTINGALE, Florence (1820-1910) 10, South Street, Mayfair, W1.
'lived and died on a house on this site'
Florence Nightingale, she never married, was named Florence because she was born there. After a tough training, she qualified as a nurse and slowly worked her way up to become a hospital matron. The war in the Crimea began in 1853 and was the first to have war correspondents attached to the troops in the field. Their published reports, described the appalling conditions the wounded suffered, and quoted their death rate as 50%. Florence Nightingale, enlisted the aid of 38 nurses and appealed to the War Office for permission to go to the Crimea and aid the sick and wounded. The General Staff were reluctant, but were finally forced to bow to pressure from newspaper editorials. She arrived in Scutari to find conditions worse than she imagined. She recognised that those suffering from cholera, typhus and dysentery would stand a chance of surviving only if sanitary conditions were improved. Again the War Office were reluctant to disturb the status quo of command and again it was newspaper pressure which forced them to allow Florence Nightingale the changes she wanted. In a short time she brought the death rate down to 2% and earnt the gratitude of the common soldier. She returned to London and South Street, a sick woman who had to be nursed. She continued her fight for better standards in hygiene and care and, in 1860, she established a nurses' training institution at St. Thomas's hospital, that became the envy of the world. In 1907 she was the first woman to receive the Order of Merit and a year later she received the Freedom of the City of London. In 1992 plans were announced to close St. Thomas's in order to keep down overall NHS costs. Plaque erected 1955. Nearest tube station = Bond Street.

NOEL-BAKER, Philip (1889-1982) 16, South Eaton Place, Belgravia, SW1.
'Olympic Sportsman. Campaigner for Peace and Disarmament lived here'
Noel-Baker, born in London, was, whilst at Cambridge both an athlete and academic. He captained the British Olympic team in 1912 and, during WW1, led an ambulance unit organised by the Society of Friends. He was on the committee of the League of Nations (1919-1922) and in 1929 became Labour MP for Coventry. He lost his seat in the General Election of 1931 but regained it for Derby in 1936 and stayed. He held several ministerial positions, including secretary of state for air (1946-7), commonwealth relations (1947-50) and minister for fuel and power (1950-51). In 1959, he was awarded the Nobel peace prize and created a life peer in 1977. He wrote several books of which "Disarmament" (1926) and "The Arms Race" (1956) are the most notable. He would probably have been terribly saddened to see his son Francis gravitate from being a Labour MP to a Tory party member, via the SDP. It has recently emerged that Philip and Megan Lloyd George, daughter of David, had an ongoing love affair that lasted some 25 years. She died a spinster. Philip was married. When his wife died in 1956 Megan expected to take her place. Philip, it would appear, thought her too old. Plaque erected 1992. Nearest tube station = Sloane Square.

NOLLEKENS, Joseph (1737-1823) 44, Mortimer Street, Marylebone, W1.
'sculptor lived and died in a house on this site'
Nollekens was born in London to parents who lived in extreme poverty. He grew up in this atmosphere and it was to affect his life until he died. By a stroke of good fortune, his expertness in modelling clay was recognised and harnessed in the right direction; so he was able to make a living. In 1770, he established a studio, in the house he rented near Oxford Street, and soon became accepted by society, so much so, he was able to command as much as £4,000 for a bust of Pitt. However, the more money he made the meaner he became. He was haunted by the sceptre of poverty and the fear that perhaps his commissions might dry up. So he became a miser and a hoarder and imposed a strict economy on his wife. He ordered her never to light the candles until it was well into the night and then never more than two. The furniture was allowed to fall to pieces and the blinds turned into rags. A single loaf of bread was made to last a week. At the annual banquet, at the Royal Academy, Nollekens, a small bow-legged man with a big head and large nose, would craftily stuff his pockets with all sorts of food uncaring what anyone watching might think. His wife refused to accept the new paper money and insisted on gold coins. She kept a hoard of over a thousand guineas in the library and her evening pleasure was counting and feeling them. The commissions however continued and, despite their eccentricities, they were not shunned by their neighbours. Nollekins died at 86 and left over £300,000. Plaque erected 1954. Nearest tube station = Goodge Street.

NOVELLO, Ivor (1893-1951) 11, Aldwych, WC2.
'composer and actor-manager lived and died in a flat on the top floor of this building'
Novello, born in Cardiff and educated at Magadalen College School, Oxford, moved here, together with his mother, the singer, Dame Clara Novello Davies, in 1914, and stayed. He gave an enormous amount of pleasure to people. His songs were the pop of the day and his stage plays toured the country. He wrote "Keep the Home Fires Burning" in 1913 and received a fortune in royalties, as it became one of WW1's most popular songs. His best known shows were "The Dancing Years" (1939), "Perchance to Dream" (1945) and "King's Rhapsody" (1949). He never married. Plaque erected 1973. Nearest tube station = Aldwych.

OATES, Captain Lawrence (1880-1912) 309, Upper Richmond Road, Putney, SW15.
'Antarctic explorer lived here'
Oates, born in Putney, London, was educated at Eton before becoming a soldier with the cavalry in South Africa (1901-2). Always fascinated by exploration, he volunteered to go with Robert Scott on his 1910 Antarctic expedition to the South Pole. On the return journey, Oates suffered the most terrible frostbite to his feet. Despite resting up his condition wouldn't improve. Realising he was endangering his comrades by delaying them, and with supplies at their lowest ebb, he celebrated his 32nd birthday, on March 17th, by hobbling out of the tent claiming, "I am just going outside and might be some time". He stumbled out into a blizzard and was never seen again. The pity was that his sacrifice was in vain; his companions died before rescue came. Plaque erected 1973. Nearest Station = Putney.

O'CASEY, Sean (1880-1964) 49, Overstrand Mansions, Prince of Wales Drive, Battersea Park, SW11.
'Playwright lived here at flat No. 49'
Born in a poor part of Dublin there was only one way O'Casey could go and that was up. He picked up an education as he went along and did labouring to keep body and soul together. He started writing for something to do on cold evenings when he didn't have the price of a pint of beer. He found success with "Shadow of a Gunman"(1923) followed a year later with "Juno and the Paycock". Much of his work was produced by the Abbey Theatre. He began his autobiography in 1939 and finished it in 1954. Plaque erected in 1993. Nearest tube station = Queenstown Road

OLDFIELD, Ann, (1683-1730) 60, Grosvenor Street, Mayfair, W1.
'actress. First occupant of this house 1725-1730'
Ann Oldfield was born in London and made her debut as an actress in 1700. She was most popular and continued on the stage until her death. Quite why a plaque should be erected to an actress, unknown after her time and some two hundred and sixty years after her death isn't readily known. But it becomes absurd when one thinks of the enormous number of well known and beloved people, more deserving of acknowledgement who have lived at some time, in this well known area of London. Plaque erected 1992. Nearest Tube Station = Bond Street.

OLIVER, Percy Lane (1878-1944) 5, Colyton Road, Peckham Rye, SE22
'founder of the first voluntary blood donor service lived and worked here'
Oliver, born in London, was a dedicated supporter and worker for the Red Cross for over twenty years. When in 1921 he was asked by King's Cross Hospital, if he knew of a blood donor who could help a patient with a rare blood group, Oliver couldn't help them; but it gave him the idea of establishing a group of doctors who would be prepared to run, on a regular basis, blood donors. In 1928 the service established itself at Colyton Road and Oliver and his wife were its first supervisors. Plaque erected 1979. Nearest Station = Peckham Rye.

ONSLOW, Arthur (1691-1768) 20, Soho Square, Soho, W1.
'Speaker of the House of Commons from 1728 to 1761 lived in a house on this site'
Onslow, born in London, lived here from 1753 to 1761 only leaving to retire into the country, following his enormously long stint as Mr. Speaker. His 33 years has never been equalled. Nor should it be assumed that the business of the House was any different from to-day. There were late sittings, two o' clock in the morning was commonplace, and all night sittings not unknown. Keeping order was a constant difficulty, when feelings ran high and tempers exploded. Nothing has changed. Onslow sought comfort and solace in the company of such people as Dr. Johnson and his friend Boswell and similar figures, unconnected with the everyday hustle of politics. Onslow, it is claimed, set the standard future Speakers have tried to live up to. Plaque erected 1927. Nearest tube station = Tottenham Court Road.

ORPEN, Sir William (1878-1931) 8, South Bolton Gardens, South Kensington, SW5.
'painter lived here'
Orpen, born in Stillorgan, County Dublin, started his career by winning the 1899 Slade Prize. It was worth £40 and the resulting publicity brought him many commissions. He was particularly popular during WW1, being asked to paint the portraits of new officers, in their pretty uniforms, before they went off to war. His prices were high, but the families didn't appear to mind. The result was that Orpen made a lot of money, drove around in a chauffeured Rolls Royce, had a large house with an opulent studio, was knighted by King George V and; was constantly miserable. His friends claimed he had stifled the talent he had shown at 21 in return for fame and fortune and, realising they were right, he hated himself for it. However, his earlier works, generally with an Irish genre, are very good and amongst the best in portrait painting. Plaque erected 1978. Nearest tube station = Gloucester Road.

ORWELL, George (1903-1950) 50, Lawford Road, Kentish Town, NW5.
'novelist and political essayist lived here'
Orwell was born Eric Arthur Blair in Motihari, India and sent to England to be educated at Eton. In 1922 he went off to Burma and served in the police force there. Returning to England, he lived here with two friends. It was cheap and they shared the chores, the food and the rent. Orwell spent his early years writing political tracts on the Socialist ideal. In 1933, he wrote "Down and Out in Paris and London" it was well received but it wasn't unti 1937 that he really came to the notice of the public, with his satirical novel, "The Road to Wigan Pier". During most of WW2 he was busy as a war correspondent, then his wife died and he returned to London and his son Richard. In 1945 came "Animal Farm" and "1984" in (1949). Orwell, during his poverty years rarely had enough money to feed himself properly, his death at 47, clearly reflected those years of neglect. Plaque erected 1980. Nearest tube station = Kentish Town.

'OUIDA' (Maria Louise de la Ramee) (1839-1908) 11, Ravenscourt Square, Hammersmith, W6.
'novelist lived here'
She was born in Bury St. Edmunds her mother English, her father French. She constantly mispronounced the name Louise and Ouida stuck. Had Boon and Mills been publishing their banal romantic books during the time Ouida was writing hers, they would have undoubtedly wanted her on their lists. Her first success was "Held in Bondage" (1863) but her only book of note was "Under Two Flags" (1867) and that was written in Florence, where she had gone to live seven years previously; never to return. She wrote much and enjoyed fame and some fortune. However, towards the end of her life the royalties dried up and she died, in poverty, in Viareggio, Italy. Plaque erected 1952. Nearest tube station = Ravenscourt Park.

PALGRAVE, Francis Turner (1824-1897) 5, York Gate, Regent's Park, NW1.
'compiler of "The Golden Treasury" lived here 1862-1875'
Palgrave was born in London, the son of Meyer Cohen a London stockbroker. He was an infant prodigy who, at the age of eight, translated "The Battle of the Frogs and the Mice" from Greek to French. When, in 1823, he married a non-Jew, he became a Christian and adopted his mother-in-law's maiden name. Many generations of children have enjoyed, and been influenced, by the "Treasury", an anthology of poetry. Palgrave published it in 1861, whilst working in the Department of Education. Palgrave had won a scholarship to Balliol College, Oxford and had been awarded a first, when he came to the notice of Gladstone, who invited him to join his staff as assistant private secretary. He was knighted in 1832. Plaque erected 1976. Nearest tube station = Regent's Park.

PALMER, Samuel (1805-1881) 6, Douro Place, Kensington, W8.
'artist lived here 1851-1861'
Palmer, born in London to a poor family, had a brief period of success that became known as his "Shoreham Period". Influenced by Blake, he produced visionary landscapes in a mystical style, that were much admired. He married the daughter of John Linnell and, because of a lack of patronage, was forced to accept his father-in-law's charity. This wasn't so uncommon, it still isn't, but Palmer's problem was that Linnell was also a painter and he felt belittled. He worked when he could, but had little confidence that he would ever regain the promise he had shown in Shoreham and, except for a few fine water colours and etchings, he never did. He died as he had lived; poor and unhappy. Much later, after WW2, he was rediscovered by those who saw something essentially English in his work with perhaps some overtures of Surrealism. Plaque erected 1972. Nearest tube station = Kensington High Street.

PALMERSTON, Henry John Temple, 3rd Viscount (1784-1865). 20, Queen Anne's Gate, St. James's, SW1.
'Prime Minister born here'
4, Carlton Gardens, St. James's, SW1.
'statesman lived here'
Naval and Military Club, 94, Piccadilly, W1.
'In this house formerly a Royal residence lived Lord Palmerston, Prime Minister and Foreign Secretary'

Three plaques to commemorate one man, is it deserved? He was born, with the proverbial silver spoon, in Westminster. He had every educational advantage but was judged an academic failure, so he became an M.P. for which no experience, expertise or education has ever been required. He was appointed to the War Office in the Conservative government of 1808 but found it difficult to get advancement. In 1828 he changed sides and became a Whig and two years later he was appointed foreign secretary (1830-41 and 1846-1851). He was a devotee of "gunboat diplomacy" A jingoist who once declared . . . "our desire for peace will never lead us to submit to affront either in language or act". He was a bully who shouted at poor underdeveloped countries, like Egypt, and fawned on those who could give Britain a bloody nose. He was the arch manipulator of his time, with some successes. However, he always made certain that what was good for Britain was even better for Palmerston. He became Prime Minister twice, (1855-8 and 1859-65). During this time there was the terrible war in the Crimea, which Palmerston enthusiastically encouraged. He ordered the Indian Mutiny to be put down in the most brutal fashion, ignoring the reasons why it had occurred, thereby storing up a lasting hatred for the British there. Palmerston was a larger than life character who, deciding he knew what was best for Britain, brooked no interference. The problem was that he pontificated over what was best for other European countries and here he met his match, in Bismark. In 1865, he was defeated in what became known as "The Schleswig-Holstein" affair. Plaques erected 1907/1925/1961. Nearest Tube Stations = St. James's and Piccadilly.

PANKHURST, Sylvia (1882-1960) 120, Cheyne Walk, Chelsea, SW10.
'campaigner for women's rights lived here'
Sylvia, born in London, was the daughter of Emmeline who, more than any other woman, typifies the Suffragette Movement. She led and her two daughters, Christabel and Sylvia, willingly followed. They formed the "Women's Social and Political Union" (1903), which didn't shrink from using arson and bombing to further their cause. They were imprisoned and suffered forced feeding, when they went on hunger strikes. They were generally treated more harshly than male prisoners. Their efforts forced parliament, at the end of WW1, to extend the vote to women over the age of 30. The government and the public knew the debt they owed to women who, during the war, took the place of men in such a variety of jobs that to deny their petition for the vote would have been undemocratic and a betrayal of the millions who thought they had died for freedom. The vote for women at 21 came in 1928, the year Sylvia's mother died. Sylvia continued the fight for equal opportunities for women, especially in the field of education and civil service. By the time she died in 1960, women's place in society, especially after WW2, had changed dramatically. However, despite laws to the contrary, women still see themselves as second class citizens in a man's world. The Pankhursts lit the torch that is still being carried. Plaque erected 1985. Nearest tube station = Sloane Square.

PARRY, Sir Charles Hubert (1848-1918) 17, Kensington Square, Kensington, W8.
'musician lived here'
It is fitting that the plaque for Parry follows that for the Pankhursts, for it was Charles Parry, born in Bournemouth and educated at Eton and Oxford whose setting of Blake's "Jerusalem", he wrote for the suffragette's meeting, at Queen's Hall, under their "Fight for Right" banner. Parry was influenced by Wagner and this is shown in his piano concerto, first performed at the Crystal Palace by Dannreuther in 1880. He wrote many choral works and was Professor of Music at the Royal College of Music and later at Oxford. Many musicians owe a debt of gratitude to Parry for it was he who improved the status of music and musicians in Victorian England. When he was knighted he declared . . . he was receiving his honour on behalf of all connected with music. Parry, who moved here in 1887, remained until his death. Plaque erected 1949. Nearest tube station = Kensington High Street.

PATEL, Sardar (1875-1950) 23, Aldridge Road Villas, Notting Hill, W11.
'Indian statesman lived here'
Patel was practising as a criminal lawyer in Bombay, where he was born, when, in 1917, he met Gandhi. Thereafter he rejected Western ideas in favour of Nationalist notions. He held various posts in the Indian National Congress Party and organised non-violent protests, for which he was often jailed by the British authorities. Following the end of WW2, he became No.2 to Pandit Nehru and accompanied him to London for independence talks. It was then that he stayed here. In 1947, following Independence, he became deputy Prime Minister. His most notable achievement was the bringing of 562 "princely states", into the Indian parliament. Until his death, he was for ever trying to bring peace between Hindu and Moslem. Plaque erected 1986. Nearest tube station = Westbourne Park.

PATMORE, Coventry (1823-1896) 14, Percy Street, Bloomsbury, W1.
'poet and essayist lived here 1863-1864'
Patmore, born in Woodford, Essex was a poet and writer who loved associating with Pre-Raphaelites. He wrote on love, mostly conjugal love, and his work included the series, "The Angel in the House" (1854-62) and a collection of odes, "The Unknown Eros", (1877). He was typical of his time, he preached Victorian morality, deplored the idleness of the poor and their drunkenness whilst he fathered six children, had three wives and a stream of mistresses and was, for the best part of the day, drunk. Why he was named Coventry isn't readily known but thankfully, it didn't start a trend. Towards the end of his life he became a Catholic, his poetry lost its sparkle and became boring and religious. So did Patmore. Plaque erected 1960. Nearest tube station = Tottenham Court Road.

PEABODY, George (1795-1869) 80, Eaton Square, Belgravia, SW1.
'philanthropist died here'
Peabody, born near Boston, USA, never forgot his impoverished upbringing. He created a financial empire, George Peabody and Co., in the States, dealing in foreign exchange and securities. In 1837 he came to London and opened a branch of his business in the City. He dedicated the latter part of his life to works of charity, that would educate and alleviate the miseries of the poor. He established many trusts in the US and in London, he established the Peabody Trust that built blocks of flats to house the poor. They were landmarks in the standards of construction that were used in mass building and a boon to the homeless. Unfortunately, in London, the Trust has not kept pace with modernity, with the result that many of the Trust's blocks are considered ugly, old fashioned and lacking in amenities. Many ought to be pulled down and rebuilt. He died, in London, in the arms of his mistress. However, he is buried in Peabody, Massachusetts, originally known as South Danvers and Peabody's birthplace; renamed in his honour. Plaque erected 1976. Nearest tube station = Sloane Square.

PEARSON, Karl (1857-1936) 7, Well Road, Hampstead, NW3.
'pioneer statistician lived here'
Pearson was born in London and became a barrister. He turned from law to mathematics, becoming professor of applied mathematics at University College, London, as well as Galton professor of eugenics. His work established a world of statistics in its own right. He founded and edited the journal, "Biometrika", (1901-1936). Plaque erected 1983. Nearest tube station = Hampstead.

PEEL, Sir Robert (1750-1830) 16, Upper Grosvenor Street, Mayfair, W1.
'manufacturer and reformer and his son, Sir Robert PEEL (1788-1850)Prime Minister, founder of the Metropolitan Police, lived here'
Robert Peel was born in Lancashire and educated privately. Via an uncle he started in the cotton mill industry. The mills were able to buy cotton cheaply from slave owning countries and the resulting products, British made, exported all over the world. Peel left his uncle and started his own mills. After some while he was successful and became very wealthy. He had a large house on the hill and in 1790 became an MP. In 1800 he was created a baronet. It was however his son, also named Robert, who became really famous. Born in Bury, but educated at Harrow and Christ Church College, Oxford, he gained two firsts. The son brought stability to Britain, by repealing the Corn Laws in 1846; this whilst serving his second term as Prime Minister. Previously, as Home Secretary, he secured the Catholic Emancipation Act (1829) and in the same year created the London police force. However he opposed the Reform Bill (1832). This would have upset his reformist father were he still alive. In 1834, whilst serving his first term as Prime Minister, he published what is known as the "Tamworth Manifesto", this policy document laid the foundations of the modern Conservative Party. On 29th June 1850, he was thrown from his horse and died from his injuries. Plaque erected 1988. Nearest tube station = Bond Street.

PEPYS, Samuel (1633-1703) 12, Buckingham Street, Strand, WC2.
'diarist and Secretary of the Admiralty, lived here 1679-1688'
Pepys was born in London the son of a tailor. He was educated at St.Paul's School and Trinity Hall, Cambridge. Two years after moving in here with his family, Pepys was lodging in the Tower of London, imprisoned on a charge of being a papist. Upon his release he moved back in. His famous diaries do not record his period of tenure in Buckingham Street. They only cover the years 1659-1669 and make very interesting reading. They give a picture of those times and an insight into Pepy's character. His diaries were written in cipher, a sort of shorthand. They were discovered, in 1825 at Magdalene College, there they were deciphered, edited and published. Plaque erected 1947. Nearest tube station = Charing Cross.

PERCEVAL, The Hon. Spencer (1762-1812) 59-60, Lincoln's Inn Fields, Holborn, WC2.
'Prime Minister lived here'
Perceval was born in London, the second son of the second Earl of Egmont and educated at Harrow and Trinity College, Cambridge. This address has long ago ceased to be the mansion it was, when Perceval lived and worked here as a barrister. Although he generally worked as an advocate, he was pleased to serve as Recorder of Northampton (1790). His main interest however was politics which was perhaps unfortunate because, having served as MP for Northampton from 1796 and as Chancellor of the Exchequer under the Duke of Portland in 1807, he succeeded Portland as Prime Minister in 1809. On May 11th 1812 a Liverpool broker, John Bellingham, shot him whilst in the lobby of the House of Commons. Bellingham, a Catholic, was upset by Perceval's opposition to Catholic claims. Inevitably Bellingham was hanged. Plaque erected 1914. Nearest tube station = Holborn.

PETRIE, Sir William Matthew Flinders (1853-1942) 5, Cannon Place, Hampstead, NW3.
'Egyptologist lived here'
The term Egyptologist, during the latter half of the 19th century, was often a euphemism for pillaging and stealing the treasures of Egypt, Greece, Palestine, Syria and Turkey and bringing them to London museums. Petrie, born in Charlton, Kent, was no exception. He was responsible for excavating Memphis, Thebesand, the 1st dynasty tombs at Abydos, and many items of discovery found their way to the British Museum. He was, however, much admired for the meticulous methods he used, which generally raised the standards of archaeology. For some forty years he served as Professor of Egyptology at University College, London and was the author of some 100 books. Renowned for his energy and spartan tastes, he continued working well into his eighties, and died in Jerusalem. Plaque erected 1954. Nearest tube station = Hampstead.

PHELPS, Samuel (1804-1878) 8, Canonbury Square, Highbury, N1.
'tragedian lived here'
Phelps, born in Devonport, lived here from 1844 to 1867. During this period he took over the management of the Aquatic Theatre, later to be known as Sadlers Wells. When he announced that he was to replace the existing light comedy and musical shows with Shakespeare, the heavier variety, he was scorned and given a few weeks at most to survive. Eighteen years later, he retired undefeated tragic actor of his time. He had survived barracking during performances, tiny houses, reluctant actors and miserable backers. Gradually, the scorners came to cheer, the actors eager to perform, and the backers wore a smile. How had Phelps transformed them? He was a superb actor and his Shakespeare was adjustable. He was a fitness fanatic, walked five miles a day and on performance days, had a light lunch and a long sleep. He retired when he discovered his wife had cancer. Phelps adored her. She was his dresser and the sicker she became the more reluctant was he to act. He gave a series of farewell performances to cheering audiences and left them wanting more. He nursed his wife until she died and then became a recluse. Plaque erected 1911. Nearest tube station = Highbury and Islington.

PICK, Frank (1878-1941) 15, Wildwood Road, Golders Green, NW11.
'pioneer of good design for London Transport lived here'
Pick, born in Spalding, Lincolnshire, became a lawyer before he joined the Underground section of London Transport. At 50, he was appointed Managing Director of the newly created London Passenger Transport Board (1928). He influenced radical changes that brought the underground system in line with other great cities. He commissioned imaginative designers to give London's transport system an individual and distinct character that has survived. Frank Pick was responsible for creating the world's largest urban transport system. He lived here, close to the Heath, from 1914 to 1941. What he would make of to-days carve-up of London's transport can only be imagined, but he would certainly have fought against breaking up what he had created and which worked so well for so long. Plaque erected 1981, Nearest tube station = Golders Green.

PINERO, Sir Arthur (1855-1934) 115a, Harley Street, Marylebone, W1.
'playwright lived here 1909-1934'
Pinero was the foremost dramatist of his day. He was able to write successful plays that covered a wide spectrum of life. He wrote farces, eg "Dandy Dick" (1887); problem plays eg, "The Second Mrs Tanquery" (1893); and sentimental comedies such as, "Trelawny of the Wells" (1898). Pinero, born in London, came from an old and respected Anglo-Jewish family. His father, a doctor, wanted his son to follow him into medicine but Arthur, although becoming a lawyer, brought him round to his way. In 1881 his first play "The Money Spinners" was performed at St. James's Theatre and exposed the gambling that went on behind the scenes of polite society and which ruined many. The play was a success and Pinero continued to enjoy success until after WW1, when audiences wanted a different type of play, one which Pinero was unable to supply. However, he is still performed. Plaque erected 1970. Nearest tube station = Goodge Street.

PISSARRO, Lucien (1863-1944) 27, Stamford Brook Road, Hammersmith, W6.

'painter, printer, wood engraver, lived here'

Lucien, the son of a French-Jewish father and a West Indian-Catholic mother, was born in France the eldest of four sons all of whom followed in their famous father's footsteps and became artists. Only Lucien achieved a modicum of fame, for his Impressionist landscapes and woodcuts and he was partly responsible for introducing Impressionist painting to England. He was educated in France and trained by his father, Camille, until in 1890, he came to London where he met such figures as William Morris, Charles Ricketts and others who interested Lucien in the art of book design. This led directly to the establishment of "The Eragny Press" which produced the earliest types of "coffee table books", beautifully illustrated books of a particular interest. Plaque erected 1976. Nearest tube station = Stamford Brook.

PITT, William, Earl of Chatham (1708-1778) 10, St. James's Square, St. James's, SW1.

'Here lived three Prime Ministers: William PITT, Earl of Chatham (1708-1778); Edward Geoffrey STANLEY, Earl of Derby (1799-1869); William Ewart GLADSTONE (1809-1898)'

Of Pitt, born in Westminster and educated at Eton and Trinity College, Oxford, Lord Chesterfield wrote ". . . has very little parliamentary knowledge; his matter is generally flimsy, and his arguments often weak; but his eloquence is superior, his actions graceful, his enunciation just and harmonious . . ." Pitt had the advantage of patronage, in his case, two women, the Queen and the King's mistress. However the King, George III, would later force him to resign. Pitt was Prime Minister 1757-1761 and during this period he was able to evict the French from both India and Canada as well as suffer considerable pain, from gout. He was particularly anxious that the American war of Independence should be settled peacefully. On the day of the debate, in the House of Lords Pitt, although ill, attended. He made a brilliant speech, won the day and fell back into the arms of his friends and died. He was given a public funeral and buried in Westminster Abbey. Pitt lived here 1759-1762. Twenty years after Pitt died Stanley, later the 14th Earl of Derby was born in Lancashire and educated at Eton and Christ Church College, Oxford. He entered parliament for Stockbridge in 1820. He was prime minister three times, all for brief periods. The original Lord Stanley became an earl, in 1485, by the shameful reneging on a promise of support made to Richard III. This betrayal secured the crown, following the battle at Bosworth Field, for Henry VII, who showed his gratitude in the usual way. Plaque erected 1910. Nearest tube station = St.James's Park.

PITT, William, the younger (1759-1806) 120, Baker Street, Marylebone, W1.
'Prime Minister lived here 1803 to 1804'
Pitt was born in Hayes, Kent and educated privately and at Pembroke Hall, Cambridge. The father died at 70, the son at 47. Both were prime ministers (the son, 1783-1801 and 1804-6) and both made their reputation against the French. There the similarity ends. The father was a Whig, the son a Tory. The father took his political problems in his stride the son worried and lived on his nerves. They both served their country during a time of intense anxiety over European problems. In the son's case it was Napoleon. He was marching all over the continent and it was hearing of his victory at Austerlitz that caused Pitt the Younger to collapse and die. Plaque erected 1949. Nearest tube station = Baker Street.

PITT-RIVERS, Lieutenant General Augustus Henry Lane Fox (1827-1900)
4, Grosvenor Gardens, Belgravia, SW1.
'anthropologist and archaeologist lived here'
Pitt-Rivers was born in Yorkshire and finished his education at Sandhurst. After an undistinguished military career, he turned his hand to digging up his Wiltshire estates and minutely recording every detail, albeit trivial. This work produced his publication "Excavations in Cranborne Chase" (1887-98). In 1882 he was appointed the first inspector of ancient monuments. Plaque erected 1983. Nearest tube station = Victoria

PLAATJE, Sol (1876-1932) 25, Carnarvon Road, Leyton, E10.
'black South African writer lived here'
Plaatje founded the first native newspaper in South Africa. The 'Tswana Gazette' first appeared in 1901 and lasted until 1908. In 1912, he became the first Secretary General of the South African National Congress, now known as the ANC. In 1919 he went to Paris, in the vain attempt to get South African native issues heard at the Peace Conference. He then travelled widely, including staying here, trying to awake the world to what was happening to Blacks in South Africa and how they were treated as little better than slaves. In 1919 he completed his novel "Mhudi". It wasn't until 1930 that he found a publisher, at which time it was the first novel published in English and written by a Black. The Indians in South Africa had Gandhi, the blacks Plaatje. Unfortunately there was very little co-operation between the two races. Plaque erected 1986. Nearest tube station = Walthamstow Central.

PLACE, Francis (1771-1854) 21, Brompton Square, Brompton, SW3.
'political reformer lived here 1833-1851'
Place was the man behind the scenes in more than one sense. Born in London and trained as a tailor, Place had a shop in Charing Cross and behind the shop was a room which served as the meeting place for like minds. These were reformers, men who disliked what they termed the unacceptable side of Victorian values. Some of them were MPs and through them, Place steered a bill through the Commons in 1824, which repealed the Combinations Act, the act which had made trade unions illegal. In 1835, whilst living with his second wife here, Place drafted the People's Charter, for the Chartists. In 1822 he wrote "The Principle of Population", a study on birth control. Plaque erected 1961. Nearest tube station = South Kensington.

PLAYFAIR, Sir Nigel (1874-1934) 26, Pelham Crescent, South Kensington, SW7.
'actor-manager lived here'
The beautiful Lyric theatre at Hammersmith owes its present day survival to Nigel Playfair. He resurrected it, from a derelict unused nuisance to the glory it had enjoyed, prior to the first world war. Playfair was born in London and trained as a barrister but the theatre was his first love. In 1919 he produced Drinkwaters' "Abraham Lincoln" which ran for nearly 500 performances. He was successful in introducing the great classics to increasingly wider audiences. He lived here, in a house built by George Basevi in 1830, from 1910 to 1922 and at one time, drove himself around London in a carriage drawn by a large silver grey horse. Plaque erected 1965. Nearest tube station = Gloucester Road.

PORTUGESE EMBASSY, 23-24, Golden Square, Mayfair, W1.
'these two houses were the Portuguese Embassy (1724-1747). The MARQUESS OF POMBAL, ambassador 1739-1744, lived here'
Later the Ear Nose and Throat Hospital came to live here; in rebuilt premises. Portugal has always been known as Britain's oldest ally and Pombal so admired what he saw of London's commercial districts that when he returned home he urged his master, Joseph I, to emulate them. Pombal was put in charge of these and other reforms, including the reduction in the power of the Jesuits. This he did with a ruthlessness that pleased the King, especially as Pombal dealt equally harshly with anyone who he thought might be a threat to the monarchy. Pombal was born in Coimbra and one of the reforms dearest to his heart, was the provision he provided, that allowed the establishment of elementary education for all. He was also responsible for the rebuilding of Lisbon, following the 1775 earthquake. Plaque erected 1980. Nearest tube station = Piccadilly.

PRIESTLEY, Joseph (1733-1804) Ram Place Hackney, E9.
'scientist, philosopher and theologian, was Minister to the Gravel Pit Meeting here in 1793-1794'
Priestly was born in Fieldhead nr Leeds, and is best known as the chemist who discovered oxygen, nitric acid, hydrochloric acid and sulphur dioxide. As well as for their individual uses, he claimed he improved methods for studying gases, in order to benefit mankind. Later, as a result of a religious experience, he became a Unitarian Minister. The Gravel Pit Meeting, was a large gathering of like minded people who supported the aims and principles of the French Revolution. Priestly, for his part, preached a like revolution for Britain, this wasn't exactly appreciated by those in power. They, via the local police, organised a mob to ransack his home and fire it. In 1794 he was persuaded to emigrate to America, where he was given a hero's welcome. Plaque erected 1985. Nearest Station = Hackney Downs.

PRIORY of St. John the Baptist, Holywell and the THEATRE. 86-88, Curtain Road, Hackney, EC2.
The site of this building forms part of what was once the precinct of the Priory of St. John the Baptist, Holywell. Within a few yards stood from 1577 to 1598 the first London building specially devoted to the performance of plays and known as "The Theatre". The Priory goes back to the beginning of the twelfth century when it was home for over a thousand nuns of the Benedictine order. During the Reformation, the Priory was dissolved and all the lands passed to the crown (1539). In order to preserve the buildings, permission was given to James Burbage, in 1576, to use the property as a theatre. Burbage was granted a twenty-one year lease and during this time he staged many of Marlowe's plays including "Dr Faustus". There is some suggestion that Burbage's troupe of actors included one, William Shakespeare, possibly because in 1599 Burbage and his brother Cuthbert, built a summer theatre called the Globe Theatre. Plaque erected 1920. Nearest tube station = Old Street.

RACKHAM, Arthur (1867-1939) 16, Chalcot Gardens, Hampstead, NW3.
'illustrator lived here'
Rackham, born in London, studied at the Lambeth School of Art. He moved here following his marriage to Edith Starkie in 1903. They stayed until 1920. As a young man, Rackham was a member of the Westminster Fire Office and illustrating was a hobby. In 1892 he turned his hobby into his livelihood and eventually became the foremost book illustrator for Edwardian writers, specialising in books for children. His work included the illustrations, in Art Nouveau style, for "Rip Van Winkle" (1905), "Peter Pan" (1906) and "Midsummer Night's Dream" (1908). He was also a watercolour artist of some note and spent a lot of time in Germany, painting and selling. Plaque erected 1981. Nearest tube station = Belsize Park.

RAGLAN, Lord Fitzroy Somerset, 1st Baron (1788-1855) 5, Stanhope Gate, Hyde Park, W1.
"commander during the Crimean War, lived here'

Raglan lived here for the twenty years preceding the famous "Charge of the Light Brigade". Raglan was a disaster. He used his position, as an aide to the Duke of Wellington during the Peninsular wars, to get kickbacks from the suppliers to the army. He wasn't bothered if the equipment he purchased and the supplies he procured were of the required quality as long as he was rewarded by the supply merchants. The war against Napoleon over, during which he lost an arm at Waterloo, Raglan dabbled in politics, becoming MP for Truro. He had many cronies who wielded power so it wasn't difficult for Raglan, when he decided that gambling and wenching was becoming boring, to persuade the War Minister to make him C-in-C of the Crimean forces, when war was declared in 1854, between England and Russia. He showed disdain for his troops, his staff of advisors and for the French, who although they were England's allies, he kept calling "the enemy". He declared Florence Nightingale's attempts to alleviate suffering ". . . a waste of her time and our concern". On 25th October 1854, at Balaklava, occurred the battle when the Light Brigade charged the Russian guns in an exploit that wasn't planned but which has given Alfred Lord Tennyson immortality, Hollywood a hit and the birth of the Victoria Cross. The key to the success, or failure, of the campaign, was the capture of Sebastopol, a vital seaport. Raglan decided a siege was the answer and refused to budge, despite pleas from his French and Turkish allies. Fortunately Raglan died in June 1855 and the port was taken shortly after. Plaque erected 1911. Nearest tube station = Green Park.

RATHBONE, Eleanor (1872-1946) Tufton Court, Tufton Street, Westminster, SW1.
'pioneer of family allowances, lived here'

Eleanor Rathbone was born in Liverpool, where her father was a prosperous merchant. After reading classics at Somerville College, Oxford, she made an extensive study of how widows managed under the poor laws and, as a result, become an advocate for family allowances. In the thirties, she became an independent MP for the Combined English Universities and came to live here. She pursued legislation that would provide better housing for working class people. She was active in India, where she fought for women's emancipation and the abolition of child marriages. She was against appeasing Hitler, non-intervention in Spain and the Italian invasion of Ethiopia. She was a dedicated Zionist, who tried to get Jewish refugees out of Germany and into Palestine. Soon after the liberation of Belsen, by the British army, she was a member of the parliamentary delegation that visited the scene. She was so shocked by what she saw, that her health suffered and never fully recovered. She died a few months later. Plaque erected 1986. Nearest tube station = Victoria.

RAVILIOUS, Eric (1903-1942) 48, Upper Mall, Hammersmith, W6.
'artist lived here 1931-1935'
Born in Sussex, Ravilious studied at Eastbourne School of Art and at the Design School of the Royal College of Art. He studied under Paul Nash and worked for J. Wedgewood, designing much of their domestic wares, such as their travel series, coronation mugs and Christmas decor. He also specialised in designing printed patterns for the textile industry. His main interest however was wood engraving, although he also found time to illustrate books. In the thirties, he turned to painting watercolours and in WW2 he was appointed an official war artist (1940). He lost his life during 1942, whilst on active service; he was aboard an RAF aircraft lost whilst on patrol off Iceland. Plaque erected 1991. Nearest tube station = Ravenscourt Park.

RED HOUSE, Red House Lane, Bexleyheath, Bexley.
'built in 1859-1860 by Philip WEBB for William MORRIS, poet and artist who lived here 1860-1865'
The Red House started life when William Morris bought a meadow, in what was then part of rural Kent, and now a high density London suburb. He engaged Philip Webb to build a house to his design. Morris, 1834-1896, was born in Walthamstow, London, the son of middle-class parents. Educated at Marlborough School and Exeter College, Oxford, he studied architecture under George Street, but it was on the advice of Dante Rossetti that he became a professional painter. Together with, Philip Webb 1831-1915, a young architect branching out on his own, they planned the Gothic arches, the high pitched roofs and the stained glass windows but it appears no-one thought about heating the place. During the cold winters and icy East winds, blowing in from Russia, the place was an iceberg. Morris stood it for 5 years, inviting all his literary and artist friends of the Pre-Raphaelite movement for weekends. Then he moved back to London and Bloomsbury. Morris had built the house for his bride, the beautiful model Jane Burden, whom he married in 1859. In 1861, Morris, together with some pre-Raphaelite friends, began the firm that came to be known as, Morris, Marshall, Faulkner & Co. They revolutionized house decoration and the style of English furniture for decades to come. Morris wrote much, did much and, more than most, deserves his commemorative plaque and probably more important, his place in English history. Plaque erected 1969. Nearest station = Abbey Wood.

RELPH, Harry (1851-1928) 93, Shirehall Park, Hendon, NW4.
' "Little Tich", music hall comedian, lived and died here'
Harry Relph, born in London, was a freak of nature who turned misfortune to advantage. 4 foot 6 inches tall and described as a miniature 'Quasimodo', Relph made a fortune acting on the music halls. He achieved fame for his act, known as the "Big Boot Dance". This meant wearing a pair of outsize boots, monstrous in shape and size, and stamping all over the stage, often leaning out in all manner of angles, the audience thinking he would fall over. In the early twenties, Relph retired and came to live here. Plaque erected 1969. Nearest tube station = Brent.

RESCHID, Mustapha Pasha (1800-1858) 1, Bryanston Square, Marylebone, W1.
'Turkish statesman and reformer lived here as an ambassador in 1839'
This imposing property was built by Joseph Parkinson in 1811 and deserved a better fate, than to be the embassy and therefore the extension, of the oppressive and cruel Ottoman Empire. Reschid, after his two stints as ambassador, returned to Turkey, where he made some small attempts at political and economic reform. Plaque erected 1972. Nearest tube station = Marble Arch.

REYNOLDS, Sir Joshua (1723-1792) Fanum House, 47, Leicester Square, WC2.
'portrait painter lived and died in a house on this site'
Reynolds was born in Plympton, Devon and attended the village school. As a young man he toured Italy and learnt all he could about portrait painting. On his return, he opened a studio in St. Martin's Lane and gradually acquired a reputation. This was enhanced by the studies he painted of the biblical Samuel, as a child, and, as an infant at prayer. The first now hangs at the Dulwich Gallery and the latter at the National. In 1760, Reynolds moved here and, like many other artists, his home incorporated his studio from where his outpourings gathered momentum. All this work didn't mean he had no time for socialising; on the contrary. He constantly entertained the stars of his time. Dr. Johnson, Edmund Burke, David Garrick and others. He was also involved in the founding of the Royal Academy of Art, of which he was the first president. He did much to raise the status of painters in the eyes of the community and this work was recognised by his appointment as "painter-in-ordinary" to George III (1784). In 1789 he became partially blind and forced to stop painting. He is buried in St. Paul's Cathedral. He is ranked amongst the finest of the English school of portrait painters. Especially fine is the manner in which he painted children. He gave them a tenderness that was quite unique e.g. "Simplicity", "The Strawberry Girl", etc. This building later became part of the headquarters of the Automobile Association. Plaque erected 1960. Nearest tube station = Leicester Square.

RICHMOND, George (1809-1896) 20, York Street, Marylebone, W1.
'painter lived here 1843-1896'
Richmond, born in London, was the first man to elope to Gretna Green to marry. His bride was an architect's daughter. When the couple returned to London they were penniless. Richmond applied to the Royal Academy School, was accepted and eventually specialised in portrait painting. He was good and soon the commissions came pouring in. Amongst them the leading actors, politicians and clerics of the day. He became rich and held open house to a wide variety of celebrities; from the Duke of Wellington upwards, as one wag put it. As far as one can tell, the Richmonds lived happily ever after. Plaque erected 1961. Nearest tube station = Baker Street.

RICKETTS, Charles (1866-1931) Landsdowne House, 80, Landsdowne Road, Notting Hill, W11.
'In these studios lived and worked the artists: Charles RICKETTS (1866-1931), Charles SHANNON, (1863-1937), Glyn PHILPOT (1863-1937), Vivian FORBES (1891-1937), James PRYDE (1866-1941), F. Cayley ROBINSON (1862-1927)'
The first artists to move in, upon completion of the building in 1904, were Ricketts and Shannon. They were joint editors of the magazine "The Dial" and Ricketts was also a theatrical stage designer of some note. Philpot was a sculptor and Pryde designed and produced posters and, under the name, Beggarstaff, introduced the technique of paper cut-outs to give striking silhouettes. Robinson was a watercolour artist who taught. Plaque erected 1979. Nearest tube station = Notting Hill.

RIPON, George Frederick Samuel Robinson Marquess (1827-1909) 9, Chelsea Embankment, Chelsea, SW3.
'statesman and Viceroy of India lived here'
Save possibly for Earl Mountbatten, Ripon, born in London and educated at Harrow, was probably the only Viceroy (1880-1888) India had, who really tried to involve the Indians in their destiny. He encouraged their participation at all levels of political life and was criticised by the Conservatives in the House of Commons for doing so. Ripon was a progressive who became Colonial Secretary (1892-1895) and later served as Lord Privy Seal retiring in 1908. In 1870, he was forced to resign the office of Freemason's grand master, upon his conversion to Catholicism. He lived here from 1890 onwards. Plaque erected 1959. Nearest tube station = Sloane Square

RIZAL, Dr Jose (1861-1896) 37, Chalcot Crescent, Camden Town, NW1.
'writer and national hero of the Philippines lived here'
Rizal, born in Calamba, Luzon, only spent a few months here, whilst on his travels trying to gather support for his countrys' independence from Spain. Following publication of his book "The Lost Eden" in 1886, he was forbidden to return to Manilla. Amidst great secrecy, he returned to the Philippines in 1895 and became one of the revolution's leaders. He was betrayed by his mistress, convicted of inciting a rebellion and executed. His death led to a general uprising and eviction of the Spanish. Plaque erected 1983. Nearest tube station = Camden Town.

ROBERTS, Earl Frederick Sleigh (1832-1914) 47, Portland Place, Regent's Park, W1.
'Field-Marshal lived here'
Roberts lived here from 1902 to 1906. He was born in Cawnpore, India and educated in England, at Eton and Sandhurst. He served in the Indian Army throughout the Mutiny and in 1858 was awarded the V.C. for conspicuous gallantry. In 1880 he made his famous march through Afghanistan to the relief of Kandahar. This brought him much popularity and from 1885 to 1893 he was C-in-C India. In 1899, following the early Boer victories, Roberts was sent to South Africa to reorganise the British army. In 1904 he retired but in 1914, he went to France to see for himself the state of the British Expedition Force; there he contracted pneumonia and died at St. Omer. Plaque erected 1922. Nearest tube station = Regent's Park.

ROBINSON, James (1813-1862) 14, Gower Street, Bloomsbury, WC1.
'Pioneer of anaesthesia and dentistry lived and worked here'
James Robinson, the son of a naval captain, was born in Hampshire and educated at Guy's Hospital and London University. After a stint as a chemist in Store Street, Holborn (1830) he became a surgeon dentist at the Metropolitan hospital, later the Royal Free (1834). In 1846, he introduced anaesthetics to the world of dentistry and never looked back. Two years later he was appointed dentist to Prince Albert and became advisor to many hospitals that included dentistry, both here and overseas. In 1862 he founded the National Dental hospital in Great Portland Street. He wrote several books on his subject including "The Surgical, Mechanical and Medical treatment of the Teeth" (1846), "A Treatise on the Inhalation of Ether" (1847) and "Causes of Irregularity of the Permanent Teeth" (1859). He lived here during his younger days, later he moved to Kenton in Harrow. One day, whilst walking in his garden, he saw a branch of a small tree had broken in the fierce wind of the previous night. He took his sharp gardening knife and started removing the broken branch. Suddenly his knife slipped and penetrated his thigh. He was unable to move and was apparently not missed with the result he died from loss of blood, whilst laying under the offending tree. He is buried in Highgate cemetery. He was only 49 and would have undoubtedly continued a distinguished career had he only left the damaged tree to his gardener. Plaque erected 1991. Nearest tube station = Euston Square.

ROE, Alliott Verdon (1877-1958) Railway arches at Walthamstow Marsh Railway Viaduct, Walthamstow Marshes, E17.
'Under these arches Alliott Verdon ROE assembled his AVRO No. 1 triplane. In July 1909 he made the first all-British powered flight from Walthamstow Marshes'
Roe was born in Patricroft, nr Manchester and when only fifteen was in Canada working on drawings for a flying machine. He returned to London five years later and went to King's College, London to study naval engineering. After many years modelling aircraft, Roe, in 1907, became the first Englishman to design, build and fly his own aircraft. Together with his brother Humphrey, married to Dr. Marie Stopes, they started A. V. Roe & Co. , (1910). Amongst many aircraft they built, the AVRO 504, a bomber/trainer that set the standard for many future aircraft. Roes' also produced the early flying boats that were used by airlines prior to WW2. During the war they produced the Lancaster, arguably the best bomber produced by any country. Plaque erected 1983. Nearest Tube Station = Walthamstow Central.

ROHMER, Sax, (Arthur Henry Ward) (1883-1959) 51, Herne Hill, Brixton, SE24.
'creator of Dr Fu Manchu lived here'
Rohmer was the pseudonym used by Ward, because his father didn't approve of him being so infatuated with things Egyptian and writing fiction about them. He was born in Birmingham and after a formal education, persuaded his maternal grandmother to fund his travelling the continent. Because her son-in-law objected, she was pleased to oblige her grandson. Ward created the character Dr Fu Manchu, whilst drunk in a Paris bar. Literary fame and fortune followed. He lived here in the late twenties. Plaque erected 1985. Nearest Station = Herne Hill.

ROMILLY, Samuel (1757-1818) 21, Russell Square, Holborn, WC1.
'law reformer. Born 1757. Died 1818'
Romilly was born in London of Huguenot descent. He became an ardent disciple of Rousseau and lived in Paris throughout the Revolution. He was called to the Bar in 1783 and was a member of Grays Inn. He became interested in politics, but from behind the scenes. He was involved with Wilberforce in the emancipation of Catholics and freedom for slaves. He was particularly involved in Law Reform and attempted to reduce the number of offences for which death was the punishment. He and his family moved here in 1805 and, when his wife died in 1818, he committed suicide, a few days later, in his library. Plaque erected 1903. Nearest Tube Station = Russell Square.

ROMNEY, George (1734-1802) Holly Bush Hill, Hampstead, NW3.
'painter lived here'
Romney was born in Dalton-in-Furness, Lancashire, where his father was a farmer. He first studied cabinet making but eventually settled for portrait painting. He came to London in 1762, leaving his wife and children behind, and spent most of his time in a studio off Cavendish Square. He lived here, in Hampstead, for only a year, after spending a fortune on renovations. In 1798 he returned to Kendall and the wife he had deserted so many years previously. During his time in London, he was the only opposition to Joshua Reynolds in the portrait painting business. Although his portrait of Lady Hamilton made him, for a while, the more famous of the two, Reynolds won their popularity battle; but only on points. Plaque erected 1908. Nearest Tube Station = Hampstead.

ROSEBERY, 5th Earl (1847-1929) 20, Charles Street, Mayfair, W1.
'Prime Minister and first Chairman of the London County Council was born here'
Although Rosebery, born in London and educated at Eton and Christ College, Oxford, was Foreign Secretary twice (1886 and 1892-4) and Prime Minister (1894-5); it was as the owner of three horses that won the Derby, that he is best known. He wrote several biographies on political characters including Pitt (1891) and Peel (1899). It is said he was a better judge of horses than he was of men. He had succeeded Gladstone as PM but his advocacy of imperialist policies in Africa estranged him from much of the Liberal Party. However, he did favour the reform of the Lord's and advocated a more equal representation. In 1878, he married Hannah, the only daughter of Baron Meyer de Rothschild and they came to live here. Plaque erected 1962. Nearest Tube Station = Green Park.

ROSENBERG, Isaac (1890-1918) Whitechapel Library, 77, High Street, E1.
'poet and painter lived in the East End and studied here'
Born in Bristol of Jewish parents, who had come to England to escape religious persecution in Czarist Russia. The family moved shortly after Isaac's birth to the East End of London, which at that time was teeming with Jews. In 1911 he went to the Slade School of Fine Arts, but felt his depth of expression could better be served by words than art. Rosenberg was one of several poets who, during WW1, died in the trenches of France. During that war he wrote his "Trench Poems" and his play "Unicorn". In 1922 the first volume of his poems were published, with an introduction from the poet Laurence Binyon. In 1937, his "Collected Works" appeared with a forward by Siegfried Sassoon. It is generally accepted that much of Rosenberg's wartime poetry is not just realistic about trench warfare, but that there is a streak of romantic lyricism and a love of beauty more reminiscent of Blake, than of any 20th century poet. Plaque erected 1987. Nearest Tube Station = Whitechapel.

ROSS, Sir James Clark (1800-1862) 2, Elliot Place, Blackheath, SE3.
'polar explorer lived here'
Ross, born in London the son of a rich merchant, has had two places named after him; Ross Island and Ross Sea, both in the Antarctic. This followed his expedition (1839-43). He was also rewarded with a knighthood. During his voyage he discovered the Great Ice Barrier and Coulman Island, which he named after his fiancee. Perhaps his greatest discovery was the position of the North magnetic pole (1831). It is all detailed in his book published 1847, "The Voyage of Discovery". Ross was fortunate that his sponsor, Felix Booth was rich and that he didn't require Ross to have 'Booth's Gin' painted on the ship's side. Plaque erected 1960. Nearest Station = Blackheath.

ROSS, Sir Ronald (1857-1932) 18, Cavendish Square, Marylebone, W1.
'Nobel Laureate discoverer of the mosquito transmission of malaria lived here'
Ross was born in Almara, India and studied medicine at St. Bartholomew's Hospital in London. For his great achievements in the world of tropical medicine in general and malaria in particular, Ross received, in 1902, the Nobel Prize for Medicine and a knighthood in 1911. Much of Ross's research was carried out in India. His motives were to help the poor of that country combat the disease that was endemic there. He later became Director-General of the Ross Institute and Hospital for Tropical Diseases in London. He wrote his memoirs in 1925. Plaque erected 1985. Nearest Tube Station = Oxford Circus.

ROSSETTI, Christina Georgina (1830-1894) 30, Torrington Square, Holborn, WC1.
'poetess lived and died here'
Christina Rossetti was born in London, the younger sister of Dante Rossetti. Educated at home, she decided, on reaching her teens, to become a poet and her grandfather published, what were considered precocious, a pamphlet of her works. In her late teens she became engaged and disengaged within a period of a month. Religious differences were given as the reason. Christina was High Anglican, her fiance a Catholic. She was twenty when her first poems were published in the first issue of "The Germ". She wrote under the pseudonym, Ellen Alleyne. She published "Goblin Market" (1862), "The Prince's Progress" (1866). "Sing Song", a nursery rhyme book with illustrations by Arthur Hughes, appeared in 1872. It was around this time that she started the illnesses that were to dog her for the rest of her life and eventually make her an invalid. She continued writing and published her final work in 1892, "The Face of the Deep". She was a technical virtuoso who used her emotions imaginatively. Plaque erected 1913. Nearest tube station = Euston Square.

ROSSETTI, Dante Gabriel (1828-1882)

'here are three plaques for Rossetti. These are given in order of erection.

110, Hallam Street, Marylebone, W1.

'poet and painter born here' Erected 1906

17, Red Lion Square, Holborn, WC1.

'In this house lived in 1851, Dante Gabriel Rossetti, poet and painter, and from 1856-1859 William MORRIS (1834-1896), poet and artist and Sir Edward BURNE-JONES (1833-1898) painter' Erected 1911

16, Cheyne Walk, Chelsea, SW3.

'poet and painter and Algernon Charles SWINBURNE (1837-1909) poet lived here' Erected 1949.

Dante's father was a Neapolitan political refugee and his mother the daughter of Gaetano Polidori. Although born in London, it is not surprising that Dante, growing up in an Italian atmosphere that was artistic and learned, became a poet. After attending King's College School and the Antique School of the Royal Academy, Dante, together with others, founded the Pre-Raphaelite Brotherhood. During his early years, he enjoyed much success with both his poetry and his painting. When his wife, Elizabeth, died from an overdose of laudanum in 1862, her grief stricken husband had his latest manuscripts buried alongside her, to keep him with her. His work, at first bright and light, now became morbid. A few years after her death, Rossetti exhumed Elizabeth's body and retrieved his manuscripts. These appeared, with others, in a volume entitled "Poems" (1870). Following a critical attack by Robert Buchanan, who called his work putrid, Rossetti attempted suicide. He failed and went on to produce "Ballads and Sonnets" (1881). His work was at variance with Victorian morality. It was open, erotic, romantic and of abiding interest and imagination. Nearest Tube Stations = a/Goodge Street; b/Holborn; c/ Sloane Square.

ROWLANDSON, Thomas (1757-1827) 16, John Adam Street, Adelphi, WC2.

'artist and caricaturist lived in a house on this site'

Rowlandson was born in London and at the age of 15 went to Paris to study art and collect a legacy. A French aunt had died and left her favourite nephew £7,000. Most of the money he used on gambling, drinking and whoring and the rest he frittered away. However, despite his debauchery, he did learn to paint and when the money ran-out, he returned to London and made a decent living as a portrait painter. Soon, he was looking for fresh pastures and he turned to watercolour caricatures. These were vigourous in style and soon developed into book illustrations for famous authors like Smollett and Goldsmith. His best known work were his satires on the social scene and his "Tours of Dr Syntax" became very popular. His political satires created enemies and much of his time was spent avoiding being provoked into fighting duels. Plaque erected 1950. Nearest tube station = Charing Cross.

ROY, Ram Mohun (1772-1833) 49, Bedford Square, Holborn, WC1.
'Indian scholar and reformer lived here'
Roy was a reformer of religion. A Bengali of high Brahman ancestry, who published many works in Persian, Arabic and Sanskrit and who tried to uproot idolatry. He assisted greatly in the abolition of suttee, although not completely and it lingers on. In 1820, he published "The Precepts of Jesus" in which he accepts Christ's teachings of morality but rejects that he is the son of God or the worker of the miracles attaching (something that is being claimed a 170 years later by present day Christians). He began the Brahma Samaj association in 1828 and in 1830, the Delhi bestowed on him the title of rajah. In 1831 he came to London and stayed in Bedford Square, whilst attending the conference on Indian affairs, to which he gave valuable authentic evidence of local conditions. Plaque erected 1985. Nearest tube station = Goodge Street.

ROY, Major-General William (1726-1790) 10, Argyll Street, Mayfair, W1.
'founder of the Ordnance Survey lived here'
Roy was born in Miltonhead, Lanarkshire and educated in Scotland. Following his training, he was appointed to survey Scotland (1747). He was then granted a commission in the army, in order to facilitate his movements, whilst mapping large areas of Britain, necessary in order to aid English troops fighting Bonnie Prince Charlie. He received no formal military training and thus reached the rank of Major-General (1781). He was elected a Fellow of the Royal Society in 1767 and he was the first to measure, accurately, specific areas, e.g. The base line of Hounslow Heath is 5 and one fifth miles long. For his works he received the Royal Society's Copley medal. In 1793, he published 'Military Antiquities of the Romans in Britain'. His greatest achievement, which led to the setting up of the Ordnance Survey, was to establish the triangulation of south-east England in order to discover the relative positions of the Paris and Greenwich observatories. Plaque erected 1979. Nearest tube station = Oxford Circus.

RUSKIN, John (1819-1900) 26, Herne Hill, Herne Hill, SE24.
'man of letters lived in a house on this site'
When Ruskin's father, a prosperous wine merchant, moved here; John was aged four and the whole area was countryside. It has changed dramatically. Now parts are termed as subject to inner city decay. He was educated at home and when he went up to Christ Church, Oxford, he was, to say the least, unworldly. At Oxford, he won the Newdigate prize for poetry. He met Turner and decided to become his "Boswell", consequently Ruskin published, in 1843, "Modern Painters", its' purpose was to rescue the great painter from what Ruskin saw as his obscurity. Ruskin's wife, Effie Chalmers Gray, left him in 1848, after a brief and unconsummated marriage, to live with Millais, with whom Ruskin was associated in the Pre-Raphaelite movement. Ruskin was the acknowledged critic of his day, following publication of "The Stones of Venice" (1851-3). He went on to write on many subjects, including a rejection of capitalism and a plea for what might be described as Christian Communism. In 1869, Oxford made him its first Slade professor of fine art. He later settled at Coniston, in the Lake District. Here he continued writing with increased vigour, claiming the air was finer for his mind. His autobiography "Praeterita" was published after his death. Ruskin wanted to emulate St. Francis and divest himself of all wealth. He failed and left his cousin, Mrs Arthur Severn and her family, with whom Ruskin spent his last years, a substantial fortune. Plaque erected 1926. Nearest Station = Denmark Hill.

RUSSELL, Lord John, 1st Earl (1792-1878) 37, Chesham Place, Belgravia, SW1.
'twice Prime Minister lived here'
John Russell born in London, was the third son of the 6th Duke of Bedford. Third sons of Earls and Dukes usually wound up as colonials, looking after overseas family interests for a pittance. Not this one. After a formal education, ending at the University of Edinburgh, he entered politics on behalf of the Whigs. He won Tavistock (1813), and his efforts at reform won many seats for the Liberals at the 1830 election. Wellington was out, Earl Grey was in and John Russell became paymaster to the forces. He was one of four ministers empowered to prepare the Reform Bill of 1832 for presentation to Parliament. Following the repeal of the Corn Laws (1846), Peel was defeated and Lord John, as he was now known, became PM. (1846-1852). His involvement in the illfated Crimean war and his bungling of the Vienna conference combined to make him unpopular and for four years he was out of office. He returned in 1859, as foreign secretary under Palmerston and when he died in 1865, Lord John once again became PM. He resigned shortly after, following defeat of his Reform Bill. However, he continued to speak and write, on current issues, until the very day he died. Plaque erected 1911. Nearest tube station = Sloane Square.

SALVIN, Anthony (1799-1881) 11, Hanover Terrace, Regent's Park, NW1.
'architect lived here'
Born in Worthing, Sussex, Salvin's father was owner of Croxdale Manor in Durham, that had been in the family since 1474. Educated at Durham School, Slavin became an architect and is generally recognised as the greatest authority on military architecture. He restored the Tower at Windsor Castle, recently damaged by fire (1992) and for 60 years, was London's chief architect of public buildings. During this period, he lived part of the time here. He restored castles all over the country, built halls of residences, restored manor houses and built new ones. He built many churches and at Peckforton, Cheshire, he built a large castle in the style of a Plantagenent favoured by Henry VIII. In order to protect their family estates, Salvin married his first cousin. He exhibited at the Royal Academy, between 1823 and 1836, a total of eight architectural subjects. He is buried at Fernhurst, one of the churches he built. Plaque erected 1990. Nearest tube station = St. John's Wood.

SAN MARTIN, Jose de (The Liberator) (1778-1850) 23, Park Road, Regent's Park, NW1.
'Argentine soldier and statesman stayed here'
San Martin, the national hero of Argentine, was born in Yapeyu. After a career as a Spanish army officer, he aided Buenos Aires and defeated Spanish forces at the battle of Chacabuco (1817). After a series of battles, that liberated Peru and Chile from Spain, San Martin was declared Protector of Peru. He resigned in 1822, following differences with Bolivar, and came to London. He stayed here a short while, before going to live in exile in Boulogne. There, five years later, accompanied by Angelina, his mistress of many years, he died. Plaque erected 1953. Nearest tube station = Baker Street.

SANTLEY, Sir Charles (1834-1922) 13, Blenheim Road, St. John's Wood, NW8.
'singer lived and died here'
Santley was born in Liverpool and lived here for the final 10 years of a long and successful career. After training in Milan, he made his debut in Haydon's "Creation" (1857). Although he preferred Italian opera, he sang the role of "Vanderdecken" in the "Flying Dutchman", the first Wagner opera given in England. He later became known for concerts and crowned it all by getting knighted, in 1907, for services to music. His last London performance was at the Mansion House in 1915, during WW1, in aid of Belgian refugees. In 1909 he published his autobiography, entitled, "Reminiscences". Plaque erected 1935. Nearest tube station = St. John's Wood.

SARGENT, Sir Malcolm (1895-1967) Albert Hall Mansions, Kensington Gore, SW7.
'Conductor lived and died in a flat in this building'
Malcolm Sargent is one of the very few beneficiaries of a blue plaque who lived "above the shop" or in his case right next door. The Royal Albert Hall, where he saw so much success. He was born in Stamford, Lincolnshire and originally trained as an organist. In 1921, his "Rhapsody on a Windy Day" was performed at a Promenade Concert. This was the first time Sargent conducted in public. Thereafter he was conductor of the Royal Choral Society from 1928 and in charge of the Liverpool Philharmonic from 1942 to 1948. His best known work is as conductor of the BBC Symphony Orchestra 1950-57. Those old enough to remember him on the last nights of the proms, will recall his witty speeches and twinkly smile. Plaque erected 1992. Nearest tube station = Kensington High Street.

SARTORIUS, John F. (c. 1775-c1830) 155, Old Church Street, Chelsea, SW3.
'sporting painter lived here 1807-1812'
Sartorius, born in London, found fame as a painter of sporting subjects, in particular horse racing. He was exhibited at the Royal Academy, for the first of many times, in 1802. Thereafter he was commissioned by many London clubs, who had large walls to fill and he wasn't expensive. Plaque erected 1979. Nearest tube station = Gloucester Road.

SAVARKAR, Vinayak Damodar (1883-1966) 65, Cromwell Avenue, Highgate, N6.
'Indian patriot and philosopher lived here'
Savarkar must have lived here prior to 1911 because in 1911 he was sentenced to life imprisonment as a conspirator in the murder of an Indian official in London. He was released in 1937 and went to India, where he became President of the Hindu Mahasabha (1937-1943). In 1948, he was one of eight people charged with the assassination of Gandhi but eventually acquitted. Plaque erected 1985. Nearest tube station = Highgate Archway.

SCAWEN-BLUNT, Wilfred (1840-1922) 15, Buckingham Gate, Belgravia, SW1.
'diplomat, poet and traveller founder of Crabbet Park Arabian stud lived here'
Born at Petworth House, Sussex, Scawen-Blunt was educated at Stonyhurst and Oscott before entering the diplomatic service. He travelled throughout Europe and the Near East, as a King's Messenger, before marrying Byron's granddaughter. After inheriting Petworth House, he turned his hand to writing poetry but didn't exactly set that world on fire. He then invested a large part of his inheritance on horses and established the Crabbett Park stud. He made many visits to Egypt, to buy horses and made an issue of Egyptian freedom, from Turkish rule, a political platform in England. He also wrote love poems which he published for private circulation. Plaque erected 1979. Nearest tube station = Victoria.

SCHREINER, Olive (1855-1920) 16, Portsea Place, Bayswater, W2.
'author lived here'
Olive Schreiner lived here for only a few months, during 1885-6. She was born into a Boer family in Wittebergen, South Africa where her father ran the Mission Station. Largely self educated, she became, at 15, the governess to a large Boer family close to the Karoo desert. She educated the children of this and other nearby families by the use of the bible, some educational books, and a whip. She left and went to live in Durban, where she started writing. She came to London in 1881 and whilst here she wrote "The Story of an African Farm" (1883). The first full story about every day life in Africa. She wrote it under the name of Ralph Iron, as a way of getting published. She was a naturally fiery and rebellious person who took great exception in having to masquerade as a man. Her temperament led her to become a passionate advocate for women's rights. She wrote many books on behalf of women, "Women and Labour" (1911) is probably the best known. She wrote on social matters , "Trooper Peter Halket" (1897) and her best known novel was "From Man to Man" (1916). An unusual feature of her life was her marriage to S. P. Cronwright who took her name and wrote her biography in 1924. Plaque erected 1959. Nearest tube station = Bayswater.

SCHWITTERS, Kurt (1887-1948) 39, Westmoreland Road, Barnes, SW13.
'artist lived here'
Schwitters was born in Hanover, Germany and became a painter in the Surrealist mode. He created collages from the most ordinary things; discarded bus tickets, old menus, receipts of all kinds, sweet wrappers, bits from old newspapers; anything and everything. During the thirties, Schwitters and the Nazi regime didn't see eye to eye about the meaning of art. Schwitters headed, first to Norway and then to England. After a brief sojourn in London, he spent the war years in the Lake District. Plaque erected 1984, Nearest Station = Barnes.

Site of SCOTLAND YARD, Ministry of Agriculture building, Whitehall Place, SW1.
'First headquarters of the Metropolitan Police, (1829-1890)'
This was the former Royal Palace of White Hall. Previous to the police occupancy, the rooms were occupied by such luminaries as Inigo Jones, Christopher Wren, Lord Nelson and Sir John Denham. A large part of the premises were used to house horses and large closed carriages; forerunners of the "Black Maria". Plaque erected 1979. Nearest tube station = Green Park

SCOTT, Sir George Gilbert (1811-1878) Admiral's House, Admiral's Walk, Hampstead, NW3.
'architect lived here'
Scott was born in Gawcott, Buckinghamshire. After a formal education, that resulted in his qualifying as an architect, he threw himself into a wave of Gothic revival. His work load was formidable. One way and another he was responsible for the building or restoration of 26 cathedrals, and over 500 churches and monuments. As if all this wasn't enough, he designed the Albert Memorial (1862-3), for which he earned his knighthood, and St. Pancras, which started off as yet another cathedral and wound up a main line railway station (1865). Other work of note included: The India Office, in the style of the Italian Renaissance (by order of Palmerston), Glasgow University (1865) and many more. He was also professor of architecture at the Royal Academy and he wrote numerous books on English medieval church architecture. He also found time for marriage and a family. If he had any time for hobbies, or walking the dog on the nearby Heath, it isn't noted. He was what is now termed, a "workaholic". Plaque erected 1910. Nearest tube station = Hampstead.

SCOTT, Sir Giles Gilbert (1880-1960) Chester House, Clarendon Place, Bayswater, W2.
'architect designed this house and lived here 1926-1960'
This is a case of, anything Granddad can do I can do better. Giles, born in London and educated at Beaumont College, Old Windsor, was the grandson of George Scott. In 1903 he won a competition to design the Anglican cathedral in Liverpool. It was consecrated in 1924 and destroyed in 1941 by German bombers. He too worked very hard and had many fine buildings to his credit. These included, during the years between two world wars, many extensions to colleges and libraries at Oxford and Cambridge. He designed Waterloo Bridge (1945) and he was responsible for the rebuilding, after bomb damage during WW2, of the House of Commons. Plaque erected 1990. Nearest tube station = Lancaster Gate.

SCOTT, Captain, Robert Falcon (1868-1912) 56, Oakley Street, Chelsea, SW3.
'Antarctic explorer lived here'
Scott of the Antarctic! A schoolboy hero and subject of at least one Hollywood film. He lived here for three years from 1905. He was born in Devonport and entered the navy in 1881. In 1900 he commanded HMS Discovery and spent four years exploring the Ross Sea area and discovering King Edward VII Land. He was promoted to captain and in 1910, started his second Antarctic expedition aboard "Terra Nova". He, together with Oates, Bower and Evans, reached the South Pole on January 17th 1912, only to discover that Amundsen's Norwegian expedition had beaten them to it by a month. Scott and his party, delayed by blizzards and sickness, eventually perished. Scott was posthumously knighted and there is a statue to him at Waterloo Place, sculptured by his wife Kathleen. Plaque erected 1935. Nearest tube station = South Kensington.

SEACOLE, Mary (1805-1881) 157, George Street, Marylebone, W1.
'Jamaican nurse heroine of the Crimean War lived here'
Mary Seacole was born Mary Jane Grant. She was the daughter of a Scots army officer and a "free" black woman, who worked as a boarding house manager, in Kingston, Jamaica. This is where Mary was born and where she received her education, at a church mission school. She trained as a nurse in London and, at the start of the Crimean war, she volunteered to go with the army as a part of their medical team. Her request was refused and, at her own expense, she travelled to the Crimea where, despite objections from senior British officers, she set up the "British Hotel", two miles from the front, at Balaclava. Here, she dispensed food and drink to weary soldiers, temporarily withdrawn from the fighting. In her spare time she rode, on horseback, to the front and administered aid and medicines to the wounded. All this was before the arrival of Florence Nightingale on the scene. In 1857 she wrote of her experiences in "Wonderful Adventures of Mrs Seacole in Many Lands". Mrs Seacole, at various times, was a businesswoman, gold prospector, traveller and writer. She lived here towards the end of her life; when she wasn't travelling to Jamaica. Plaque erected 1985. Nearest tube station = Baker Street.

SHACKLETON, Sir Ernest Henry (1874-1922) 12, Westwood Hill, Sydenham, SE26.
'Antarctic explorer lived here'
Shackleton was born in Kilkee, Ireland and lived here from 1884 until his marriage in 1904. He was with Scott, when he commanded the 'Discovery' on the 1901-3 expedition. Later, in 1908-9, he commanded an expedition that visited the Falklands. He saw great potential for sheep farming and mining and, upon his return, obtained land at giveaway prices. He returned to the area several times, once he was involved in rescuing survivors marooned on Elephant Island. His last trip was in 1920, which took him to South Georgia. Here in 1922 he died and it was left to his family to profit from his land investments. Plaque erected 1928. Nearest station = Sydenham.

SHARP, Cecil (1859-1924) 4, Maresfield Gardens, Hampstead, NW3.
'collector of English folk songs and dances lived here'
Sharp was born in London but, after qualifying as a lawyer, he went to live and work in Australia, working first as a lawyer and later as an organist. Recognising his first love was music, he returned to England in 1892 and, in 1896, upon his appointment as principal of Hampstead Conservatory, came to live here. His accumulated collection is kept at Cecil Sharp House, home of the English Folk Dance society, which he founded in 1911. Plaque erected 1985. Nearest tube station = Finchley Road.

SHAW, George Bernard (1856-1950) 29, Fitzroy Square, Bloomsbury, W1.
'lived in this house from 1887-1898. "From the coffers of his genius he
enriched the world" '
Shaw was born in Dublin of Protestant parents. His mother was a singing teacher
and Shaw inherited his love of music from her. A series of short stints at various
schools left Shaw, at 15 looking for a job. He tried to obey the routine of an estate
agency, but it wasn't for him. His parents had split up and young Shaw followed
his mother and sister Lucy, a musical comedy actress, to London. He began
writing, but to no avail, the five novels he wrote, between 1879 and 1883, were all
rejected. Shaw had a hard time making ends meet. He read Karl Marx and his
thinking was influenced accordingly. He had begun writing music criticisms for
various journals and managed to afford to rent here. He stayed until his
marriage, to Charlotte Payne-Townsend in 1898. Although busy working as a
journalist, novelist and playwright, he found time to serve as a socialist
councillor in St. Pancras. Gradually Shaw found his place as the foremost
playwright of his day. Many of his works have been turned into musicals and
films. "Pygmalion", famous in its own right, has become even more so under its
adapted title of "My Fair Lady". In 1925, he was awarded the Nobel Prize for
Literature. It was probably because of his criticism of WW1, as told in "Common
Sense About the War" (1914), that he was refused the peerage, or some other
honour, he so richly deserved. He once said that the work he was most pleased
with was "The Intelligent Woman's Guide to Socialism" written in 1928 and as
valid today as it was then. Plaque erected 1951. Nearest tube station = Warren
Street.

GRIMS DYKE, Old Redding, Harrow Weald, Harrow, Middlesex.
'This house, designed by R. NORMAN SHAW, architect for Frederick
GOODALL, painter was later the home of W. S. GILBERT, writer and
librettist'
This is an odd plaque, as it appears to commemorate a house first and three
people second. The house is decidedly strange, as though the designer wanted to
be all things to all clients. It's a bit Traditional English, a bit Gothic and vaguely
Victorian. Frederick Goodall, born in London, was a painter of moderate talent
and only able to afford to commission the building of Grims Dyke, because of a
fortunate marriage and an inheritance from his father. W. S Gilbert, Gilbert
Schwenk born in London, of course needs no introduction, the "words part of the
duo, Gilbert and Sullivan", he made a fortune and displayed it, when in 1890, he
moved here and played the part of "The Squire". Had he been more circumspect
he might have lived longer. He died in 1911, trying to save a guest who had fallen
into his lake. He was however, 75 at the time and Sullivan had been dead 11 years,
so perhaps he welcomed this heroic exit. The house is now used as a hostelry
where fans can eat, drink and hear their favourite Gilbert and Sullivan arias
sung by well meaning artists. Plaque erected 1976. Nearest Station = Headstone
Lane.

SHELLEY, Percy Bysshe (1792-1822) 15, Poland Street, Soho, W1.
'poet lived here'
Shelley, born in Field Place, Sussex, came to live here when he was sent down from Oxford in March 1811. His fall from grace followed the essay he sent to the bishop of University College, Oxford, entitled "The Necessity of Atheism". Shelley pranced around London society acting as though everyone owed him a living. It was as if he had a death wish. He did everything to antagonise those who might have helped him. He thrived on the sobriquet of "Mad Shelley", that had been given to him at Eton. His elopement, with 16-year-old Harriet Westbrook, succeeded in causing a rift with his family which never healed. Shelley on his part, figuratively stuck two fingers up, and told them what they could do with his inheritance. His writings were admired but didn't sell. Harriet, after giving him two children, he found to be ageing, so he left her and went off to Italy with 16 year old Mary Godwin. He never stopped writing and produced a variety of work. He had many friends in the literary world and they inspired one another. In 1816, Harriet drowned herself in Hyde Park's Serpentine and Shelley promptly married Mary. Between 1819 and 1821, Shelley found a great burst of creative energy and produced some of his best work, including the completion of the fourth part of "Prometheus Unbound", probably his most famous work. His last effort was, "Hellas", concerning the war of Greek Independence being waged by, Lord Byron, amongst others. Out sailing, in the schooner, "Ariel", off Livorno, Italy, he, and two companions, drowned when a sudden storm came up. His body was washed ashore a month later and cremated, on the beach where it was discovered, by his friends Trelawny, Leigh-Hunt and of course Byron. Plaque erected 1979. Nearest tube station = Tottenham Court Road.

SHEPARD, E. H. (1879-1976) 10, Kent Terrace, Regent's Park, NW1.
'Painter and Illustrator lived here'
Ernest Howard Shepard was born in London and from an early age made it clear he wanted to be an artist when he grew up. He kept his word although it was as the illustrator of A. A. Milne's "Winnie the Pooh" and Kenneth Grahame's "The Wind in the Willows" that he made his name. Shepard lived here in the latter part of a very long life. Plaque erected 1993. Nearest tube station = Regent's Park

SHEPHERD, Thomas Hosmer (1793-1864) 26, Batchelor Street, Islington, N1.
'artist who portrayed London lived here'
Mr and Mrs Shepherd lived here from 1818 until 1841. They saw the area change from rural to urban. Shepherd, born in London, was probably the best, and best known, topographical artist of his time, specialising in every day London. His major work was "Metropolitan Improvements" which he began in 1826 and for which he made over 150 engravings. It was published in 41 parts and was a great success. Its appeal to a wide audience, many of whom couldn't read, was for its' pictures and the ease of being able to recognise the sites. Shepherd's last work was, "Mighty London" (1853). Plaque erected 1976. Nearest tube station = Angel

SHERATON, Thomas (1751-1806) 163, Wardour Street, Soho, W1.
'furniture designer lived here'
Sheraton, born in Stockton-on-Tees, arrived in London in 1790 and came to live here in 1791. He stayed until 1794, before moving to Golden Square. He was forever poor and unrecognised for the genius designer he was. His elegant neo-classical designs only became really appreciated long after his death. He enjoyed writing and his major work "The Cabinet-Maker and Upholsterer's Drawing Book" published, whilst living here, was a success, but didn't provide much money. In 1800, he chucked it all in and became ordained. Plaque erected 1954. Nearest tube station = Tottenham Court Road.

SHERIDAN, Richard Brinsley (1751-1816) 14, Savile Row, Mayfair, W1.
'dramatist lived here'
10, Hertford Street, Mayfair, W1.
'dramatist and statesman lived here 1795-1802'
Sheridan was born in Dublin and educated at Harrow. In 1773 he married Elizabeth Linley and suddenly realised, that instead of playing at writing, he best work hard at it, in order to feed and clothe his bride, himself and the domestics. He wrote "The Rivals" in 1775 and two years later "The School for Scandal". "The Critic" (1779) was Sheridan's last work of note. In 1780, he entered Parliament as member for Stafford and held a series of Government appointments. In 1787 he made a five hour speech in support of the impeachment of Warren Hastings. He was a friend and supporter of Charles Fox throughout his time in politics. He moved to Savile Row but was plagued by debt, due to his investment in the Drury Lane Theatre. Uninsured, it was destroyed by fire in 1809. He died in great poverty but was buried in Westminster Abbey, after a glorious funeral paid for by his friends. Plaques erected 1881 and 1955. Nearest tube stations = Bond Street and Hyde Park.

SHORT, Sir Frank (1857-1945) 56, Brook Green, Hammersmith, W6.
'engraver and painter lived here'
Short lived here from 1893 to 1944. He was born in Stourbridge and came to London to be educated at St. Pauls School. He was a great master of the engraving process and became a teacher and authority on the subject. As well as an established engraving artist, he was Head of the Engraving School at the Royal College of Art and President of the Royal Society of Painter Etchers (1910-1939). He lived here, together with his family, from 1893 to 1944. Plaque erected 1951. Nearest tube station = Hammersmith.

SICKERT, Walter (1860-1942) 6, Mornington Crescent, Camden, NW1.
'painter and etcher lived and worked here'
Sickert lived and worked here for some twenty years, from 1907. He was born in Munich, Germany, of Dutch and Danish parents. He spent three years on the English stage before going to the Slade School of Art to study under Whistler. He worked in Paris, where he was much influenced by Degas and used his technique to illustrate London's low life. He founded the London Group in 1910, which introduced post-impressionism onto the British art scene. His famous 'Ennui' in the Tate, belongs to this period. His autobiography, "A Free House!", was published five years after his death. In November 1992, an exhibition of Sickert's work was held at the Royal Academy, organised by enthusiast Wendy Baron who claimed " . . . Sickert is the greatest British painter since Turner". Plaque erected 1977. Nearest tube station = Camden Town.

The SILVER STUDIO, 84, Brook Green Road, Hammersmith, W6.
'established here in 1880. Arthur SILVER, (1853-1886), Rex SILVER, (1879-1965), Harry SILVER, (1881-1971), designers lived here'
Arthur Silver was born in Reading, the son of a cabinet maker. After studying at Reading Art School, Arthur was apprenticed to HW Batley and soon became a versatile professional designer. In 1880, he opened his studio and prospered. He designed interior schemes for private customers and wallpapers for manufacturers, including Jeffery & Co. In 1889, he published the Silver Series of Photographs, which represented textiles at the South Kensington Museum (now the V&A). Rex and Harry were Arthur's sons, who were young children when their father died. The studio however continued and as soon as the brothers had finished their training they took over. The business of advising and creating all aspects of design work continued throughout two world wars and only closed in 1962. Plaque erected 1981. Nearest tube station = Hammersmith Broadway.

SIMON, Sir John (1816-1904) 40, Kensington Square, Kensington, W8.
'pioneer of public health lived here'
Simon, born in London, lived here from 1868 to 1904. After qualifying as a doctor, John Simon became a pathologist. In 1848, he was appointed London's first medical officer for health and later became chief medical officer to the Privy Council. His book, "English Sanitary Institutions" remains an authority on the subject of public health. Simon was one of the youngest men ever elected to the Royal Society; he was 29, and had written a paper on the thyroid gland. Plaque erected 1959. Nearest tube station = Kensington High Street.

SLOANE Sir Hans (1660-1753) Kings Mead, King's Road, Chelsea, SW3
'The ground to the West of this building was given to the Parish of Chelsea in 1733 by Sir Hans Sloane, President of the Royal Society. Born 1660. Died 1753'
4, Bloomsbury Place, Bloomsbury, WC1.
'physician and benefactor of the British Museum lived here 1695-1742'
Sloane born in Killyleagh, County Down in Ireland, studied in France and London and became a doctor. In 1685, whilst physician to the governor of Jamaica, he collected a herbarium of some 800 species. In 1716 he was knighted on becoming the number one physician to George II. In 1721 he created the famous Chelsea Physic Garden, still going strong and well worth a visit. He is remembered for his book, "The Natural History of Jamaica" (1707-25). Plaques erected 1977 and 1965. Nearest Tube Stations = Sloane Square and Russell Square.

SMILES, Samuel (1812-1904) 11, Granville Park, Lewisham, SE13.
'author of "Self Help" lived here'
Smiles was born in Haddington, Scotland and studied medicine at Edinburgh. He practised in Haddington and then went to live in Leeds, where he gave up medicine and became editor of the "Leeds Times". He then met George Stephenson and fell in love with railways. He became secretary to two, Leeds and Thirsk in 1845 and the South Eastern Railway in 1846. In 1854 he came to London and lived here for several years. In 1857, he wrote a book on the life of Stephenson, but his most famous piece was "Self Help", published in 1859. It gave potted biographies of great men with the admonishment to readers to do likewise. It was the ideal Victorian school prize. He went on to write further pieces of gratuitous advice "Character" (1871), "Thrift" (1875) and "Duty" (1880). He was an advocate of social and political reform, state education and public libraries. Plaque erected 1959. Nearest Station = Lewisham

SMIRKE, Sir Robert (1781-1867) 81, Charlotte Street, W1.
'architect lived here'
Smirke was born in London, his father a well known painter and illustrator who lived to see his architect son achieve his finest creation. The British Museum was started in 1823 and completed in 1847. His father died two months later. Other well known buildings were Covent Garden Theatre (1809), The General Post Office (1824) and the College of Physicians (1825). His style of design was generally divided in two. Classical, if it was a public building and Gothic if it were a domestic commission. Later in life he teamed up with his brother, Sydney, and they built amongst others, King's Library; Oxford and Cambridge Club House and The Carlton Club. He lived in Charlotte Street 1805-1810. Plaque erected 1979. Nearest tube station = Goodge Street.

SMITH, E. Earl of Birkenhead (1872-1930) 32, Grosvenor Gardens, Belgravia, SW1.
'lawyer and statesman lived here'
Smith, born in Birkenhead attended the local grammar school and won a scholarship to Wadham College, Oxford. He was a character who, when a he became a fashionable lawyer, was loved by cartoonists for he was over 6ft tall, well built, wore his hat at the back of his head, smoked large cigars and always wore a red rose in his buttonhole. Before WW1 he, together with Carson, had talks with German officials in Berlin, over possible German support in the event Home Rule for Ireland, any part of Ireland, became a reality. He was accused of being a traitor but the government played it down. He moved here in 1915 and stayed. He had entered parliament in 1906 and had became Attorney General in 1915. The irony over his accord with the Germans, was that in 1916, he prosecuted Sir Roger Casement for treason. Smith hated Casement because Casement wanted Home Rule. Smith brought false evidence and secured a conviction. Casement was hanged. In 1919, Smith became Lord Chancellor, was created Earl of Birkenhead in 1922 and Secretary of State for India in 1924. Then it all went wrong. He was recalled from India in 1928, for embezzlement. Fortunate not to be prosecuted, it was said he had something on every member of the cabinet, he left politics. He spent some time in the city, before retiring to write on famous trials, biographies and modern history. Plaque erected 1959. Nearest tube station = Victoria.

SMITH, Sydney (1771-1845) 14, Doughty Street, Holborn, WC1.
'author and wit lived here'
Smith lived here for three years, from 1803 and then moved, following the death of his infant son, who fell out of an upper storey window. Smith was born in Woodford, Essex and educated at Winchester and New College, Oxford, where he later became a fellow. Although ordained, he appeared to have a love/hate relationship with the Church. He started the 'Edinburgh Review' in 1802 and then became a lecturer, at the Royal Institution, on moral philosophy, where he caused problems, by his outspoken support for Catholic emancipation. He at various times wrote outspoken pamphlets on many of the contentious subjects of his day including; American independence, gaming laws and prison abuse. Plaque erected 1906. Nearest tube station = Russell Square.

SMITH, William, MP. (1756-1835) 16, Queen Anne's Gate, St. James's, SW1.
'pioneer of religious liberty lived here'
Smith, born in London, lived here from 1794 to 1819. He inherited a fortune when his father died, and was able to afford to work for the disadvantaged. This he did by supporting anti slavery and, for non-Anglicans, to have freedom of worship and citizenship. He fathered ten children and one of his granddaughters was Florence Nightingale. Plaque erected 1975. Nearest tube station = St. James's Park

SMITH, W. H. (1825-1891) 12, Hyde Park Street, Bayswater, W2.
'bookseller and statesman lived here'
This Smith was the grandson of the man who started the family newsagency business in the Strand. Smith, born in London, entered parliament in 1868 but always made sure his business came first. He held some high positions in government, including being First Lord of the Admiralty under Disraeli. He took advantage of his position to prosper his firm. On this basis he was able to secure the advantage for W. H. Smith to have the sole right to bookstalls at railway stations; proof that the adage 'it isn't what you know but who you know' works. He died at Walmer Castle, whilst Lord Warden of the Cinque Ports. Plaque erected. 1966. Nearest tube station = Paddington.

SPURGEON, Charles Haddon (1834-1892) 99, Nightingale Lane, Clapham, SW12.
'preacher lived here'
Spurgeon, born in Kelvedon, Essex, was a born rabble rouser. His platform was as an evangelist Baptist. At one time he had as many as 14,000 people, standing in a field listening to him spouting how their poverty, sickness and deprivation would come right in the world hereafter. However, he, like present day mass preachers, made sure he didn't share their poor standard of life in this world. He had this house built for him, in a most desirable part of London, and in 1857 he and his family moved in. In 1868, he had it rebuilt and extended. In 1869 he published a collection of pithy sayings entitled "John Ploughman's Talk". Plaque erected 1971. Nearest Station = Wandsworth Common.

STANFORD, Sir Charles (1852-1924) 56, Hornton Street, Kensington, W8.
'musician lived here 1894-1916'
Stanford was born in Dublin and studied at Cambridge, Leipzig and Berlin, before his appointment as organist to Trinity College, in 1872. He became a professor at the Royal College of Music and generations of young British composers were most fortunate to have him as their teacher. He was an outgoing man, who was most happy having a drink with his students, rather than with his colleagues. He was proud of being Irish and named the opera he wrote in 1896 "Shamus O'Brien"; it enjoyed a long run in London before it opened in Dublin. Plaque erected 1961. Nearest tube station = Kensington High Street.

STANHOPE, Charles, 3rd Earl (1753-1816) 20, Mansfield Street, Marylebone, W1.
'reformer and inventor lived here'
Stanhope was born in London and educated at Eton and Geneva. In 1774, he married Lady Hester Pitt, the sister of Pitt, the Younger. A man of science, he invented a microscope lens that bears his name, as well as various items that were used in the printing trade. He entered parliament in 1780, but broke with his brother-in-law, the Prime Minister, because Stanhope supported the French Revolution and advocated peace with Napoleon. He became a minority of one and in 1794, a mob attacked this house, where he lived from 1785 to 1795. Plaque erected 1951. Nearest tube station = Oxford Circus.

STANLEY, Sir Henry Morton (1841-1904) 2, Richmond Terrace, St. James's, SW1.
'explorer and writer lived and died here'
What an amazing life Henry Stanley had. He was born of unmarried parents, in Denbigh, Wales and abandoned, when he was only a few weeks old. His real name was John Rowlands and he was brought up in a workhouse that doubled as an orphanage. When he was 18 he went to the local docks and begged an American ship's captain to give him any sort of job, so long as it took him away from Britain. He eventually landed in New Orleans, where he was befriended by a cotton-broker named Stanley. In gratitude, Rowlands took his name and joined first, the Confederate Army and then the U.S. navy. By this time he was writing the odd article for various journals. After the civil war, he got a job on the New York Herald and over the years, became its roving reporter in Africa and Europe. In October 1869, he received the terse order from his editor, Gordon Bennett, "find Livingstone". After a very tough journey, through some of the world's most inhospitable country, and confrontations with some very hostile natives, Stanley, on November 10th 1871, uttered the immortal words, "Dr Livingstone, I presume". He returned to London and published, in 1872, "How I Found Livingstone". In 1874, financed by the "New York Herald" and "The Daily Telegraph", Stanley left to complete Livingstone's work. He made later trips to Africa, including setting up the Congo Free State, which Britain had refused to assist, but which the King of the Belgians quickly took on; when he realised the enormous potential that existed in diamonds, gold and minerals. Stanley rounded off his amazing life by representing Lambeth in parliament, (1895-1900), marrying Dorothy Tennant in 1890 and coming to live here in 1902. He was knighted the same year. Plaque erected 1987. Nearest tube station = St. James's Park.

STANLEY W. F. R. (1829-1909), Stanley Halls, 12, South Norwood Hill, South Norwood, SE25.
'Inventor, Manufacturer and Philanthropist founded and designed these halls and technical schools'
William Ford Robinson was born in Buntingford, Hertfordshire and received a scanty education at a local private school. He left to go to work for his father, a jobbing builder, who went bankrupt six months later. Stanley went to London and got a job as a plumber and joiner with time off to go to classes at Birbeck Institute. He later rejoined his father in an engineering works in Whitechapel and turned his hand to inventing. He introduced the steel wired spider wheel for bicycles and went on to invent and make mathematical and drawing instruments. He invented and exhibited and became wealthy. Amongst his more novel inventions was the "penny in the slot" machine. In 1894 he became a member of the Royal Astronimcal Society. He began dabbling in design and became an accomplished artist and architect. He designed and built Stanley Halls in 1903 and on his death he left large legacies to hospitals, schools and a childless wife to whom he was married for over fifty years. Plaque erected 1993. Nearest station = Annerley

STEER, Philip Wilson (1860-1942) 109, Cheyne Walk, Chelsea, SW10.
'painter lived and died here'
Steer was born in Birkenhead and studied painting in Paris. He soon became attracted to Impressionism and added an English dimension. A founder of the New English Art Club, he taught at the Slade and was a significant influence on modern painters, who have made their name in the latter half of this century. He excelled as a portrait artist as for example, "The Music Room" (Tate) and "Self-Portrait" (Pitti). He lived here from 1898 until his death. He had a heart attack during an air raid on London. Plaque erected 1967. Nearest tube station = Sloane Square.

STEPHEN, Sir Leslie (1832-1904) 22, Hyde Park Gate, Knightsbridge, SW7.
'scholar and writer lived here'
Stephen was born in London and was brought up in the 'Clapham Sect', a radical Christian group. He was educated at Eton and Trinity College, Cambridge. He became ordained in 1864 but six years later he left the church and became an agnostic. In 1873 he published his reasons in "Essays on Free Thinking and Plain Speaking" and later "An Agnostic's Apology". He part founded the "Pall Mall Gazette". In "English Men of Letters" he wrote a series of biographies on the famous; Samuel Johnson, Pope, Swift and George Eliot. This became the basis for his "Dictionary of National Biography". In 1902 he was knighted. Stephen and his family lived here from 1890 and, one of his eight children, would later find fame as Virginia Woolf. Plaque erected 1960. Nearest tube station = South Kensington.

STEPHENSON, Robert (1803-1859) 35, Gloucester Square, Bayswater, W2.
'engineer died here'
Stephenson spent his final twelve years here. He was born in Willington Quay, son of George Stephenson, the locomotive designer. After serving his apprenticeship, he assisted his father in organising the Stockton and Darlington Railway. He later worked abroad; constructing railways in Egypt, artificial lakes in Norway and bridges, of all types, all over the world. His major works were the Britannia Tubular Bridge and the Royal Border Bridge at Berwick, in 1850. In 1847, he entered parliament and served on various parliamentary commissions and committees. He is buried in Westminster Abbey. Plaque erected 1905. Nearest tube station = Paddington.

STEVENS, Alfred (1817-1875) 9, Eton Villas, Hampstead, NW3.
'artist lived here'
Here Stevens lived from 1865 until he died. He was born in Blandford, Dorset and studied in Rome, under Thorvaldsen. From 1845 to 1847 he taught architectural design at Somerset House in London. He then spent the next ten years designing a whole range of household furniture and porcelain. His was a most varied career; from mosaics at St. Pauls, to the lions at the British Museum. In his younger days, whilst living in Florence, he existed by copying paintings in the Uffizi. These were sold as genuine by a crooked art dealer. Plaque erected. 1924. Nearest tube station = Chalk Farm.

STILL, George Frederic, (1868-1941), 28, Queen Anne Street, W1
'Paediatrician lived here'
Still, born in London, was educated at Merchant Taylors and Caius College, Cambridge where he gained a first class degree. He joined Guy's Hospital and later transferred to the Hospital for Sick Children in Great Ormond Street. In 1906 he became the first professor for diseases of children at King's College Hospital and stayed until 1935. He became an expert on chronic rheumatoid arthritis in children and wrote "Common Disorders and Diseases of Childhood" (1909). Whilst living here he was knighted in 1937. Plaque erected 1993. Nearest tube station = Great Portland Street.

STOKER, Bram (1847-1912) 18, St Leonard's Terrace, Chelsea, SW3.
'author of "Dracula" lived here'
Stoker, born in Dublin, lived here from 1896 to 1906. Educated at Trinity College, Dublin, he studied law and science before entering the Civil Service. Bored with moving paper around, he turned to the theatre and joined Henry Irving in running London's Lyceum theatre. In 1897, he published the classic horror story, "Dracula". It has recently been turned into a film, with Anthony Hopkins in the star part. It's reputed to be one of the most scary films ever made. Dracula has become a household name for someone who looks and acts in an evil way. Stoker wrote other, more gentle books, as well as Henry Irving's biography, "Personal Reminiscences of Henry Irving" in 1906. Plaque erected 1977. Nearest tube station = Sloane Square.

STOTHARD, Thomas (1755-1834) 28, Newman Street, W1.
'painter and illustrator lived here'
Stothard, born in London, was a run of the mill artist. He showed early promise, when several of his paintings were exhibited at the Royal Academy, but then he turned to becoming a jobbing engraver. In all, some 3000 of his designs became everyday household items. There were exceptions to the humdrum, these included engravings, depicting "Canterbury Pilgrims" and "Flitch of Bacon". He moved here, with his family, in 1810; they remained in residence for 13 years after his death. Plaque erected 1911. Nearest tube station = Goodge Street.

STRACHEY, Lytton (1880-1932) 51, Gordon Square, Bloomsbury, WC1.
'critic and biographer lived here'
Strachey was born in London, the son of an Indian army officer, and educated at Leamington College, Liverpool University and Trinity College, Cambridge. He entered the world of literature, as a critic for "The Spectator", and began his writings during the ten years he was with the magazine. He was a Francophile and his "Landmarks in French Literature", published in 1912, was well received. In WW1 he registered as a conscientious objector; this caused a great stir, which resumed, following publication in 1918, of "Eminent Victorians", which demolished the stuffy, self important figures of society. He moved here in 1919 and was immediately at the centre of what became known as "The Bloomsbury Set". His work then became solely biographical, racy and punchy, and covered a wide spectrum. Plaque erected 1971. Nearest tube station = Euston Square.

STRANG, William (1859-1921) 20, Hamilton Terrace, St. John's Wood, NW8.
'painter and etcher lived here 1900-1921'
Strang was born in London. After studying at the Slade School of Art, he became a student of Alphonse Legros, the leading figure in the British etching movement. It is strange that whilst there is a commemorative plaque to Strang, the averagely talented pupil, there isn't one to Legros, the master. Plaque erected 1962. Nearest tube station = St. John's Wood.

STREET, George Edmund (1824-1881) 14, Cavendish Place, Marylebone, W1.
'architect lived here'
Street was born in Woodford, Essex. He was a teacher to student architects who would make their mark in later years; Philip Webb, Norman Shaw, William Morris and others. Street restored Christ Church in Dublin, designed the Law Courts in London and scores of churches up and down the country. His love of architecture took him all over Europe and he wrote about what he saw in Italy and Spain. Plaque erected 1980. Nearest tube station = Oxford Circus.

STRYPE STREET, 10, Leyden Street, Whitechapel, E1.
'Formerly Strype's Yard derives its name from the fact that the house of John STRYPE, silk merchant, was situated there. At that house was born in 1643 his son John STRYPE historian and biographer who died in 1737. '
The son was a great man of letters, amongst his biographies were those of Cranmer, Aylmer, Cheke and Grindal, all ecclesiastical figures of their time. He was educated at St. Pauls School and Cambridge. He will be particularly remembered for completely re-editing and enlarging Stow's "Survey of London" (1720). Plaque erected 1929. Nearest tube station = Aldgate East.

STUART, John McDouall (1815-1866) 9, Campden Hill Square, Kensington, W8.
'first explorer to cross Australia, lived and died here'
Stuart was born in Dysart, Fife. He emigrated to Australia in 1838 and worked as a surveyor. He spent much time exploring the interior and, in 1860, he crossed the country from North to South with the purpose of eventually erecting a continuous telegraph line as well as planning for future road and railway links. His efforts drained his health and he returned to London in 1864 for medical treatment. He spent his final years here, with relatives. In 1942, because of the threat of a Japanese invasion, the Australian government ordered a road to be built from North to South, along the route originally proposed by Stuart. It is known as the Stuart Highway. Plaque erected 1962. Nearest tube station = Holland Park.

SWINBURNE, Algernon Charles (1837-1909) 11, Putney Hill, Putney, SW15.
'poet and his friend Theodore WATTS-DUNTON (1832- 1914), poet, novelist, critic, lived and died here'
Swinburne was born in London, the son of an Admiral who wanted his son to follow in his footsteps. The son however had other ideas. At Eton he had been cruelly beaten, which affected him all his life. He left Oxford, without a degree, and travelled the continent. In France he was housed by Victor Hugo, before eventually returning to London and a literary crowd. He fell in with some who, whilst sharing their friend's homosexual needs, also drank to excess. It reached the stage when, in 1879, his friend, and later lover, Watts-Dunton, had cause to rescue him and bring him here, where he spent the rest of his life. In 1866, Swinburne had his great success with "Poems and Ballads". Now safe, in the house of his friend, Swinburne was again able to write. Some regard "Studies in Prose and Poetry" (1894), as the best thing he ever wrote. The last of the Romantic movement, he was most prolific and successful. Watts-Dunton was born in St. Ives, Cambs and became a solicitor. He discovered the world of Ford-Maddox, Rossetti, Morris and others. He gave up the law and became a writer. His best known book is probably "Alwyn" (1898), a novel about gypsy life. Plaque erected 1926. Nearest Station = Putney.

SZABO, Violette, GC (1921-1945) 18, Burnley Road, Stockwell, SW9.
'secret agent lived here. She gave her life for the French Resistance'
Szabo was her married name, Bushell her maiden one. Her husband, an officer in the French Foreign Legion, was killed at El Alamein. Although the mother of a small child, she offered her services to the Free French forces in London. She joined the resistance as a courier, under the auspices of the SOE. In June 1944 she was captured, by the Germans just after D-Day, whilst taking important plans to the various Maquis groups in the Limoge region. She was tortured by the German gestapo and the French police and later moved to Ravensbruck, where she, together with two other British girls, were shot. The posthumous award of the George Cross, received by her daughter in 1946, praised her courage and spoke of how dignified she was in the face of overwhelming suffering. It is ironic that the National Front, a fascist party of the order Violette Szabo hated so much, is today an important factor in French political life. Plaque erected 1981. Nearest tube station = Stockwell.

TAGLIONI, Marie (1809-1884) 14, Connaught Square, Bayswater, W2.
'ballet dancer lived here 1875-1876'
Taglioni was an Italian dancer born in Stockholm. Her father, Filippo was a master of the ballet. The odd thing about the daughter was, that although she was born with a physical deformity, she danced with astonishing grace. She came to London in 1829 and danced "Les Sylphide" at Covent Garden to rave reviews. She married Count de Voisins in 1832, gave up dancing and taught deportment to the British royal family. Plaque erected 1960. Nearest tube station = Marble Arch.

TAGORE, Rabindranath (1861-1941) 3, Villas on the Heath, Vale of Health, Hampstead, NW3.
'Indian poet stayed here in 1912'
Tagore was born in Calcutta, the son of a rich Hindu religious reformer. He came to London in 1878, to study law, before returning to India and the vast family estates. He spent his time, away from the family business, writing tales and legends of his world: "A Poet's Tale" (1878), followed by a novel, "Karuna" (1878) and a drama, "The Tragedy of Rudachandra" (1888). He developed the Visva-Bharati university and received the Nobel prize for literature in 1913, the first Asiatic to do so. In 1915 he was knighted but, in 1919, he returned the honour in protest at British conduct and policy in the Punjab. Plaque erected 1961. Nearest tube station = Hampstead.

TALLEYRAND, Prince (1754-1838) 21, Hanover Square, Mayfair, W1.
'French statesman and diplomatist lived here'
Talleyrand's full name was Charles Maurice de Talleyrand-Perigord, Prince of Benevento and he lived here for four years from 1830. Born in Paris, he'd been educated for the Church. Instead, he was elected to the States General and given the task of being one of the Assembly to draw up the Declaration of Rights. He proposed the seizure of church property, to help the state cater for the poor. In February 1790 he was elected President of the Assembly. He first came to London to meet with Pitt, but they were unable to come to mutually satisfactory terms. Under a new regime, Talleyrand's name was placed on a list of emigres and he was forced into exile. He came to London, but was forced to leave, because of the Alien Act of 1794. He went to the United States and only returned to France, in 1796, when Robespierre was defeated. Under Barras, he was made foreign secretary. During the period he was French ambassador to the Court of St. James, he lived here and was most influential in securing the independence of Belgium and re-aligning other European states. After his term of office, he retired to his family chateau in South West France, where he died, surrounded by his children and grandchildren. Plaque erected 1978. Nearest tube station = Bond Street.

TALLIS, John (1816-1876) 233, New Cross Road, New Cross, SE14.
'publisher of "London Street View" lived here'
Tallis lived here for the final six years of his life. Born and educated in London, he joined his father's bookshop business before branching out into publishing. He launched the "Illustrated News of the World" but it failed to attract readers from the well established "Illustrated London News". High costs in production and distribution, caused the magazine to close and Tallis was made bankrupt. Plaque erected 1978. Nearest Station = New Cross Gate.

TATE, Harry, (Ronald MacDonald Hutchinson) (1872-1940) 72, Longley Road, Tooting, SW17.
'music hall comedian lived here'
Tate, born in Alfreton, started work in the local iron works, before becoming a music hall artist. He was a born mimic and created sketches from all walks of life. He performed at four Command Performances and was one of the first comedians to appear regularly on radio. He made several films, that were regional rather than national. He had many hobbies, all expensive; flying, motor rallying, yachting and living the high life. Plaque erected 1984. Nearest tube station = Tooting.

TAWNEY, Richard Henry (1880-1962) 21, Mecklenburgh Square, Bloomsbury, WC1.
'historian, teacher and political writer lived here'
Tawney lived here for the final decade. His was a well fulfilled life. He was born in Calcutta and educated at Rugby School and Balliol College, Oxford, where, in 1918, he was elected a fellow. He was most critical of WW1 in which, at the battle of the Somme (1916), he was severely wounded. After Oxford, he worked for a time at Toynbee Hall, in London's poor East End, before getting involved with the Workers Educational Association and becoming president (1928-1944). A socialist and Christian, he wrote much on social and political affairs, including "Religion and the Rise of Capitalism" (1926), "The Acquisitive Society" (1928) and "Business and Politics Under James I" (1958). He witnessed both World Wars and wrote on them. In the post war Labour government of 1945, he was offered a peerage; he turned it down. In 1909 he married Annette Jeanie, her brother was Lord Beveridge, whose "Report" led to the National Health Scheme. Plaque erected 1980. Nearest tube station = Russell Square.

TELEVISION, Alexandra Palace, Wood Green, N22.
'The world's first regular high definition television service was inaugurated here by the BBC 2nd November 1936' Open to the public.

TEMPEST, Dame Marie (1864-1942) 24, Park Crescent, Regent's Park, NW1.
'actress lived here 1899-1902'
Marie Tempest, born in London, was the first actress, of the non-classical genre, to be made a Dame. She excelled in what were known as, 'drawing room comedies'. She began as a singer, but soon turned to the stage. She was involved in the introduction of plays written by the "new and up and coming playwrights" e.g. Somerset Maugham and Noel Coward. Coward wrote "Hay Fever" for her and she was a favourite of the Royal Family. Her real name was Mary Susan Etherington. Plaque erected 1972. Nearest tube station = Regent's Park.

TERRY, Dame Ellen (1847-1928) 22, Barkston Gardens, South Kensington, SW5.

'actress lived here'

Ellen Terry lived here from 1888 to 1910. She was born in Coventry, the daughter of touring actor. She had a turbulent life, which resulted in three failed marriages and two wild love affairs, one resulting in two children, yet she was honoured with a DBE in 1925; at a time when her conduct was considered most outrageous. The reason was, that Ellen Terry, on stage from the age of eight, was the greatest actress of her time. Her partnership, with Henry Irving, electrified the gaslit theatres of London. In Shakespearean productions she was Portia or Juliet or Kate or Ophelia or Lady Macbeth and so on. Irving was jealous of her fame, which is probably the highest praise she could achieve. In 1903 she went into theatre production, without Irving, but with her son, Edward Craig, in charge. She left Shakespeare and went for Ibsen, Barrie and Shaw. Her third marriage, was in 1907, to an American. It lasted until 1910, when they divorced and she left the English stage. She lived the rest of her life alone, and suffering from diminishing memory and failing sight. It was probably because of her poor health and old age that she was created a Dame, but she wasn't accorded the burial in Westminster Abbey that she deserved; that would really have caused ructions. Plaque erected 1951. Nearest tube station = Gloucester Road.

THACKERY, William Makepeace (1811-1863) 2, Palace Green, Kensington, W8.

16, Young Street, Kensington, W8.

36, Onslow Square, South Kensington, SW7.

'novelist lived here'

Not at all three places at one time of course. The list given is in order of when the plaques were erected. However, Thackery lived at Young Street from 1846 until 1855. Then he and the family went off to Onslow Square, where they remained until 1862. Then because of his failing health, the air at Palace Green was considered better for him. He was born in Calcutta, where his father worked for the East India Company. He went to Charterhouse School and Trinity College, Cambridge, but couldn't face his finals and left. A mixture of journalism, art study, writings and a stay in Paris, failed to provide any sort of living and, as he had married Isabella Shaw in 1836 and she was expecting their first child, regular employment became a must. He joined "The Times" and for many years, alongside his daily work, tried his hand at writing books, but without success; his "Notes of a Journey from Cornhill to Grand Cairo" written in 1846, was scorned by critics and mocked by Charles Dickens, who resented its anti-semitic tone. It wasn't until his pieces for "Punch" were noticed, that he was able to devote his full time to novels of which "Vanity Fair" (1850) is the most famous. He became the first editor of "Cornhill Magazine" (1854). He wrote much but still found time to conduct well paid lecture tours in Britain and America. His tour of the New World resulted in "The Virginians" (1860). Plaques erected. 1887/1905/1912. Nearest Tube Stations = Kensington High Street (1 and 2) and South Kensington (3).

THOMAS, Dylan (1914-1953) 54, Delancey Street, Camden Town, NW1.
'poet lived here'
Dylan Marlais Thomas, born in Swansea, the son of a schoolmaster, worked for a time as a reporter on the South Wales Evening Post. In 1934, he published "Eighteen Poems" and followed with "Twentyfive Poems". He continued writing and publishing his poetry and receiving mixed reviews, mainly because his poetry was so obscure of meaning. In 1954 came "Under Milk Wood" and great deserved success. Then he turned to alcohol. Why isn't readily known, perhaps he felt he couldn't write anything that would match "Milk Wood", anyway, it killed him. He died whilst on an American lecture tour. He was only 39. How much more he might have given the world, can only be guessed at. Plaque erected 1983. Nearest tube station = Camden Town.

THOMAS, Edward (1878-1917) 61, Shelgate Road, Wandsworth, SW11.
'essayist and poet lived here'
Born in London of Welsh parents, Thomas was educated at St. Pauls School and Lincoln College Oxford. On the last day of his finals he celebrated, by getting married. In order to keep his wife, he took on a job as hack writer and general critic, for a local paper. Thomas was one of those who found fame as a war poet. He had been writing poetry for many years and had a novel, 'The Happy Go-Lucky Morgans' published in 1913. All the time he continued working as a journalist. During WW1 he wrote "Six Poems" (1916) and in 1917 "Poems". He was killed in action, during the battle for Arras. After his death he was rated a poet in the class of Keats and Hardy. Plaque erected 1949. Nearest tube station = Clapham Junction.

THORNE, Will (1857-1946) 1, Lawrence Road, West Ham, E13.
'trade union leader and Labour MP lived here'
Thorne was born in Birmingham. He started work when he was only six years old, as a sweeper in a barber's shop. In 1889 he co-founded the National Union of General and Municipal Workers. From 1906 to 1945, he was MP for West Ham, one of parliament's longest serving members. In 1925 he wrote "My Life's Battles". Plaque erected 1987. Nearest tube station = West Ham

THORNYCROFT, Sir Hamo (1850-1925) 2a, Melbury Road, Kensington, W14.
'sculptor lived here'
Thornycroft lived here from 1878 onwards. Born in London, he knew from the time he was a small child, that he wanted to be a sculptor. He first studied with his father, then onto the Royal Academy. By the time he was 26 he had made his name with "Warrior Beasino: A Wounded Youth". There followed more sculptures, many of which were exhibited including "Artemis" (1880). Then he started on statues. General Gordon in Trafalgar Square (1885), Cromwell in Westminster (1899) and many others all over the country. Both he and his brother John, a naval architect, were knighted in the same honours list of 1920. His maternal grandfather, his mother and father, were all well known sculptors. Plaque erected 1957. Nearest tube station = Kensington High Street.

TILAK, Lokamanya (1856-1920) 10, Howley Place, Bayswater, W2.
'Indian patriot and philosopher lived here 1918-1919'
Tilak trained as a mathematics teacher but the attitude and antagonism of the British, involved him in Indian politics. He founded a newspaper, of which he was editor and, as a result of his anti British editorials, he was imprisoned by the British in 1897 and again from 1908 to 1914 and only freed in order to help unite Indian war efforts during WW1. In 1916, he became President of the Indian Home Rule League, and at that time he made a pact with Jinnah for Hindu and Muslim accord. This was known as the Lucknow Pact. Following the war, he attended the ongoing conferences held to halt the Hindu/Muslim disturbances and to seek a platform, for independence discussions, with the government. On his empty handed return to India, he organised a boycott of British made goods and turned passive resistance into a national philosophy. Plaque erected 1988. Nearest tube station = Warwick Avenue.

TOWNLEY, Charles (1737-1805) 14, Queen Anne's Gate, Belgravia, SW1.
'antiquary and collector lived here'
Townley was born in Towneley, Lancs. During his youth, whilst travelling abroad, he deliberately dropped the first 'e' from his name in order not to let it be known his family owned the village in which he was born. On the death of his father, he inherited Towneley Hall and set about improving the estate generally and the Hall in particular. In 1765, he left for Italy and stayed until 1772. During this time he studied ancient art in Rome and Florence. Upon his return, he bought this large house in Belgravia, and created space to house his huge collection of ancient art and memorabilia. In 1786 he was made a member of the Society of Dilettanti, an exclusive club for the devotees of ancient cultures. In 1791, he was made a trustee of the British Museum. He was well known for the lavish dinner parties he held for his friends. These were always held on a Sunday, with the result that his family, all connected with the Church, could safely be invited because they wouldn't attend. He never married and when he died, his brother Edward, inherited the lot and the dinner parties ceased. Plaque erected 1985. Nearest tube station = St. James's Park.

TREE, Sir Herbert Beerbohm (1853-1917) 31, Rosary Gardens, South Kensington, SW7.
'actor-manager lived here'
Tree only lived here for two years, from 1886, whilst manager of both the Comedy and Haymarket theatres. Born in London, he received a commercial education in Germany, which probably stood him in good stead in his later management years. He started his theatrical career as an actor and achieved some success, as Spalding in "The Private Secretary". He also appeared in the roles of Svengali, Falstaff, Hamlet, Fagin, Shylock, Malvolio and Micawber. A very varied portfolio that was surpassed, as Professor Higgins, in the first production of Shaw's "Pygmalion" (1914), the year he was knighted. His wife, the actress Helen Maud, who he married in 1883, lived on for a long time after Tree died. Her last professional appearance was in the 1932 film, "The Private Life of Henry VIII". Plaque erected 1950. Nearest tube station = South Kensington.

TROLLOPE, Anthony (1815-1882) 39, Montagu Square, Marylebone, W1.
'novelist lived here'
Trollope moved here in 1873 and stayed until he died. He was born in London, the son of an unsuccessful barrister who had difficulty meeting his son's school fees. As a result, Trollope's days at Harrow and Winchester were miserable. Later, when funds were even lower, the family went to live in Belgium, where his father died. In 1834, the family returned to London, where his mother, Francis, earned some money as a writer and Anthony got a job with the General Post Office. Twenty years later he left the service, having introduced the idea of the letter-box, for the whole country. Whilst he was in the Civil Service he had started writing, but his first three novels, written between 1847 and 1850, met with little success. It was with "The Warden", written in 1855, the first of the Barchester novels, that Trollope knew he was on the right road. After the Post Office, he travelled to Australia, before returning to stand for parliament. He failed to get elected and so concentrated all his talents on writing. He wrote some 47 novels, travel books, biographies, plays, short stories and literary sketches; but he started work at 5.30 am and continued right through the day. He isn't considered one of the greats; but pretty close. Plaque erected 1914. Nearest tube station = Marble Arch

TURNER, Charles (1774-1857) 56, Warren Street, W1.
'engraver lived here'
Turner, born in London, lived here from 1799 to 1803. He and his wife moved in on the day they were married to an area that is, today, the centre of the second hand car trade. Turner learnt his trade in Italy and worked on a variety of materials but especially mezzotint. He produced many etchings, aquatints and engravings and his work was in much demand for everyday application. Plaque erected 1924. Nearest tube station = Warren Street.

TURNER, J. M. W. RA (1775-1851) 40, Sandycombe Road, Twickenham.
'painter, designed and lived in this house'
J. M. W. = Joseph Mallord William and he was born above his father's barber shop in Covent Garden. Having bought a plot of land in 1843, known as Sandycombe Lodge, he designed, built and moved in two years later. Turner was one of the great masters of landscape painting. At 14 he was at the Royal Academy school, the following year he was exhibiting there. He worked in oils and watercolour and toured the country for suitable subjects to paint. His output was prolific, some 300 oil paintings and around 20,000 watercolours. All these he left to the nation. He never married, but lived for a time with Lord Egremont at Petworth, an area often featured in his work. He was a loner, who often lived in obscure taverns, picking up men as the fancy took him. He died in a small lodging house in Chelsea, where he used the name of Booth. Plaque erected 1977. Nearest tube station = Kew

TWAIN, Mark, (Samuel Langhorne Clemens) (1835-1910) 23, Tedworth Square, Chelsea, SW3.
'American writer lived here in 1896-1897'
Twain, the author of those two great adventure books; "Tom Sawyer" and "Hucklebury Finn", lived a wonderfully fulfilling life. At various times, he was a journalist, printer, river pilot, goldminer, businessman, traveller, bankrupt, inventor and probably much more. He was born in Florida, Missouri and adopted his pen name from the call of the man sounding the depth of the river (mark twain meaning by the mark of two fathoms). He married in 1871, Olivia Landon, a rich lady who indulged his passion for travel. Other well known titles are "A Tramp Abroad" (1880) and "A Connecticut Yankee in King Arthur's Court" (1889). In 1896 his daughter Susy died and Twain spent his year in London in seclusion. The picture he presents, of the 19th century scene in America, is considered unique. In 1835 "Tom Sawyer" was the first manuscript to be written on a typewriter. Plaque erected 1960. Nearest tube station = Sloane Square.

TWEED, John (1863-1933) 108, Cheyne Walk, Chelsea, SW10.
'sculptor lived here'
Tweed, born in London, specialised in working on war memorials and statues to famous soldiers. All over England, South Africa and Rhodesia (Zimbabwe), can be seen evidence of his work. He covered the Boer wars, the Zulu wars and the First World war. Plaque erected 1985. Nearest tube station = Sloane Square.

TYBURN TREE, Traffic Island at the junction of Edgware Road, and Bayswater Road, Marble Arch, W2.
'site of Tyburn Tree'
For some 500 years before 1783, when they were removed for use at Newgate prison, Tyburn Tree gallows stood here. This was a permanent site for public hangings. They took place every six weeks or so and some ten to fifteen men, women and children were put to death for crimes that were often no more than petty thieving. The gallows were removed, following complaints from nearby newly built residential areas, who objected to the crowds and death carts passing their doors. Plaque erected 1965. Nearest tube station = Marble Arch.

UNDERHILL, Evelyn (1875-1941) 50, Campden Hill Square, Kensington, W8.
'Christian philosopher and teacher lived here 1907-1939'
Born in Wolverhampton, to an agnostic family, Evelyn, after graduating from King's College London, became a friend and disciple of Hugel and found her way to intellectually accepting Christianity. She became a lecturer, on religious philosophy, at Manchester College, Oxford (1921) before embarking on a career as a poet. She wrote "The Life of the Spirit" in 1922. In 1907 she married Herbert Moore, a barrister. In 1911 she wrote the novel "Mysticism" which attracted a lot of attention at the time. Plaque erected 1975. Nearest tube station = Holland Park

UNWIN, Sir Stanley (1884-1968) 13, Handen Road, Blackheath, SE12.
'publisher was born here'
It is hard to understand just why a businessman, who contributed little, except make vast profits for his company and obtaining a knighthood for political reasons, should be commemorated here. Sufficient to state that he was a publisher who, in 1960, wrote his autobiography "The Truth About a Publisher". Plaque erected 1984. Nearest Station = Hither Green.

VAN BUREN, Martin (1782-1862) 7, Stratford Place, Mayfair, W1.
'eighth US President lived here'
Van Buren, born in Kinderhook, New York, came to London in 1881 as US ambassador. However, he returned home a few months later, because it would appear his appointment was made before the Senate ratified it. It therefore must have been some consolation to him to become President (1837-1841), albeit by only a majority of some 25,000 votes. His four year term was undistinguished, he was reluctant to end the slave trade that still lingered, there were ongoing financial problems and he was more interested in wining and dining girls from the chorus, than attending to matters of state. He didn't serve a second term. Plaque erected 1977. Nearest tube station = Oxford Circus.

VAN GOGH, Vincent (1853-1890) 87, Hackford Road, Stockwell, SW9.
'painter lived here 1873-1874'
Van Gogh lived here, whilst working at the London branch of his brother's art gallery in Southampton Street. He was born in Groot-Zundert, Holland, where his father was the Lutheran pastor. Taking into account that he only lived to 37, he spent, pro rata, quite a long time in England. Besides living here, he was a teacher at schools in Ramsgate, Kent and Isleworth, Middlesex (1876). He also had a love affair with an English schoolmistress, which left him with recurring headaches and an inferiority complex. Women, it would appear, didn't gell well with Van Gogh. In Brussels, in 1881, he fell in love with a cousin who didn't appreciate his advances and threw him aside. He settled for a whore in The Hague and devoted the rest of his short life to his wonderful paintings. Perhaps if he had had a normal family life he might not have committed suicide, might have sold some paintings and given the world more of his talent. What is certain is that he would have laughed his head off, had anyone suggested he would become immortal and achieve the highest price ever paid for a painting. The setting for his painting "Cornfields with Flight of Birds" was where, on July 27th, he chose to shoot himself. Plaque erected 1973. Nearest tube station = Stockwell

VANE, Sir Harry, the younger, Vane House, Rosslyn Hill, Hampstead, NW3
(House demolished but plaque remains on surviving gate pier)
'statesman lived here. Born 1612 beheaded 1662'
Born in Hadlow, Kent and educated at Westminster School and Magdalen Hall, Oxford, Vane made the mistake of being a staunch Republican after it was no longer fashionable. During Cromwell's time he was, from 1643 to 1653, the civilian head of the goverment but then came the Restoration and Harry didn't know when to keep quiet. Besides, the knives were out over his part in having Strafford beheaded, some years previously. When it was his turn to mount the scaffold, he mocked the King and praised the memory of Cromwell. Plaque erected 1897. Nearest tube station = Belsize Park.

VAUGHAN WILLIAMS, Ralph (1872-1958) 10, Hanover Terrace, Regent's Park, NW1.
'composer lived here from 1953 until his death'
Vaughan Williams moved here following his second marriage. He was born in Down Ampney, Gloucestershire, where his parents encouraged his emerging musical prowess. He was fortunate that whilst at Charterhouse School, there was a music teacher who further encouraged him. He went on to the Royal College of Music and studied under Stanford. He enlarged his range by studying under Bruch in Berlin and Ravel in Paris. Despite his foreign teaching, Vaughan Williams is quintisentially an English composer. His first success was the choral "Sea Symphony" (1910) then, under the influence of Gustav Holst, he for a time concentrated on folksongs. He wrote "Fantasia on a Theme of Tallis" in 1909, only to have it performed quite regularly outside Britain. He served in WW1, both in the RAMC and the Artillery. In 1935 he was awarded the Order of Merit. Despite his large output and heavy workload he found time to write the music for two well known films; "The 49th Parallel" and "Scott of the Antarctic". The absence of a peerage or knighthood only serves to increase the mystery surrounding the 'honours system'. Plaque erected 1972. Nearest tube station = Baker Street.

VENTRIS, Michael (1922-1956) 19, North End, Hampstead, NW3.
'architect and decipherer of Linear B script, lived here'
Ventris was born in Wheathampstead. Whilst just a teenager, he became interested in undeciphered Minoan scripts, found on tablets excavated in Crete and brought to the British Museum, by Arthur Evans. Ventris was later able to prove that the langauge, on what were known as the Linear B tablets, was a form of ancient Greek. Ventris was killed in a road accident shortly before publication of his major work; "Documents in Mycenaean Greek" Plaque erected 1990. Nearest tube station = Golders Green.

VON HUGEL, Baron Friedrich (1852-1925) 4, Holford Road, Hampstead, NW3.
'theologian lived here 1882-1903'
Hugel was born in Florence where his father was Austrian ambassador. He settled in England in 1871 and founded the London Society for the Study of Religion in 1905. He had been educated, in Brussels by a Protestant tutor, under a Catholic supervisor, and this appeared to affect him all his life as he wasn't able to decide which creed to follow. He tried to take an intellectual and mystical approach to the problem and wrote various books on the subject, as well as subjecting himself to self-flagellation, but there is no evidence that he came to any conclusion. In any event, it wasn't terribly important to the world at large, constantly engaged in horrific wars and probably only mattered to himself and a few devoted followers. Plaque erected 1968. Nearest tube station = Hampstead.

WAINWRIGHT, Lincoln Stanhope (1847-1929) Clergy House, Wapping Lane, E1.
'Vicar of St. Peter's London Docks, lived here 1884-1929'
Wainwright, born in Lincoln of working class parents, decided early on, he would like to become a missionary. Instead, after ordination and several minor posts, he came here at a time when the poor were in great need of charity and understanding. Wainwright took up the challenge and did his best to relieve their suffering and give them hope for the future. He founded the Church of England Working Men's Society, which attempted to provide medicine, clothes and education, but they were always short of money. Appeals to the Church of England fell, to the most part on deaf ears, despite their rich coffers from the sale of land to satisfy increasing urban development. Altogether, Wainright gave over 50 years of his life to helping the poor and disadvantaged; surely a great charitable donation. Plaque erected 1961. Nearest tube station = Wapping.

WAKELEY, Thomas (1795-1862) 35, Bedford Square, Bloomsbury, WC1.
'reformer and founder of "The Lancet", lived here'
Wakeley lived here from 1828 to 1848, during this time he was MP for Finsbury. Born in Membury, Devon he became a doctor and set up practise in the Strand. He founded "The Lancet" in 1823 and used it to denounce abuses in the practise of medicine. He exposed practises in food preparation, that led to the 1860 "Adulteration of Food and Drink Act". In 1839, he became coroner for West Middlesex and was instrumental in stopping soldiers being flogged to death as a routine punishment. Whilst an MP, he helped secure a free pardon for the Tolpuddle martyrs, organise affordable housing for working people , the opening of free museums and art galleries and higher wages for the lower paid. Despite all this activity he was never rewarded by so much as a knighthood. During his days as a coroner, Charles Dickens was a frequent visitor to the court, gleaning material for his novels. Plaque erected 1962. Nearest tube station = Tottenham Court Road.

WALKER, Sir Emery (1851-1933) 7, Hammersmith Terrace, Hammersmith, W6.
'typographer and antiquary lived here 1903-1933'
In 1886 Walker, born in London, founded his typographic etching company in Clifford's Inn and went on, together with William Morris, Walter Crane and others to found The Arts and Crafts Exhibition Society. He also met up with Sidney Webb and became involved with the birth of the Labour Party, for which he became the first secretary of the Hammersmith branch. His house, which faces onto the River Thames, was purchased from the profits he made in Dove Press, which he co-founded in 1903. He produced very fine books with fine clear type drawings. Plaque erected 1959. Nearest tube station = Hammersmith.

WALLACE, Alfred Russel (1823-1913) 44, St. Peter's Road, Croydon.
'naturalist lived here'
Wallace only spent about a year here, probably because he was so busy travelling the world in pursuance of his work. Wallace was born in Usk, Gwent. He became a teacher in Leicester, before joining Henry Bates on his voyages to the Amazon basin. He then journeyed on to the Malayan Archipelago, before returning to London, where he assisted Charles Darwin in his research prior to the publication of "The Origin of the Species". Darwin was aided by Wallace's research as illustrated in his "Contribution to the Theories of Natural Selection" (1870). He and Darwin formed the "Linnaean Society" in 1858 and this became a haven for those interested in all aspects of evolution by natural selection. Wallace wrote many works on this subject, as well as the scientific foundations of zoogeography. In his later years Wallace became associated with some odd theories, that appeared to claim that white supremacy was inherent in mankind. This was well after the death of Darwin who, Wallace knew, would have disassociated himself from these views, some of which the Germans would use a quarter of a century later, with chilling effect. Plaque erected 1979. Nearest Station = South Croydon.

WALLACE, Edgar (1875-1932) 6, Tressillian Crescent, Lewisham, SE4.
'writer lived here'
Wallace lived here from 1908 to 1915. Born in London, he was found abandoned in Greenwich, just 9 days old. He was brought up by a Billingsgate fish porter and his wife, given an elementary education and turned out into the world at large. Wallace, a born gambler, tossed a coin, as a result he enlisted in the army and sent to South Africa and the Boer War. There, in 1899, he left the army and became a journalist on a Natal newspaper that sent Wallace's despatches on to Fleet Street. This resulted in an appointment on the "Daily Mail" and an opportunity to write novels in his spare time. "The Four Just Men" appeared in 1905 and was successful, then followed "Saunders of the River" (1911) and "Bones" (1915). He was most prolific, and wrote over 170 novels. He should have been rich but he still had his habit of gambling and the habit became an obsession. He worked to pay off his gambling debts. It was these debts that lured him to Hollywood as a scriptwriter, there he died from a mixture of alcohol and neglect. Plaque erected 1960. Nearest Station = St. Johns.

WALPOLE, Sir Robert (1676-1745) 5, Arlington Street, St. James's, SW1.
'Prime Minister and his son Horace WALPOLE (1717-1797), connoisseur and man of letters lived here'

Walpole lived here from the time he left Downing Street in 1742 and his death three years later. Walpole was born in Houghton, Norfolk and educated at Eton and King's College Cambridge. Originally meant for the Church, he gravitated to politics. Following the untimely death of his two elder brothers, which meant a large estate, lots of money and time to do as he wished, he entered parliament in 1701, as Whig member for King's Lynn. He progressed rapidly, and after some junior appointments, became Chancellor of the Exchequer (1715). As George I couldn't speak English, it was left to Walpole to speak and act on his behalf and by so doing, he established the post of Prime Minister and chaired a small group of Ministers, the forerunner of today's Cabinet. Walpole was the longest serving PM (1721-1742) and he saw the realignment of Europe as either a cause for hope or war. His ambition was for peace in Europe, and his alliances with France were towards that end. His efforts were rewarded by being created Earl of Orford and the gift of 10, Downing Street in Whitehall; this property he willed for the future use of Prime Ministers. His youngest son Horace, the 4th Earl of Orford was quite a different man from his father. The son, who went to Eton and Cambridge was a politician in name only. He was an observer who chronicled the events of his day. His first hand accounts of the Jacobite trials, following the 1745 Uprising, and of the Gordon riots are invaluable. He inherited his title from his brother in 1791 and the estates that went with it. Plaque erected 1976. Nearest tube station = Green Park.

WALTER, John (1739-1812) 113, Clapham Common North Side, SW4.
'founder of 'The Times' lived here'

John Walter was born in London and started his working life as a coal merchant. All went well and he became prosperous. He moved here with his family, in 1774, and continued to prosper until, one day he was persuaded to become a Lloyds underwriter and in 1782 he went bankrupt. Familiar? A while later, Walter bought a patent for a new method of printing, known as logotype and, at a printing shop in Blackfriars in 1785, he started up a scandal sheet called "The Daily Universal Register". Three years later it was renamed "The Times". It is probably apposite that today both the "Times" and "The Sun", presently the number one scandal sheet, are owned by the same company. Walter's son John took "The Times" into the big league. In 1803, the paper published official reports, employed correspondents overseas and soon became the daily newspaper that reflected the views of the establishment. Plaque erected 1977. Nearest Station = Clapham Common.

WARLOCK, Peter (Philip Arnold Hesseltine) (1894-1930) 30, Tite Street, Chelsea, SW3.
'composer lived here'
Peter Warlock, born in London of Dutch parents, came to live here soon after WW1. At the commencement of the war, he volunteered for the army but was rejected, because of his suspected homosexual leanings. He turned to composing music and under the influence of Delius and van Dieren, produced "The Curlew" a song cycle (1920-22). He founded the musical magazine "The Sackbut", in the early twenties, but it foundered when Warlock became ill. In 1923, he wrote a biography of Frederick Delius and in 1926 his autobiography was published, "The English Ayre". Plaque erected 1984. Nearest tube station = Sloane Square.

WATERHOUSE, Alfred (1830-1905) 61, New Cavendish Street, Marylebone, W1.
'architect lived here'
Waterhouse was born in Liverpool and is known as the man who led the Gothic revival. He designed Manchester Town Hall, several Assize courts, refurbished a few Cambridge colleges and built Owens College, Manchester. He was also the designer of the Natural History Museum in London (1873-1881). In later years, whilst living here, he started using terracotta and brick, when designing new universities and colleges, thus giving rise to the term for new universities, as "Redbricks". Plaque erected 1988. Nearest tube station = Baker Street.

WAUGH, Benjamin (1839-1908) 26, Croom's Hill, Greenwich, SE10.
'founder of the National Society for the Prevention of Cruelty to Children, lived here'
Waugh was born in Settle, Yorkshire and educated at Airedale College, Bradford. He lived here, together with his family, whilst director of the NSPCC 1889 - 1908. He was editor of the "Sunday Magazine" 1874 to 1896. He was an ardent advocate of not sending juveniles to prison and supported the establishment of Borstals, where a useful trade could be taught. Plaque erected 1984. Nearest tube station = Greenwich.

WAUGH, Evelyn (1903-1966), 145, North End Road, Golder's Green, NW11.
'Writer lived here'
He didn't live here for very long; it was after all the wrong end of Hampstead Heath. Waugh was born in London and educated at Lancing and Hertford College, Oxford where he killed time reading history. "Decline and Fall" appeared in 1928 a couple of years after he attempted suicide whilst working as a schoolteacher. Following an unsuccessful marriage he travelled and survived by sending articles to leading newspapers. He went on to become a popular writer in the humourous vein and publisher of "Scoop". Probably his best known work is the ever-lasting "Brideshead Revisited" (1945). Waugh reckoned the most important event of his life was becoming a Roman Catholic in 1930. Plaque erected 1993. Nearest tube station = Golders Green.

WEBB, Sidney (1859-1947) 10, Netherhall Gardens, Hampstead, NW3.
'and Beatrice WEBB (1858-1943), social scientists and political reformers lived here'
The Webbs lived here for a few months, following their marriage in 1892. Sidney was born in London, the son of an accountant. He got a law degree from London University in 1885 and soon became immersed in radical politics. Both the Webbs were leading members of the Fabian Society, forerunner to the establishment of the Labour Party. Sidney was involved in the setting up of the London School of Economics and Political Science (1895). Here he became professor of public administration (1912-27). In 1913 both the Webbs founded "The News Statesman". Sidney entered parliament in 1922 and later became President of the Board of Trade. In 1929 he was created Lord Passfield and awarded the OM in 1944. Plaque erected 1981. Nearest tube station = Finchley Road.

WEIZMANN, Chaim (1874-1952) 67, Addison Road, Kensington, W14.
'scientist and statesman. First President of the State of Israel, lived here'
Weizmann lived here from 1917 to 1920, during which time the house was also used as the offices for the British wing of the world Zionist movement. Weizmann was born in Pinsk, Russia and educated in Germany, where he later lectured on chemistry. He came to Manchester university in 1910, where he was Reader in Biochemistry. He became involved in the Zionist movement, during the 1894 trial of Dreyfus in France and realised a home for the Jewish people was a must, if they were to survive pogroms and anti-semitism. During WW1, he discovered an improved method of producing acetone, an essential ingredient in the manufacture of explosives. In 1915 he made his discovery available to the Admiralty and moved to London. In 1917, after extensive lobbying of Balfour and Lloyd George the "Balfour Declaration" of 1917 was made that promised a Jewish National Home in Palestine. It wasn't until 1948, and the death of 6 million Jews in German gas chambers, that the promise of 1917 was fulfilled; following the intersession of the UN. In May 1948, Chaim Weizmann was elected the State's first President and within hours he was involved in the war that followed. Plaque erected 1980. Nearest tube station = Holland Park.

WELLCOME, Sir Henry (1853-1936) 6, Gloucester Gate, Regent's Park, NW1.
'pharmacist, founder of the Wellcome Trust and Foundation, lived here'
Wellcome, the son of a clergyman, was born in Minnesota the middle of America's bible-belt. He started a pharmaceutical business in the States but came to Britain in 1880 because he thought the opportunities better. The business grew so well and so quickly that Wellcome, shortly before he died, and because of a failed marriage, decided to create the Wellcome Trust. In 1994 that trust has assets in excess of £6 billion, gives away some £400 million a year around the world for medical research. The influence of the Wellcome Trust comes from Hank Wellcome's grave and the conditions contained in his will. In 1901 Wellcome married Syrie, the younger daughter of Dr. Barnado, she was 27 years younger than him. Objecting to the frequent whippings she received, Syrie left Wellcome and turned to Somerset Maugham for company and a child. Wellcome was furious. Not only was he upset his wife had left him but to leave him for a homosexual was more than he could take. He indulged himself in every way including building an ediface to himself in the shape of his HQ at 183, Euston Road. He probably became naturalised because he was knighted, by George V and delighted in using the title bestowed. Wellcome, outside of his business, had a varied and interesting life. He pioneered aerial photography and doing so aided the discovery of architecturial digs. He received many doctorates, from all over the world and made a Fellow of the Royal Society. In 1885, he was awarded the Royal Humane Society's Medal for saving someone from drowning. Plaque erected 1989. Nearest tube station = Baker Street.

WELLS, H. G. (1866-1946) 13, Hanover Terrace, Regent's Park, NW1.
'writer lived and died here'
There was nothing easy in Wells' life. The third son of an unsuccessful draper in Bromley, Kent, he grew up counting the pennies. His education didn't really start until he won a scholarship to The Normal School of Science at South Kensington and studied biology under T. H. Huxley. Here in 1890, he got a BSc and worked as a tutor and lecturer at Universal Tutorial College. Gradually his short stories began earning money, until he was able to devote himself full time to his writing. He was also passionate about politics and threw his hat into the socialist arena. His marriage to his cousin in 1890, ended in divorce. His second wife, in 1895, was Amy Robbins who eventually lost count of his mistresses. In all he wrote over 100 books. "The Time Machine" (1895), "The Island of Dr. Moreau" (1896), "The Invisible Man" (1897), "The War of the Worlds" (1898), and so on until, in 1905, he started on comic novels, "Kipps" (1905), "The History of Mr Polly" (1910), etc, etc. In 1935 he wrote "The Shape of Things to Come" a warning about the menace of fascism. He quarrelled with other literary Fabians, Shaw and the Webbs, but he kept faith with himself. In 1936 he wrote his obituary, but this was premature by ten years. During the whole of WW2 he remained here, despite the air raids. In November 1992, Michael Coron, writing a new biography of Wells, reveals that a dark side has been hidden, that in fact Wells was anti-semitic, a plagiarist and quotes examples of how he admired Adolf Hitler. Plaque erected 1966. Nearest tube station = Baker Street.

WESLEY, Charles (1707-1788) 1, Wheatley Street, Marylebone, W1.
'divine and hymn writer lived and died on a house on this site and his sons, Charles, (1757-1834), and Samuel, (1766-1837), musicians also lived here'
Wesley was the younger of the Wesley brothers who were in the evangelist business. He was born in Epworth, Lincolnshire and studied at Christ Church College, Oxford, where he gathered around him the like minded and formed "The Oxford Methodists". He later assisted his brother John, in running the Methodist Church. He wrote over 5000 hymns, the majority of which were instantly forgettable. An exception is "Hark, the Herald Angels Sing". Plaque erected 1953. Nearest tube station = Regent's Park.

WESLEY, John (1703-1791) 47, City Road, Islington, EC1.
'evangelist and founder of the Methodism lived here'
John was altogether a far better educated man than his brother Charles. After Charterhouse and Christ College Oxford, he became ordained a priest in 1728. He was much interested and influenced by religious scholars. Following an unfortunate love affair, he decided he wanted to bring religion to the masses. The church wasn't big enough for him, so he started mass gatherings in fields close to the large cities and towns. At Bristol, in 1739, he founded the first chapel. Later he bought an ex-foundry in Moorfields and turned it into his H.Q. He was a magnetic speaker and upwards of 30,000 people would gather to hear his message. He always claimed his movement was within the Church of England and, during his lifetime, it remained so. In 1751 he married a widow, Mary Vazeille, who left him in 1776 claiming . . . "a body can only stand so much". Plaque erected 1926. Nearest tube station = The Angel.

WESTMACOTT, Sir Richard (1775-1856) 14, South Audley Street, Mayfair, W1.
'sculptor lived and died here'
Westmacott, born in London, followed in his father's footsteps. After learning his trade under Canova in Rome, he returned home and set up a studio where, it is reputed, he had so much work that he earned some £100,000 in 10 years. Later he became a professor of sculpture at the Royal Academy. He was knighted by Queen Victoria, ever thankful that the work he did of her and her consort Prince Albert, showed them in a good light. Plaque erected 1955. Nearest tube station = Bond Street.

WHALL, Christopher Whitworth (1849-1924) 19, Ravenscourt Road, Hammersmith, W6.
'stained glass artist lived here'
Whall was born in Northamptonshire the son of a clergyman. After training at the Royal Academy School he met Arthur Mackmurdo, two years his junior, who introduced him to what is acknowledged as the forerunner to Art Nouveau. Whall however, was busy flirting with religion and in 1878 converted to Catholicism. This conversion led him directly to the art of stained glass windows and, in 1880, he designed the first modern stained glass window at St. Ethelreda, Ely Place. In 1888 he showed examples of his work at the Arts and Crafts Exhibition held at the Liverpool Art Congress and designed the main glass window at Holy Trinity, Sloane Street in 1889. He taught at the Arts and Crafts Central School from 1896, and wrote "Stained Glass Work" in 1905 for the Artistic Crafts Series. In 1912 he became Master of the Arts and Crafts Guild and continued to show at many exhibitions. He now began collaborating with his daughter Veronica (1887-1970) who had become a very talented stained glass designer. Whall now became affectionatly known as Daddy Whall. His style evolved from Pre-Raphaelite to expressionism. Plaque erected 1983. Nearest tube station = Ravenscourt Park.

WHEATSTONE, Sir Charles (1802-1875) 19, Park Crescent, Regent's Park, NW1.
'scientist and inventor lived here'
Wheatstone lived here from 1866. He was born in Gloucester. Probably his main claim to fame is that he invented the concertina (1829). Following his experiments in sound, he was appointed professor of experimental philosophy at King's College London (1834). In 1837 he, together with William Cooke, took out a patent on what they termed as, an electric telegraph. Later he invented a sound magnifier which he called a microphone. Plaque erected 1981. Nearest tube station = Regents's Park.

WHEELER, Mortimer (1890-1976) 27, Whitcomb Street, WC2.
'Archaeologist lived here'
Robert Eric Mortimer Wheeler was born in Glasgow and educated at Bradford and London. When only 30 he became director of the National Museum of Wales. In 1926 he was appointed Keeper of the London Museum and stayed here throughout the war. His television programmes made him a star. His passionate posturings endeared him to the public and more importantly introduced, the majority of viewers, to the pleasures and mysteries of archaeology. He was knighted in 1952 and wrote his autobiography "Still Digging" in 1955. Plaque erected 1993. Nearest tube station = Leicester Square

WHISTLER, James Abbot McNeil (1834-1903) 96, Cheyne Walk, Chelsea, SW10.
'painter and etcher lived here'
The time he spent here (1866-1878) was where some of his most important work was done. Born in Lowell, Massachusetts, he spent five informative years in St. Petersburg (Leningrad) where his father worked as a railway engineer. After failing West Point, he left the States and never returned. He spent time in Paris, studying art under Gleyre and later Courbet. He became moderately successful and when, in 1863, his mother came over to live with him he flourished as a portrait painter. "Whistler's Mother" is now in the Louvre. In 1877 he brought a libel action against Ruskin, who had expressed vitriolic criticism over Whistler's contribution to the Grosvenor Gallery exhibition. The result was, an award of a farthing damages and Whistler went bankrupt, unable to pay the high legal costs. Plaque erected 1925. Nearest tube station = South Kensington.

WHITE, William Hale (Mark Rutherford) (1831-1913) 19, Park Hill, Carshalton, Surrey.
'novelist lived here'
Hale moved here in 1868, following completion of the house he designed, together with the architect Charles Vinall. White was born in Bedford, the son of William White who spent thirty years (1850-1880) as the doorman of the House of Commons and wrote "Inner Life of the House of Commons", published in 1897, by his son. White used the name of Mark Rutherford, rather than his own, because he was working in the Civil Service at the time his books were published. The best known are "The Autobiography of Mark Rutherford" (1881), "Mark Rutherford's Deliverance" (1885) and "The Revolution in Tanner's Lane" (1887). Earlier he had wanted to become an Anglican Minister, but was expelled for his radical views on Christianity. Plaque erected 1979. Nearest Station = Carshalton.

WILBERFORCE, William (1759-1833) 111, Broomwood Road, Battersea, SW11.
'On the site behind this house stood, until 1904, Broomwood House-formerly Broomfield-where William Wilberforce resided during the campaign against slavery which he successfully conducted in Parliament' Plaque erected 1906
WILBERFORCE, William (1759-1833) Holy Trinity Church, Clapham Common, SW4.
'and the Clapham Sect worshipped in this church. Their campaigning resulted in the abolition of slavery in the British Dominions 1833'. Plaque erected 1984
WILBERFORCE, William (1759-1833) 44, Cadogan Place, Belgravia, SW3.
'opponent of slavery died here' Plaque erected 1954
Wilberforce was born in Hull, the son of a wealthy merchant. Educated at St. John's College, Cambridge, he was elected MP for Hull in 1780. He was a close friend of William Pitt the Younger, who was of great assistance in later years. During a tour of the continent in 1785, he became an evangelical Christian and embarked on his 19 year crusade against slavery. In 1807, the trade in slaves was made illegal, but slavery continued until, in 1833, a few months before Wilberforce died, it was abolished in all British territories. Wilberforce, through ill health, was forced in 1831 to move to his cousin's house in Belgravia. Nearest Tube Stations = Wandsworth Common/Sloane Square/Clapham Common.

WILDE, Oscar O'Flahertie Wills (1854-1900) 34, Tite Street, Chelsea, SW3. 'wit and dramatist lived here'

Wilde moved in here in 1885 — ten years later he moved to Reading Gaol. Wilde's plays have been translated and performed all over the world. He was born in Dublin, his father Sir William Wilde, his mother Lady Jane. At the age of 9, he was sent to Portora Royal School in Enniskillen, then to Trinity College Dublin and finally Magdalen College, Oxford; where he was dandified, openly homosexual, contemptuous of conventions and existing moralities. He was an explosion waiting to happen. It happened in the shape of the Marquis of Queensbury. Queensbury, who organised the rules for boxing, objected violently to his son Alfred and Wilde being lovers. Instead of Wilde, who was by now famous following the production of such plays as "Lady Windermere's Fan", "A Woman of No Importance", and of course "The Importance of Being Earnest", conducting his affairs in a more private way, he flaunted himself even more openly. At this time Wilde was a married man with two children, he didn't have to present such a public pageant. The truth was that Wilde's success had gone to his head, he had become an egocentric. On his lecture tour of America in 1882, the customs officer asked "what he had to declare" Wilde responded "only my genius". Wilde sued Queensbury for libel, following Queensbury's visit to Wilde's club where he left his card addressed to Wilde; "To Oscar Wilde posing as a Somdomite". Wilde lost the case he should never have brought, then the authorities brought a charge of, practising homosexuality, against him. Wilde was found guilty and given a two year sentence which he served in Reading Gaol. On his release, he went to France where he published the "Ballad of Reading Gaol" in 1898. It was the last thing of note he wrote. He spent his last years wandering and idling on the continent. Plaque erected 1954. Nearest tube station = Sloane Square.

WILLAN, Dr. Robert (1757-1812) 10, Bloomsbury Square, WC1. 'dermatologist lived here'

Willan died in Madeira, but he lived here from 1800 until 1811. He was born in Bath, where his father was a doctor at the Spa. After qualifying as a doctor, Willan worked with his father and noted how many patients had skin disorders. Later, these observations, plus much more from his work as a physician to London's public dispensary, combined for Willan to produce the first classification of diseases of the skin. He published his work on the subject in "The Description and Treatment of Cutaneous Disease" (1798-1808). Plaque erected 1949. Nearest tube station = Holborn.

WILLIS, 'Father' Henry (1821-1901) 9, Rochester Terrace, Regent's Park, NW1.

'organ builder lived here'

Henry Willis was born in London. After a basic education he was apprenticed to an organ maker, during which time, he is credited with the invention of special manual and pedal couplers. In 1842 he worked for Evans of Cheltenham, who at that time were the leading organ builders in Britain. He left in 1845 and started his own business in London and came to live here. During his time he rebuilt the organ at Gloucester Cathedral and, for the Great Exhibition at Crystal Palace in 1851, he built the largest ever organ. For this achievement he was awarded the Council Medal and after the exhibition, the organ was installed in Winchester Cathedral. He went on to build and install the great organ in St. Georges Hall, Liverpool. He became known as 'Father' Willis following the arrival in the business of his two sons, Vincent and Henry. His masterpiece is the organ installed, in 1891, in St. Pauls, London. Plaque erected 1986. Nearest tube station = Kentish Town.

WILLOUGHBY, Sir Hugh, King Edward Memorial Park, Shadwell, E1.

'This plaque is in memory of Sir Hugh WILLOUGHBY (d. 1554), Stephen BOROUGH, (1525-1585), William BOROUGH, (1536-1599), Sir Martin FROBISHER, (1535?-1594), and other navigators who in the latter half of the sixteenth century set sail from this reach of the River Thames near Ratcliffe Cross to explore the Northern Seas'

Going to sea in those far off days was more than just an adventure, it was probably the only way even the humblest sailor had of making his fortune. The world of India, Japan and China was opening and their treasures were for the taking. But there were many hazards. Willoughby, whose boats were fitted out in a deal with London merchants, never arrived, he died when his boat sheltered in a cove in Lapland and everyone on board died of cold and scurvy. The following year Russian fishermen found the boats, surrounded by frozen corpses. They also found the commander's journal and this was eventually published by The Hakluyt Society in 1903. STEPHEN BOROUGH, born in Northam, Devon was more fortunate. In 1553 he commanded "The Searchthrift" the first English ship to reach Northern Russia via North Cape. He later discovered the entrance to the Kara Sea. His brother WILLIAM, became controller of the navy and responsible for charting the Northern ocean in 1560, and the North Atlantic in 1576. He was vice-admiral to Drake, during the Cadiz adventure. During the battle with the Spanish Armada in 1588, he commanded a warship. FROBISHER was born in Altofts, near Wakefield. On the way to find the North-West passage to Cathay, he reached Labrador and discovered Frobisher Bay. He was knighted whilst commanding the "Triumph" fighting in the Armada. He was later mortally wounded at the seige of Crozon, near Brest. Plaque erected 1922. Nearest tube station = Wapping.

WILSON, Edward Adrian (1872-1912) Battersea Vicarage, 42, Vicarage Crescent, Battersea, SW11.
'Antarctic explorer and naturalist lived here'
Wilson moved here in 1886, whilst attending St. George's Hospital learning to become a doctor. Born in Cheltenham, where his father was a vicar, Wilson joined Scott on his first Antarctic expedition in the "Discovery" (1900-4). On his return, he published his illustrations of the birds and mammals he had seen. He accepted Scott's invitation to take part in his second Antarctic trip from which no-one returned. Plaque erected 1935. Nearest Station = Clapham Junction

WINANT, John Gilbert (1889-1947) 7, Aldford Street, Mayfair, W1.
'United States Ambassador 1941-1946 lived here'
Both Winant and his predecessor, Joseph Kennedy, were appointed by Roosevelt. Kennedy was recalled because of his suspected links with the Mafia, and because of the biased reports he sent home claiming Britain was going to lose the war and for the US to back Hitler. Kennedy made no secret of his support for the Germans and the British were glad to see him go. In 1941, at the height of the blitz on London, Winant saw a different Britain and reported to Roosevelt to help as much as possible. Winant was loaned this house by Churchill, after living in one of the flats above the US embassy. Winant made friends with the press, he broadcast on radio and was as supportive as a neutral could be. After December 1941 and Pearl Harbour, the gloves were off and Winant became an open Anglophile. Roosevelt's death upset him and on a trip home to Concord in 1947, he took his own life during a great bout of depression. Kennedy's son John, later became President and was assassinated, probably by the very Mafia who controlled his father. Plaque erected 1982. Nearest tube station = Green Park.

WINGFIELD, Major Walter Clopton (1833-1912) 33, St. George's Square, Belgravia, SW1.
'father of lawn tennis lived here'
Wingfield belonged to one of the oldest families in Britain. They lived in Castle, Suffolk, long before William the Conqueror arrived. Wingfield invented the modern version of lawn tennis whilst serving in H. M. Bodyguard of Gentleman at Arms. He was rewarded with the MVO in 1902. There doesn't appear to be any plaque or similar, at Wimbledon. Plaque erected 1987. Nearest tube station = Victoria.

WODEHOUSE. P. G. (1881-1975) 17, Dunraven Street, Bayswater, W1.
'writer lived here'

Wodehouse was born in Guildford, Surrey and educated at Dulwich College. After two years working in a bank, he decided to make his living as a writer. He went to America, just before WW1 and started writing short stories for "The Saturday Evening Post". For a quarter of a century, all his stories appeared first in that journal. Besides his stories, he was co-author and lyric writer to 18 musical comedies. His writings fall into three periods. The school stories 1902-1906. The American period 1915-1921 and lastly the country house period, that produced such characters as Jeeves, Lord Emsworth and Bertie Wooster. Unfortunately he blotted his copybook. During WW2, whilst on holiday in Le Touquet, France, he was captured by the Germans and interned in Germany until the end of the war. During the war, he was asked, never threatened, to make propaganda broadcasts, he agreed and, as a result, was branded a traitor. After the war he went to live in America where, in 1955, he became a citizen. He indulged his passion for golf and waited for time to forgive him. He only resumed his British nationality when, toward the end of his life, he was awarded a knighthood. Plaque erected 1988. Nearest tube station = Marble Arch.

WOLFE, General James (1727-1759) Macartney House, Greenwich Park, Greenwich, SE10.
'victor of Quebec lived here'

Wolfe spent the last 8 years of his life here. When one realises he only lived 32 years, his time here was a large percentage. Not that he was home much of the time. A restless fellow, he was born in Westerham, Kent the son of a general. At 15, he was an ensign, fighting the Scots at Dettingen, Falkirk and at Culloden. He didn't stop fighting until 1747, when he was wounded and he spent two years doing garrison duty. In 1758, he was a colonel and the following year Pitt, in pursuance of his policy of getting rid of the French in Canada, made Wolfe a General, gave him an army of 9000 men and saw him off in February 1759. In response to Montcalm's implacable defence, Wolfe found an unguarded point in a remote area. On September 13th Wolfe, and his army surprised Montcalm, on the Plains of Abraham. There was a brief battle, Montcalm was killed, Quebec was taken and Wolfe later died of wounds received in battle. However, as any visitor to Quebec province will confirm, the war is still going on. Wolfe is buried at Greenwich church. Plaque erected 1909. Nearest station = Maze Hill.

WOLSELEY, Garnet, 1st Viscount (1833-1913) Rangers House, Chesterfield Walk, Blackheath, SE10.
'Field-Marshall lived in this house' (open to the public)
Wolseley lived here at the invitation of Queen Victoria. It was a free 'grace and favour' residence. A royal 'thank you' for work done. In Wolseley's case it was merited from the service point of view but not from a financial one. He was born in County Dublin of English parents and entered the army in 1852. He was wounded at Crimea and lost an eye. He was involved in the Indian Mutiny (1857-9) and the Chinese wars of 1860. He put down a mutiny in Canada waged by Louis Riel, who wanted Quebec restored to France. In the Ashanti wars (1873-4), he was in command and on his return, was voted £25,000 by parliament. Various other commands as general, in various parts of the world, rewarded him equally as well; from Rajahs in India to Kings in Egypt. From 1890-5 he was commander in chief of the British army. During his years of service, as well as being responsible for thousands of deaths, he wrote books on soldiering and from these, he made a lot of money. During his years of retirement, he continued to write, mostly biographies, and on his death left a fortune to his family. Plaque erected 1937. Nearest Station = Blackheath.

WOOD, Sir Henry (1869-1944) 4, Elsworthy Road, Hampstead, NW3.
'musician lived here'
Wood lived here during a large part of his life, 1905-1937. He was born in London and there was little in his life other than music. His reputation was made following his appointment as conductor and musical director of the Queens Hall (1894). Together with Robert Newman, the manager of Queen's Hall, they founded the Promenade Concerts, which have run annually since 1895 and which Wood conducted every year until his death. In 1911, Wood was knighted and Newman, the driving force of this great and imaginative idea, overlooked. Plaque erected 1969. Nearest tube station = Swiss Cottage.

WOOLF, Leonard and Virginia, Hogarth House, Paradise Road, Richmond.
'lived in this house, 1915-1924, and founded the Hogarth press'
Virginia Stephen (Virginia Woolf) (1882-1941) 29, Fitzroy Square, NW1.
'novelist and critic lived here 1907-1911'
Virginia Stephen born in London, together with her brother Adrian, moved to Fitzroy Square on the death of their father. It was previously the home of George Bernard Shaw. Here she began her first novel "The Voyage Out" she also worked as a reviewer for the "The Times" and "Guardian". In August 1912, she married Leonard Woolfe. Woolfe, born in London of Jewish parents and educated at St. Pauls School and Trinity College, Cambridge, worked in the Ceylon Civil Service (1904-11) and his early novels such as "The Village and the Jungle" (1913), have Ceylon as a backdrop. The marriage was stormy, Virginia often made anti-semitic remarks then begged for forgiveness. A year after their marriage she attempted suicide. The Woolfs moved to Richmond and in 1917, started their own publishing company, the Hogarth Press; partly for therapeutic reasons and partly to publish their own work. In 1919, there appeared Virginia's best considered work "Night and Day". It made her a celebrity. The Woolfs moved to Bloomsbury in 1924 and the legend of the "Bloomsbury Group" was born. Besides publishing their own work, they published at times, T. S. Eliot and Katherine Mansfield. In 1916, Leonard joined the Fabian Society and supported the Socialist cause for the rest of his life. In 1941 Virginia successfully accomplished what she had often promised — suicide. She weighed herself down with stones and fell into the River Ouse, near her home in Rodmell, Sussex. She had once written, "A woman must have money and a room of her own if she is to write fiction". In a six year period, 1925-1931, she wrote three great novels. "Mrs Dalloway", "To The Lighthouse", and "The Waves". She wrote much else, even though she suffered long bouts of depression. After her death, Leonard wrote his autobiography in five parts, 1960-1969, each with its own title. Their Hogarth Press however, made a classic mistake; they turned down James Joyce's "Ulysses". Plaques erected 1974 and 1976. Nearest Tube Stations = Richmond and Warren Street.

WYATT, Thomas Henry (1807-1880) 77, Great Russell Street, Holborn, WC1.
'architect lived and died here'
Wyatt was born in Colchester, Essex but lived most of his life in London. He was educated at Dulwich College, at a special rate because his father was a London police magistrate and considered a civil servant. After many years of training as an architect, and working for Hardwick, Wyatt set up his own practise and designed anything he could get paid for. He built houses in Wales, factories in Liverpool, military barracks and churches anywhere plus. the Assize Courts in Cambridge. Plaque erected 1980. Nearest tube station = Tottenham Court Road.

WYATVILLE, Sir Jeffry (1766-1840) 39, Brook Street, Mayfair, W1.
'architect lived and died here'
Jeffry Wyatville was born in Burton-on-Trent, to a family involved in building and architecture. He was apprenticed to his Uncle Sam and became an architect. In 1799, he started his own practise, at Avery Row in London and his first job was designing and supervising, the building of the extensions to Longleat in Wiltshire. Nearer home, in Cheam Surrey, he built Nonsuch Park House for Sam Farmer in the style of a Henry VIII palace (1802-1806). From 1824 onwards, he transformed Windsor Castle, much of it destroyed or damaged in the 1992 great fire. He was knighted in 1828. Altogether, Wyatville was responsible for building and restoring over a 100 buildings and is buried in St. Georges Chapel, Windsor. Plaque erected 1984. Nearest tube station = Bond Street.

WYNDHAM, Sir Charles (1837-1919) 20, York Terrace East, Regent's Park, NW1.
'actor-manager lived and died here'
Wyndham lived here for just over a year. He was born in Liverpool and trained as a doctor. He went to America and worked as a surgeon, during the civil war. Then he decided an acting career was preferable to blood and bandages. He received some training and appeared on the stage for the first time in 1861. He returned to England and made his London debut in 1866. His best part was the title role in Robertson's, "David Garrick". In 1889, he opened his first theatre, Wyndhams in Charing Cross Road and in 1903, the New Theatre in St. Martin's Lane. He was knighted in 1902. Plaque erected 1962. Nearest tube station = Regent's Park.

YEATS, William Butler (1865-1939) 23, Fitzroy Road, Regent's Park, NW1.
'Irish poet and dramatist lived here'
Yeats lived here from 1867 to 1873. He was born in Sandymount, a suburb of Dublin. His father was the artist, John Butler Yeats. His mother came from Sligo and Yeats spent much of his infancy there. When he was nine, the family moved to London and Yeats attended the Godolphin School, Hammersmith. In 1880, he returned to Ireland and completed his schooling at the High School, Howth. He had thought of becoming an artist, but in 1884, some poetry was accepted by The Dublin University Review and the matter settled. He returned to London and found success, with his poetry being accepted by English magazines. He was also in demand, as a literary correspondent, by Irish-American journals. He had a large gathering of friends, including George Bernard Shaw and Oscar Wilde. Despite his success, he was homesick for Ireland, and he returned, to live with Lady Gregory at her estate in Galway. Then came his long association with the Abbey Theatre in Dublin. He was also involved in politics and made no secret of his support for an independent Ireland. He entered the Irish senate in 1922. In 1923 he was awarded the Nobel prize for literature. Unfortunately his reputation is tainted by his flirtation with fascism. In 1938, he moved to Cap Martin, near Monte Carlo, where he died a year later, leaving behind a great wealth of 20th century literature. Plaque erected 1957. Nearest tube station = Chalk Farm

YOUNG, Thomas (1773-1829) 48, Welbeck Street, Marylebone, W1.
'man of science lived here'
Young practised as a physician here from 1800-1825; specialising in physiological optics. He was born in Milvington, Somerset and studied medicine at Cambridge and Edinburgh. Besides running his practise he was a scientific researcher. He was professor of natural philosophy to the Royal Institution and an expert linguist. He spoke six languages by the time he was 21. He was also famed as an Egyptologist and is known for deciphering the inscription on the Rosetta Stone. Plaque erected 1951. Nearest tube station = Baker Street.

ZANGWILL, Israel (1864-1926) 288, Old Ford Road, Bethnal Green, E2.
'writer and philanthropist lived here'
Zangwill lived here for three years from 1884. He was born in London and went to schools in Plymouth and Bristol. Later, he graduated from London University with triple honours. After a spell of teaching, he became a journalist and editor of the comic journal "Ariel". He turned to writing novels and in 1892 published "Children of the Ghetto" which brought him instant fame. Other novels followed, a book of essays and two plays, one of which, "The Melting Pot" (1905) was translated and performed in many countries. He was a committed leader of the Zionist cause and founded the Jewish Territorial Organisation. Plaque erected 1965. Nearest tube station = Bethnal Green.

ZOFFANY, Johann (1733-1810) 65, Strand-on-the-Green, Chiswick, W4.
'painter lived here 1790-1810'
Zoffany was born in Frankfurt, Germany and after studying for some time in Rome, came to London (1758). He was fortunate to secure royal patronage from George II and Queen Charlotte and painted most of the royal family. Zoffany became a founder member of the Royal Academy, in 1768 and, from 1783-1790, he made considerable money, working in India and painting portraits of Maharajahs and their families. The house has been known as Zoffany House since the mid 19th century. Plaque erected 1873. Nearest Station = Kew Bridge.

ZOLA, Emile (1840-1902) Queen's Hotel, 122, Church Road, Upper Norwood, SE19.

'French novelist lived here 1898-1899'

Zola was born in Paris the son of an Italian engineer. He started his working life, as a clerk at Hatchettes, the booksellers. He then turned to journalism. Before he started writing his novels there came a series of short stories, that led to "Attaque de Moulin" (1880). Following the French-Prussian war, Zola established himself as a novelist with "Les Rougon-Macquart" a novel depicting a family with continuous additions, a sort of a novel soap. Beside this family novel, were many more, all having some morality or political base. In 1898, came Zola's great moment. He had become increasingly angry over the terrible treatment suffered by Captain Alfred Dreyfus, at the hands of the right wing anti-semitic General Staff. He wrote "J'accuse", which assailed the government and the judiciary as well as the powerful high command of the French army. The result was he was accused of impeaching the military authorities and sentenced to imprisonment. Instead, on September 20th 1893, Zola escaped to London and a hero's welcome. He stayed here a year and returned to a different political atmosphere. He died in Paris the following year, having been accidentally suffocated by charcoal fumes in his bedroom, whilst asleep. A hundred years later and still France hasn't forgiven Zola's attack on the establishment and his defence of the Jew, Dreyfus. Today, near Paris, Zola's house is neglected and visited by less than 10,000 people a year. In marked contrast, Monet's house, is lovingly preserved and visited by over 400,000 people annually. Plaque erected 1990. Nearest Station = Anerley.

Index by Birth

HAMPSHIRE
Besant
Brunel
Davies
Dickens
Hall
Jellicoe
Meredith
Millais
Robinson

HEREFORD
Garrick

HERTFORDSHIRE
Cecil
Manning
Stanley
Ventris

HOLLAND
Alma Tameda
Mondrian
Van Gogh

HUMBERSIDE
Johnson
Wilberforce

HUNGARY
Klein
Kossuth

INDIA
Bairnsfather
Gandhi
Jinnah
Kipling
Lugard
Nehru
Orwell
Patel
Roberts
Ross
Roy Ram
Savarker
Tagore

Tawney
Thackery
Tilak

IRAN
Nicolson

IRELAND
Balfe
Barnado
Beaufort
Burke
Castleragh
Harmsworth
Jordan
Joyce
Kitchenor
Lavery
Lecky
Lucan
Malone
Moore
Moore
O'Casey
Orpen
Shackleton
Shaw
Sheridan
Sloane
Stanford
Stoker
Wilde
Wolseley
Yeats

ITALY
Canal
Clementi
Marconi
Mazzini
Montefiore
Nightingale
von Hugel

JAMAICA
Seacole

JERSEY
Langtry

KENT
Arnold
Dadd
Grote
Hazlitt
Morgan
Petrie
Pitt
Sackville-West
Vane
Wells
Wolf

LANCASHIRE
Arkwright
Beecham
Booth
Burnett
Caldecott
Chadwick
Crane
de Quincy
Eddington
Ewart
Fenton
Ferrier
Fildes
Fleming
Gladstone
Handley
Laski
Lloyd George
Mallon
Peel
Peel
Rathbone
Roe
Romney
Santley
Smith
Steer
Townley
Waterhouse
Wyndham

LEICESTERSHIRE
Macaulay
Macaulay

LINCOLNSHIRE
Flinders
Newton
Pick
Sargent
Wainwright
Wesley
Wesley

LONDON
Allenby
Arne
Attlee
Avebury
Baden-Powell
Baillie
Banks
Barlow
Barnett
Barry
Basevi
Bax
Baylis
Bazalgette
Beard
Beerbohm
Bentley
Besant
Bliss
Blumlein
Bradlaugh
Bridgeman
Brooke
Brummell
Burgoyne
Burns
Butt
Butterfield
Canning
Cecil
Chamberlain
Chamberlain
Chesterfield

Chesterton
Chevalier
Clarkson
Cockerell
Coleridge-Taylor
Collins
Collins
Cons
Cripps
Crookes
Cruikshank
Dale
Dance
Defoe
de Morgan
Devine
Dickenson
Dilke
Disraeli
Dobson
du Maurier
Earnshaw
Edwards
Elen
Faraday
Forster
Forbes
Fox
Frampton
Franklin
Freake
Gaitskill
Gaskell
Gertler
Gibbon
Gilbert
Glaisher
Godley
Godwin
Gosse
Gosse
Gray
Greaves
Greenaway
Greet
Grey
Grimaldi

Grossmith
Grossmith
Hawkins
Heath Robinson
Herbert
Herford
Hess
Hill
Hodgkin
Hogg
Holme-Hunt
Hood
Hopkins
Hore-Belisha
Horniman
Howard
Howard
Hughes
Hughes
Hughes
Hyndman
Innes
Isaacs
Keats
Kelly
Kingsley
Lamb
Lawrence
Lear
Leno
Linnell
Lloyd
Lovelace
Lutyens
McGill
Manby
Marryat
Mathay
Mayhew
Meynell
Mill
Milne
Montgomery
Morrell
Morrison
Muirhead
Nash

Newman
Noel-Baker
Nollekins
Oates
Oldfield
Oliver
Onslow
Palgrave
Palmer
Palmerston
Pankhurst
Pearson
Pearson
Pepys
Perceval
Pinero
Pitt
Place
Playfair
Pryde
Rackham
Raglan
Relph
Richmond
Ricketts
Ripon
Robinson
Romilly
Roseberry
Ross
Rossetti
Rossetti
Rowlandson
Ruskin
Russell
Sartorius
Scott
Shannon
Sharp
Shepard
Shepherd
Simon
Smirke
Smith
Smith
Stanhope
Stephen

Still
Stothard
Strachey
Strang
Strype
Swinbourne
Szabo
Tallis
Tempest
Thomas
Thorneycroft
Tree
Trollope
Turner
Turner
Tweed
Unwin
Walker
Wallace
Walter
Warlock
Waugh
Webb
Westmacott
Willis
Willoughby
Wood
Woolf
Woolf
Zangwill

MIDDLESEX
Arnold
Hunt
Huxley

MORAVIA
Freud

NEW ZEALAND
Low
Mansfield

NORFOLK
Borrow
Burney
Cavell

Haggard
Nelson
Walpole
Walpole

NORTHAMPTONSHIRE
Chisholm
Dryden
Whall

NORTHUMBERLAND
Cobden-Sanderson
Eldon
Leybourne

NOTTINGHAMSHIRE
Knight
Lawrence
Mee

OXFORDSHIRE
Churchill
Churchill
Green

PHILIPINNES
Rizal

POLAND
Ben-Gurion
Chopin
Conrad

RUSSIA
Astafieva
Herzen
Karsavina
Kropotkin
Weizman

RUTLAND
Flecker

SCOTLAND
Adam
Baird
Ballantyne

Barrie
Boswell
Campbell
Campbell-Bannerman
Carlyle
Cochrane
Conan Doyle
Douglas
Fleming
Grahame
Haldane
Henderson
Hunter
Hunter
Irving
Lang
Lauder
London
Macdonald
Manson
Maxwell
Roy
Smiles
Stuart
Wheeler

SHROPSHIRE
Baldwin
Darwin

SRI LANKA
Fisher

SOMERSET
Bagehot
Fielding
Irving
Knee
Young

SOUTH AFRICA
Plaatje
Schreiner

STAFFORDSHIRE
Bennett
Dyson

Jerome
Underhill
Wyatville

SUFFOLK
Anderson
Constable
Fawcett
Fitzroy
Gainsborough
Garrett
Maurice
"Ouida"
Wingfield

SURREY
Ellis
Ford
Galsworthy
Wodehouse

SUSSEX
Beardsley
Blunt
Bridge
Cobden
Ravilious
Salvin
Scawen-Blunt
Shelley

SWEDEN
Lind
Taglioni

SWITZERLAND
Fuseli

TURKEY
Reschid

URUGUAY
Johnston

USA
Adams
Astor
Eliot

Franklin
Harte
Hawthorne
Irving
James
McMillan
Maxim
Morse
Peabody
Twain
van Buren
Wellcome
Whistler
Winant

WALES
Hughes
John
Jones
Lawrence
Novello
Stanley
Thomas
Wallace

WARWICKSHIRE
Cox
Eliot
Galton
Rohmer
Terry
Thorne

WILTSHIRE
Jefferies

WORCESTERSHIRE
Caslon
Elgar
Hill
Houseman
Huskinsson
Johnson
Short

YORKSHIRE
Asquith

Brailsford
Cayley
Chippendale
Cook
Flaxman
Frith
Frobisher

Gissing
Hammond
Hanson
Harrison
Hutchinson
Jackson
Laughton

Leighton
Marsden
May
Pitt-Rivers
Priestly
Waugh

Index by Train and Tube Station

BRIXTON
Chamberlain
Ellis
Leno

BROMLEY NORTH
Kropotkin

CAMDEN TOWN
Engels
Rizal
Sickert
Thomas

CARSHALTON
White

CHALK FARM
Mondrian
Stevens
Yeats

CHANCERY LANE
Maxim

CHARLTON
Barlow

CHARING CROSS
Curzon
Dadd
Franklin
Gladstone
Heine
Kipling
Kitchenor
Pepys
Rowlandson

CLAPHAM COMMON
Barry
Bentley
Burns
Knee
Macalley
Walter
Wilberforce

CLAPHAM JUNCTION
Henty
Thomas
Wilson

CLAPHAM NORTH
Henderson

CLAPHAM SOUTH
Hobbs

COVENT GARDEN
Johnson

CROYDON SOUTH
Wallace

DALSTON JUNCTION
Gosse

DENMARK HILL
Ruskin

EDGWARE ROAD
Balfe

ELTHAM
Jefferies
Morrison

EMBANKMENT
Adam
Arkwright

EUSTON SQUARE
Fawcett
Herford
Hughes
Keynes
Mazzini
Morrell
Robinson
Rossetti
Strachey

FARRINGDON
Grimaldi

FINCHLEY ROAD
Edwards
Freud
Karsavina
Webb

FOREST HILL
Horniman

FROGNAL
Sharp

FULHAM BROADWAY
Coleridge
Dobson
Gaudier-Brzeska

GLOUCESTER ROAD
Allenby
Arnold
Booth
Borrow
Franklin
Freake
Gilbert
Meredith
Millais
Orpen
Playfair
Sartorious
Terry

GOLDERS GREEN
Barnett
Hess
Linnell
Pick
Ventris
Waugh

GOODGE STREET
Furseli
Hodgkin
Hutchinson
Morse
Nollekens
Pinero

Rossetti
Roy
Smirke
Stothard

GREAT PORTLAND
STREET
Flaxman
Still

GREEN PARK
Ashfield
Brummell
Burgoyne
Burney
Canning
Cayley
Chopin
Clive
Fox
Gainsborough
Isaacs
Maugham
Raglan
Roseberry
Walpole
Walpole
Winant

GREENWICH
Chesterfield
Glaisher
McMillan
Waugh

GYPSY HILL
Besant

HACKNEY DOWNS
Lloyd
Priestley

HAMMERSMITH
Brangwyn
Short
Silver
Walker

HAMPSTEAD
Baillee
Besant
Bliss
Constable
Dale
du Maurier
Ferrier
Gaitskell
Galsworthy
Greenaway
Hammond
Hill
Hyndman
Keats
Lawrence
Macdonald
Mansfield
Malhay
Pearson
Petrie
Romney
Scott
Tagore
von Hugel

HAMPTON
Beard
Garrick

HANGER LANE
Blumlein

HARROW-on the-HILL
Ballantyne

HERNE HILL
Rohmer

HIGHBURY
Chamberlain
Leybourne
Phelps

HIGHGATE
Houseman
Kingsley
Savarker

HITHER GREEN
Flecker
Unwin

HOLBORN
Disraeli
du Maurier
Earnshaw
Dickens
Harrison
Lethaby
Marsden
Perceval
Rossetti
Williams

HOLLAND PARK
Crookes
Leighton
May
Stuart
Underhill
Weizman

HYDE PARK
Bagehot
Bentham
Campbell-Bannerman
Disraeli
Sheriden

ILFORD
Mansbridge

KENSINGTON HIGH
STREET
Baden-Powell
Beerbohm
Bridge
Chesterton
Churchill
Clementi
Crane
Dickenson
Eliot
Fildes
Grahame

Hall
James
Joyce
Lang
Low
Macaulay
Maxwell
Mill
Palmer
Parry
Sargent
Simon
Stanford
Thackerey
Thorneycroft

KENSINGTON OLYMPIA
Holman-Hunt

KENTISH TOWN
Orwell
Willis

KEW
Turner
Ziffany

KINGS CROSS
Nash

KNIGHTSBRIDGE
Alexander
Bairnsfather
Bennett
Galton
Lind

LADBROKE GROVE
Nehru

LAMBETH NORTH
Bligh
Greet

LANCASTER GATE
Barrie

Brooke
Harte
Scott

LEICESTER SQUARE
Arne
Chippendale
Clarkson
Cobden
Eastlake
Hazlitt
Reynolds
Wheeler

LEWISHAM
Smiles

MAIDA VALE
Bazalgette
Fleming
Frith
Klein

MARBLE ARCH
Browning
Churchill
Cons
Faraday
Garrett-Anderson
Grossmith
Milner
Montefiore
Reschid
Taglioni
Trollope
Wodehouse

MANOR HOUSE
Howard

MARYLEBONE
Grossmith
Haydon

MAZE HILL
Dyson
Wolf

MERTON PARK
Innes

MOORGATE
Gertler

MOTTINGHAM
Grace

MILE END
Cook

NEW CROSS GATE
Tallis

NOTTING HILL GATE
Carlile
Forbes
Ford
Hudson
Kossuth
Lewis
Morgan
Pryde
Ricketts
Robinson
Shannon

OLD STREET
Caslon

OVAL
Cox
Montgomery

OXFORD CIRCUS
Asquith
Handel
Hogg
Hughes
Irving
Lutyens
Malone
Ross
Roy
Pearson
Stanhope

Street
van Buren

PADDINGTON
Handley
Lawrence
Manby
Smith
Stephenson

PECKHAM RYE
Oliver

PICCADILLY
Astor
Basevi
Burke
Canal
de Gaulle
Dryden
Grote
Hunter
Hunter
Huskisson
Newton
Palmerston

PINNER
Heath Robinson

PUTNEY EAST
Benes
Oates
Swinbourne

QUEENSWAY
Hill
London
Meynell

QUEENSTOWN ROAD
O'Casey

RAVENSCOURT PARK
Cobden-Saunders
Devine
Herbert

Johnston
"Ouida"
Ravilious
Whall

REGENTS PARK
Adams
Boswell
Browning
Burnett
Cockerell
Cruickshank
Hallam
Jones
Lister
Maurice
Mayhew
Palgrave
Roberts
Shepard
Tempest
Wesley
Wheatstone
Wyndham

RICHMOND
Chadwick
Hughes
Newman
Woolf

ROYAL OAK
Herzen

RUSSELL SQUARE
Howard
Lethaby
Romilly
Sloane
Smith
Tawney

St.JAMES'S PARK
Blunt
Fisher
Grey
Haldane

Hore-Belisha
Lovelace
Napoleon 111
Palmerston
Pitt
Smith
Stanley
Townley

St.JOHN'S WOOD
Alma Tameda
Beecham
Cochrane
Davies
Frampton
Hood
Huxley
Knight
Kokoschka
Salvin
Santley
Strang
Wallace

SELHURST
Coleridge-Taylor
Conan-Doyle

SHORTLANDS
Muirhead

SLOANE SQUARE
Astafieva
Avebury
Baldwin
Brunel
Carlyle
Cecil
Chamberlain
Cubitt
du Morgan
Dilke
Douglas
Eliot
Ewart
Fleming
Gaskell

Gissing
Granger
Greaves
Hunt
Jellicoe
Jerome
John
Jordan
Kingsley
Langtry
Metternich
Milne
Mozart
Nicolson
Noel-Baker
Pankhurst
Peabody
Ripon
Rossetti
Russell
Sackville-West
Sloane
Steer
Stoker
Twain
Tweed
Warlock
Wilberforce
Wilde

SOUTH KENSINGTON
Belloc
Bonar-Law
Cole
Cripps
Fitzroy
Froude
Godwin
Hanson
Lavery
Lecky
Lugard
Mallarme
Place
Scott
Stephen
Tree

Thackerey
Whistler

STAMFORD BROOK
Pissarro

STEPNEY EAST
Groser

STEPNEY GREEN
Barnado

STOCKWELL
Bayliss
Szabo
van Gogh

STOKE NEWINGTON
Defoe

STREATHAM
Bax

SWISS COTTAGE
Butt
Fenton
Wood

SYDENHAM
Baird
Shackleton

TOOTING BROADWAY
Lauder
Tate

TOTTENHAM COURT
   ROAD
Baird
Banks
Bridgeman
Butterfield
Caldecott
Cavendish
Coleridge
Eldon

Hawkins
Laughton
Marx
Onslow
Patmore
Shelley
Sheraton
Wakely
Wyatt

TUFNELL PARK
Brown

TULSE HILL
Mee

TURNHAM GREEN
Forster

VICTORIA
Arnold
Beardsley
Conrad
Gray
Manning
Moore
Pitt-Rivers
Rathbone
Scawen-Blunt
Smith
Wingfield

WALTHAMSTOW
Plaatje
Roe

WANDSWORTH COMMON
Lloyd George
Spurgeon
Wilberforce

WARREN STREET
Cecil
Dance
Darwin
Flinders
Shaw

Index by Trade and Profession

Lavery
Leighton
Lewis
Linnell
May
Millais
Mondrian
Nash
Orpen
Palmer
Pissarro
Ravilious
Reynolds
Richmond
Romney
Rowlandson
Sartorious
Schwitters
Shannon
Shepherd
Short
Sickert
Steer
Stevens
Stothard
Strang
Turner
van Gogh
Whall
Whistler
Zoffany

ASTRONOMERS
Dyson
Glaisher

AVIATORS
Johnson
Roe

BIOGRAPHERS
Boswell

BIOLOGISTS
Huxley

BOTANISTS
Bentham

BUILDERS
Cubitt
Freake
Innes

CALLIGRPHERS
Johnston

CAMPAIGNERS
Pankhurst

CARTOONISTS
Bairnsfather
McGill
Low

CHRONOMETER MAKERS
Earnshaw

CHURCHMEN & PREACHERS
Herford
Hughes
Irving
Manning
Newman
Priestlly
Spurgeon
Underhill
von Hugel
Wesley
Wesley

CIVIL SERVANTS
Brooke

CLOWNS
Grimaldi

COLLECTERS
Townley

COMEDIANS
Handley

COMPOSERS
Arne
Balfe
Bax
Benedict
Berlioz
Bliss
Bridge
Chopin
Clementi
Coleridge-Taylor
Elgar
Gounod
Granger
Handel
Mozart
Novello
Parry
Vaughan-Williams
Warlock

CRICKETERS
Grace
Hobbs

CRITICS
Strachey

CRUSADERS
Wilberforce

DANCERS
Astafiena
Karsevnia
Taglioni

DESIGNERS
Brummell
Chippendale
Pick
Rickets
Sheraton

DIPLOMATS
Scawen-Blunt
Winant

DIARISTS
Pepys

DOCTORS
Bright
Garrett-Anderson
Hodgekin
Hunter
Hunter
Lister
Marsden
Sloane
Still

ECONOMISTS
Keynes

EDUCATORS
Cole
Hogg
Mansbridge

ENGINEERS
Barlow
Bazalgette
Brunel
Manby
Muirhead
Stephenson

ENTERTAINERS
Chevalier
Elen
Lauder
Leno
Leybourne
Lloyd
Lucan
Relph
Tate

ENGRAVERS
Turner

ETHNOLOGISTS
Kingsley

EXPLORERS
Scott
Shackleton
Cook
Flinders
Oates
Ross
Wilson
Stuart

GARDENERS
Bridgeman

HISTORIANS
Adams
Carlyle
Fronde
Gibbon
Green
Grote
Hallam
Hammond
Lecky
Maucauley
Strype
Tawney

HORTICULTURALISTS
Loudon

HUMANISTS
Dickenson

HYDROGRAPHERS
Beaufort
Fitzroy

ILLUSTRATORS
Rackham
Heath Robinson
Shepard

IMPRESSARIOS
Baylis
Collins

INOVATORS
Wingfield

INVENTORS
Arkwright
Baird
Blumlein
Creed
Friese-Green
Harrison
Hansom
Hughes
Hill
Marconi
Maxim
Morse
Stanhope
Stanley
Wheatstone

JOURNALISTS
Edwards
Harmsworth

KING
Napoleon 111

LAWYERS
Bradlaugh
Smith

MAPMAKERS
Roy

MATHAMATICIANS
Eddington

MUSICIANS
Beecham
Hess
Mathay
Parry
Sargent
Sharp
Stanford
Wood

NATURALISTS
Banks
Darwin

Jefferies
Wallace

NURSES
Cavell
McMillan
Nightingale
Seacole

ORGANISERS
Ashfield
Lugard

ORGAN MAKERS
Willis

PATRIOTS
Kossuth
Mazzini
Szabo
Tilak

PATRON OF ARTS
Morrell

PHILANTHROPISTS
Peabody
Cons
Horniman
Macauley

PHILOSOPHERS
Cavendish
Coleridge
Engels
Gandhi
Marx
Maurice
Mill
Newton
Savarkar

PHYSICISTS
Maxwell

PIONEERS
Barnado

Howard
Knee
Lovelace
Simon
Smith
Wellcome

PLAYWRIGHTS
Galsworthy
Gilbert
O'Casey
Pinero
Sheridan
Wilde

POETS
Arnold
Arnold
Baillie
Belloc
Blunt
Browning
Dobson
Dryden
Flecker
Heine
Hood
Hopkins
Houseman
Keats
Kipling
Lang
Mallarme
Meredith
Meynell
Moore
Palgrave
Patmore
Rosenberg
Rossetti
Rossetti
Shelley
Swinbourne
Tagore
Thomas
Thomas
Yeats

POLITICIANS
Asquith
Astor
Attlee
Baldwin
Benes
Ben-Gurion
Bonar-Law
Burns
Campbell-Bannerman
Canning
Castleragh
Cecil
Cecil
Chamberlain
Chamberlain
Chesterfield
Churchill
Churchill
Cobden
Cripps
Curzon
de Gaulle
Dilke
Disraeli
Eldon
Fox
Franklin
Gaitskell
Gladstone
Grey
Haldane
Henderson
Herzen
Hore-Belisha
Huskinson
Isaacs
Jinnah
Laski
Lloyd-George
Macdonald
Metternich
Milner
Morrison
Nehru
Noel-Baker
Palmerston

Patel
Pearson
Peel
Perceval
Pitt
Pitt
Rathbone
Reschid
Ripon
Roseberry
Russell
Smith
Talleyrand
Thorne
van Buren
Vane
Walpole
Weizman

PRINTERS
Caslon
Cobden-Sanderson

PUBLISHERS
Mayhew
Tallis
Unwin
Walter

PSYCHOANALYSTS
Dale
Jones

PSYCHIATRISTS
Freud
Klein

REFORMERS
Chadwick
Chisholm
Ewart
Fawcett
Groser
Hill
Howard
Hughes

Knee
Lawrence
Mallon
Peel
Place
Romilly
Roy
Wainright
Wakely
Waugh
Webb

REVOLUTIONISTS
Kossuth

SAILORS
Beatty
Bligh
Burough
Cochrane
Fisher
Frobisher
Jellicoe
Nelson
Willoghby

SCHOLARS
Malone

SCIENTISTS
Avebury
Banks
Cayley
Crookes
Ellis
Faraday
Fleming
Fleming
Franklin
Galton
Gray
Hutchinson
Jackson
Manson
Robinson
Ross

Willan
Young

SCULPTORS
Dobson
Flaxman
Frampton
Gauder-Brzeska
Nollekens
Thorneycroft
Tweed
Westmacott

SILVERSMITH
Silver

SINGERS
Beard
Butt
Ferrier
Lind
Santley

SOCIAL WORKERS
Oliver

SOCIALISTS
Hyndeman

SOCIOLOGISTS
Barnett
Besant
Blunt
Booth
Carlile
Davies
Drysdale
Godley

SOLDIERS
Allenby
Baden-Powell
Burgoyne
Clive
Kitchenor
Montgomery

Raglan
Roberts
San Martin
Woolf
Wolsely

SPEAKER
Onslow

TYPOGRAPHERS
Walker

WRITERS
Bagehot
Ballantyne
Barrie
Beerbohm
Bennett
Besant
Borrow
Brailsford
Burke
Burnett
Burney
Chesterton
Collins
Conan-Doyle
Conrad
Defoe
de Quincy
Dickens
Douglas
du Maurier
Eliot
Eliot
Fielding

Ford
Forester
Forster
Gaskell
Gissing
Gosse
Grahame
Haggard
Hall
Hardy
Harte
Hawkins
Hawthorn
Hazlitt
Henty
Herbert
Hudson
Hunt
Irving
James
Jerome
Johnson
Joyce
Kingsley
Kipling
Lamb
Lang
Lawrence
Lawrence
Lear
Mansfield
Marrayat
Maughan
Mayhew
Mee
Milne

Moore
Morgan
Nicolson
Orwell
"Ouida"
Plaatje
Rizal
Rohmer
Ruskin
Sackville-West
Schreiner
Shaw
Smiles
Smith
Stanley
Stephen
Stoker
Thackery
Trollope
Twain
Wallace
Walpole
Waugh
Wells
White
Woodehouse
Woolf
Woolf
Zangwill
Zola

WIGMAKER
Clarkson

ZOOLOGISTS
Gosse